WAR IN THE FALKLANDS, 1982

∘∘⊰⊱∘∘

uncovered editions

Series editor: Tim Coates

Other titles in the series

uncovered editions

WAR IN THE
FALKLANDS, 1982

London: The Stationery Office

Applications for reproduction should be made in writing to
The Stationery Office Limited, St Crispins, Duke Street,
Norwich NR3 1PD.

ISBN 0 11 702458 9
First published by HMSO as *Falkland Islands Kerguelen* (1920);
Falkland Islands Review: Report of a Committee of Privy Counsellors
(Cmnd. 8787, 1983); *The Falklands Campaign: The Lessons*
(Cmnd. 8758, 1982); and *The Falklands Campaign: A Digest of
Debates in the House of Commons 2 April to 15 June 1982* (1982).
© Crown copyright

A CIP catalogue record for this book is available from the
British Library.

Cover photograph © Imperial War Museum, FKD 2818
(Y Company of the 1st Battalion the Royal Hampshire
Regiment with Prime Minister Margaret Thatcher and Chief
of Naval Staff).

Typeset by J&L Composition Ltd, Filey, North Yorkshire.
Printed in the United Kingdom for The Stationery Office by
Biddles Ltd, Guildford, Surrey.
TJ3039 C30 2/01

CONTENTS

About the series

Uncovered Editions are historic official papers which have not previously been available in a popular form. The series has been created directly from the archive of The Stationery Office in London, and the books have been chosen for the quality of their story-telling. Some subjects are familiar, but others are less well known. Each is a moment of history.

About the series editor, Tim Coates

Tim Coates studied at University College, Oxford and at the University of Stirling. After working in the theatre for a number of years, he took up bookselling and became managing director, firstly of Sherratt and Hughes bookshops, and then of Waterstone's. He is known for his support for foreign literature, particularly from the Czech Republic. The idea for *Uncovered Editions* came while searching through the bookshelves of his late father-in-law, Air Commodore Patrick Cave OBE. He is married to Bridget Cave, has two sons, and lives in London.

Tim Coates welcomes views and ideas on the *Uncovered Editions* series. He can be e-mailed at timcoatesbooks@yahoo.com.

On 2 April 1982, Argentina invaded the Falkland Islands, a British sovereign territory. How did Britain come to have sovereignty over these remote islands in the South Atlantic? What were the events leading up to the invasion, and why was Britain caught so unprepared? How was the campaign mounted at a distance of over 8,000 miles? And why did the Foreign Secretary resign?

Starting with the official government history of the Falkland Islands (up to 1904), this book then gives the full text of Lord Franks' report, who was appointed to investigate the events leading up to the invasion, and to review the way in which the Government discharged its responsibilities. A full description of the operation as submitted to Parliament is included, and also the text of some famous debates in the House of Commons during this turbulent period, featuring interchanges between Margaret Thatcher, the then Prime Minister, and the leaders of the other parties.

The South Atlantic showing the Falkland Islands
and the Falkland Islands Dependencies

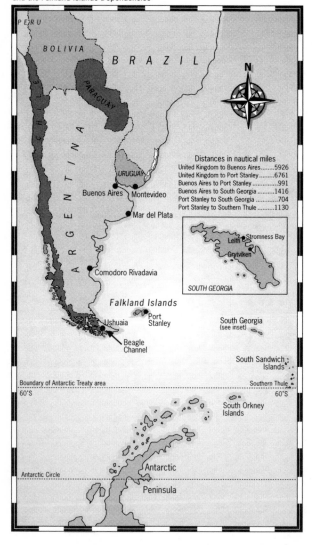

Distances in nautical miles
United Kingdom to Buenos Aires........5926
United Kingdom to Port Stanley.........6761
Buenos Aires to Port Stanley 991
Buenos Aires to South Georgia 1416
Port Stanley to South Georgia 704
Port Stanley to Southern Thule 1130

PART I

∞◦◦◦∞

HISTORY OF THE FALKLAND ISLANDS
1592–1904

NAMING OF THE ISLANDS

The Falkland Islands have been variously named. They are referred to in old books as John Davis's Southern Land or Southern Islands, from their first discoverer. Richard Hawkins called the land he sighted, in 1594, after himself and Queen Elizabeth, "Hawkins's Maiden Land". They gained the name of "The Sebaldines" from the Dutch sailor, Sebald de Weert, who sighted them in 1599. Captain Strong, who visited the islands in January 1690, named the wide strait between them Falkland Sound, after Lord Falkland,

CHRONOLOGICAL SUMMARY

1592	Islands sighted by Davis.
1594	Hawkins sights "Hawkins's Maiden Land".
1599	Sebald de Weert sights "The Sebaldines".
1690	Falkland Sound named by Strong.
1748	Anson suggests British settlement; Spain protests.
1764	Bougainville colonises Port Louis.
1765	Port Egmont founded by British.
1766	French settlement sold to Spain.
1770	British occupants of Port Egmont ejected by Spaniards.
1771	Restitution agreed to by Spain.
1774	British garrison withdrawn, but signals of possession left.
1775	South Georgia claimed by Captain Cook.
1810	The islands deserted.
1820	Buenos Aires settlement formed in Falklands.
1831	Buenos Aires settlement broken up by US.
1832–3	British sovereignty established and Port Louis occupied.
1843	Falkland Islands become a British Crown colony.
1844	Port Stanley made headquarters.
1851	Falkland Islands Company founded.
1904	Development of whaling in South Georgia.

then Treasurer of the Navy. The name afterwards passed on to the islands themselves; and Woodes Rogers, who visited them in December 1708, spoke of them as Falkland's Land. Woodes Rogers's ship had Dampier on board, Dampier having already sighted the islands in January 1684. The French name for them was "Îles Malouines", after visits from St Malo ships; and the name was confirmed by the fact that Bougainville's colony started from St Malo. The Spaniards adopted the French name, and knew them as Las Malvinas.

DISCOVERY AND EARLY HISTORY

In view of the remoteness of these islands it is curious how much history attaches to them and how many well-known names—some already mentioned—occur in their story. The first chapter of the Annual Register for 1771, written at the time of the friction between England and Spain in regard to the islands, tells what was known at that date on the subject. They were marked on old maps of the sixteenth century, and their first discovery was vaguely attributed to Magellan or Vespucci; but the first recorded discovery was made by an

Englishman, the Elizabethan sailor John Davis, who sighted them in August 1592. As already indicated, "Hawkins's Maiden Land" is generally identified with the Falkland Islands; but there is no doubt that the Dutchman, Sebald de Weert, sighted the small islands to the north-west of the group.

The history of the islands really begins after Lord Anson's famous voyage round the world in 1740–4, and the publication of the narrative of that voyage in 1748. The need for a British station and port of call in these seas was suggested; and, while Lord Anson was at the Admiralty, it was proposed to send out an expedition to make a report upon the islands, with a view to forming a station; but, according to the Annual Register, the scheme was given up owing to protests from Spain, though there appears to be no official record of such protests.

Nothing more was done until the end of the Seven Years' War and the Peace of 1763. In the summer of that year, Bougainville, the French explorer, organised at St Malo an expedition for forming a settlement in the Falklands. The ships sailed in September, carrying a few Acadian★ families as settlers, and livestock of all kinds. The Falklands were sighted on 31 January 1764, and Bougainville landed on 3 February. He chose a site for his settlement at the head of Berkeley Sound, and called it Port Louis. He went back to France in the same year to report to the French Government, and arrived again in the Falklands, with some more settlers, in January 1765. But his colony was short-lived. The French and Spanish Governments became involved in a dispute over the

★ Of or native to Nova Scotia (French derivative).

French settlement. An angry correspondence took place between the Spanish Prime Minister and the Duc de Choiseul, and the two countries were actually beginning to prepare for war, when Louis XV intervened, and proposed to the King of Spain that the French should withdraw from Port Louis on the payment of compensation by Spain. Bougainville was sent to Madrid; and an agreement on these lines was arrived at (1766), France receiving a sum of money equivalent to £24,000. Port Louis was renamed by the Spaniards Port Soledad.

Meanwhile, in 1764, the British Government, inspired probably by the action of the French, had at length carried out their intention of sending an expedition to report upon the Falkland Islands, with a view to establishing a station there, the royal instructions to that effect being given in June of that year. The commodore in charge was the Hon. John Byron, who, as a midshipman, had been wrecked on the coast of Chile in a ship belonging to the squadron in which Anson made his famous voyage. On 15 January 1765, Byron sailed into a harbour on the north coast of West Falkland, which he called Port Egmont, or Egmont Harbour, after the Earl of Egmont, then at the head of the Admiralty. "Of this harbour," he wrote, "and all the adjoining islands I took possession for His Majesty King George the Third of Great Britain under the name of Falkland's Island." On his report, Captain MacBride was immediately sent out in HMS *Jason* (whence the Jason Islands, adjoining this part of the Falklands), to form a settlement, which was begun at Port Egmont early in 1766, the site of the station being on Saunders Island, near the mouth of the inlet.

CONTROVERSY BETWEEN GREAT BRITAIN AND SPAIN

The existence of the station was not at first known to Spain, and the British were not molested for two or three years. But in 1769 the British and Spanish commanders warned each other off as trespassers; and in the next year, on 10 June 1770, a fleet of five Spanish frigates, with a strong armed force on board, obliged the small English garrison to capitulate and return to England. It should be noticed that during these proceedings, in 1769 and 1770, the protests of the British commander laid great stress on the first discovery of the islands by Great Britain. The ejected settlers reached England in September 1770; and the action of Spain roused strong public feeling there. Lord Weymouth, the Secretary of State, demanded the immediate restoration of the colonists to Port Egmont and reparation for the insult offered to the British Crown. At the same time he began with vigour to prepare for war. The King of Spain appealed to the King of France for assistance in virtue of the "Family Compact". The matter was referred to the Duc de Choiseul, who endeavoured to arrange a settlement between the two countries on the same lines as that arrived at between France and Spain. Lord Weymouth refused to negotiate on this basis; whereupon the Duc de Choiseul promised the Spanish Government the support of France in the event of war with Great Britain.

At this point, however, it became clear that Lord Weymouth was unable to carry his Government with him in his warlike schemes, and he was obliged to resign office. At the same time, Louis XV again intervened, dismissing the Duc de Choiseul, and declaring to the King of Spain his intention of preserving peace with other Powers if possible. Negotiations were reopened between Great Britain and France, and eventually, by a Convention of 22 January 1771, the Spanish Government agreed to make complete restitution, but with a reservation that the engagement "to restore to His Britannic Majesty the possession of the fort and port called Egmont cannot nor ought any wise to affect the question of the prior right of the sovereignty of the Malvinas Islands, otherwise called Falkland Islands".

Lord Rochford, the new Secretary of State, in his reply, took no notice of this reservation, which therefore stood on record without being controverted. On this ground mainly Lord North's Government was strongly attacked in Parliament and outside. Lord Chatham, among others, took a hand in Parliament, declaring that Port Egmont alone had been restored, and not the Falkland Islands; while outside Parliament "Junius" wrote against the Ministry, who were defended by Dr Johnson in "Thoughts on the late Transactions respecting Falkland Islands".

A British ship of war, the *Juno*, was forthwith sent out, with two smaller vessels, to have the Agreement duly carried into effect; and on 16 September 1771, the commander of the *Juno* was formally placed in possession of the station by the Spanish officer on the spot. A sloop, with some seamen and marines, was left to hold it; but the number of the garrison was reduced in the next year; and in 1774 the garrison was withdrawn altogether, while leaving behind "the proper marks or signals of possession and of its belonging to the Crown of Great Britain". Port Egmont was abandoned on 20 May 1774, but the British flag was left flying; and the commanding officer affixed to the door of the blockhouse an inscription engraved in lead, in the following terms:

> BE IT KNOWN TO ALL NATIONS
>
> That Falkland Islands, with this fort, the storehouses, wharfs, harbours, bays, and creeks thereunto belonging, are the sole right and property of His Most Sacred Majesty, George the Third ... In witness whereof this plate is set up, and His Britannic Majesty's colours left flying as a mark of possession.

It should be added that, in 1775, Captain Cook took possession of South Georgia, and gave it its name.

It is not clear how long the Spaniards remained at Port Soledad; they are said to have used the Falklands as a place for deportation of convicts; but, at any rate, there is no question that by 1810 the islands were left without any European garrison or permanent inhabitants. In 1820 the Republic of Buenos Aires established a settlement at Port Louis (or Soledad). By this time the development of the seal fishery had led to the islands being frequented by ships of various nations, especially American. In 1829, Louis Vernet, the Governor of the settlement at Port Louis, in virtue of the exclusive right to the seal fishery which he claimed, warned off American vessels; and in 1831 he followed this up by seizing some of the ships and detaining their officers and crews. Thereupon the commander of an American ship of war, the *Lexington*, sailed from Buenos Aires to Port Louis, and on 31 December 1831, broke up the settlement.

GREAT BRITAIN TAKES POSSESSION

At the end of November 1832, HM sloop *Clio* was sent from the British squadron on the South American station. She reached Port Egmont on 20 December 1832, and during his stay the commander set up an inscription on a board:

> Visited by HBMS *Clio* for the purpose of exercising the right of sovereignty over these islands, December 23, 1832.

After ten days' stay the *Clio* sailed on to Port Louis; and on 3 January 1833, the British flag was hoisted and possession was taken. At the same date another British ship, the *Tyne*, visited Port Egmont, and a similar ceremony took place. Since that time the Falkland Islands have remained continuously and without interruption a British possession.

In March 1833, almost immediately after the visit of the *Clio* and the hoisting of the British flag, the *Beagle*, under the command of Captain Robert FitzRoy, and having on board Charles Darwin (whose name is perpetuated in Port Darwin), arrived at Port Louis, paying a second visit to the islands in March of the following year, 1834. FitzRoy's instructions included an order to make a sketch or running survey of the Falklands and to note the best harbours. The instructions were duly carried out; and the map, which is given in the Parliamentary Papers of 1841 and 1843, relating to the Falklands, was based upon the surveys which were made in 1834. FitzRoy's narrative of his memorable voyage gives a full description of the islands and an excellent account of their history and the political controversies up to date, as well as a notice of the Vernet settlement, which appears to have been a praiseworthy and substantial effort to form a colony.

For a few months after the British occupation Port Louis was left in charge of Mr Matthew Brisbane, Vernet's partner or agent, who had accompanied Weddell on his Antarctic expedition. He was murdered by a gang of Gauchos and Indians on 26 August 1833, as is told in FitzRoy's narrative. In January 1834 a naval officer was placed in authority, and the islands remained under the Admiralty until 1842. A body of opinion grew up in favour of taking steps to colonise the islands; concessions were sought for; a Falkland Islands Association was formed; and the need for a fully constituted Government on the spot to administer law and keep order became more and more apparent. The question was referred to the Colonial Land and Emigration Commissioners, whose report, dated 22 August 1840, enumerated four grounds upon which the establishment of a regular colony had been urged—the usefulness of having a port of refuge for merchant ships plying round Cape Horn, the expediency of a port roughly halfway between the two oceans for the South American Squadron, the advantages of the islands for a penal station, and their general fitness as a settlement for agricultural and commercial purposes. The first three reasons were fully endorsed; as to the fourth, the Commissioners were in doubt, their final conclusion being that "the Falkland Islands would be able to support a small body of colonists of frugal and industrious habits". Settlers from the Orkneys and the Hebrides were suggested. The Colonial Office was opposed to the idea of a penal station, but favoured the establishment of a colony, and recommended a Parliamentary grant to cover the expenses of government. The Admiralty concurred; so did the Treasury; and in the first instance a Lieutenant-Governor was appointed under the Colonial Office in August 1841. This was Lieutenant Moody, RE, who reached Port Louis in January 1842.

After some hopeful reports from Moody, the Government took further action. On 11 April 1843, an Act of Parliament was passed "to enable Her Majesty to provide for the government of her settlements on the coast of Africa and in the Falkland Islands". Under this Act, Letters Patent and Royal Instructions were issued in the following June; Moody was appointed Governor; provision was made for a Legislature; and the Falkland Islands became a Crown colony of the ordinary type, with Governor, Executive

Council, and Legislative Council, as they have since remained.

FitzRoy had noted the excellence of Port William; and the question arose as to whether Port Louis or Port William should be made the chief centre. In 1842 Captain James Ross, on his Antarctic expedition, visited the islands in his ship, the *Erebus*, having, like FitzRoy, on board his vessel a scientist, afterwards of high distinction, the late Sir Joseph Hooker. Hooker was consulted as to the respective merits of the two ports, and unhesitatingly preferred Port William. Moody held that the country surrounding Port Louis, which was renamed Anson, was far more favourable for settlement than the vicinity of Port William, and recommended that the seat of government should be kept for the time at Port Louis, though he recognised that Port William must become the chief port of the islands. On hearing these views, Lord Stanley, Secretary of State for the Colonies, decided in favour of Port William, and on 23 March 1843, sent instructions to move the headquarters to that place as soon as possible. This was done, and in 1844 the capital of the colony was fixed at Stanley Harbour in Port William inlet, the name Stanley superseding the older name.

ECONOMIC PROGRESS OF THE COLONY

The Blue Book report for 1846 gave a population of only about 270, including 106 immigrants introduced by Mr Lafone, a rich merchant resident in Montevideo. By a contract with the Crown, dated 16 March 1846, Lafone was granted, for the sum of £60,000, payable in instalments, the concession of a very large tract in East Falkland, estimated at first at about one-third of the whole island, and the possession for six years of all the wild cattle and stock in the islands. This agreement was modified by a new contract of 9 January 1850, and shortly afterwards Lafone transferred his rights to a company, the Falkland Islands Company, whose charter dates from 23 December 1851, and which has since played an outstanding part in the history and the life of the colony.

From about 1867 onwards sheep-farming became more and more the predominating industry of the Falklands. Sheep took the place of wild cattle, Scotsmen of South American Gauchos; and at the end of the nineteenth century wool was the one export of the colony.

Meanwhile South Georgia was visited by sealers and also by scientific expeditions; and, as the result of the Swedish Antarctic expedition of 1902, Captain Larsen, a Norwegian, succeeded in 1904 in forming a company in Buenos Aires and establishing a whaling station in South Georgia. This was followed by other companies, mostly Norwegian, for exploiting the whale fisheries in these seas, with the result that the whale oil and produce, which comes from or through the Falklands, represents something like half the output of the world, and the trade returns of the colony show an enormous increase on former years. For some years prior to 1906 the chief British company, Messrs Salvesen and Co., of Leith, operated in West Falkland as well as in the Dependencies, but the Dependencies supply the main bulk of the trade.

PART II

✦

THE FALKLAND ISLANDS REVIEW

REPORT OF A COMMITTEE
OF PRIVY COUNSELLORS

CHAIRED BY

LORD FRANKS

JANUARY 1983

INTRODUCTION

On 6 July 1982, the Government decided to appoint a committee of Privy Counsellors, under the chairmanship of Lord Franks, with the following terms of reference:

> To review the way in which the responsibilities of Government in relation to the Falkland Islands and their Dependencies were discharged in the period leading up to the Argentine invasion of the Falkland Islands on 2 April 1982, taking account of all such factors in previous years as are relevant; and to report.

The Committee met for the first time on 26 July and held 42 meetings, and was provided with the following documents:

(i) folders of all the relevant papers that the Prime Minister personally saw from the time the present Government took office to 2 April 1982;

(ii) all relevant Cabinet and Cabinet Committee papers and minutes of meetings from 1965 onwards;

(iii) detailed memoranda prepared by the Foreign and Commonwealth Office Research Department on the history of the dispute from 1965, various other papers and, for the period from the beginning of 1976 onwards, a comprehensive set of documents;

(iv) a comprehensive set of Ministry of Defence documents covering the period from 1965;

(v) comprehensive sets of Treasury, Department of Energy, Home Office and Department of Trade documents;

(vi) every report from the intelligence agencies relating to the Falkland Islands from the beginning of 1981 until 2 April 1982, and a large number of reports from previous years, including all those circulated in 1976 and 1977; and

(vii) every assessment on Argentina and the Falkland Islands made by the Joint Intelligence Organisation since 1965, together with any relevant minutes of meetings.

In addition, at the Committee's request, all relevant Foreign and Commonwealth Office and Ministry of Defence files for the first three months of 1982 were placed in the

Committee's offices for the duration of the review. They also asked for, and received, papers on a number of specific aspects of their remit, and were provided with reports from the intelligence agencies received after 2 April that threw light on the events leading up to the invasion. Any files for previous years were freely available for their inspection, and they took advantage of this facility to obtain a number of documents that they thought relevant. They received every assistance from all Departments in their review, and all their requests for additional papers and information were met.

On 26 July the Committee invited anyone who had information which might assist it in considering its remit to submit evidence in writing by 30 August 1982. The Committee also wrote to the editors of all the national newspapers, to the Secretary of the Newspaper Society, and to several periodicals asking whether they had any specific information in the first three months of the year which indicated the possibility of Argentine action against the Falkland Islands.

The Committee decided that, in addition to reading the documents, they should talk to those principally involved, both Ministers and officials, in the development of the present Government's Falkland Islands policy; to some Ministers of previous administrations, including all the former Prime Ministers for the period covered by the review; to persons with a special knowledge of and interest in the area; to representatives of the broadcasting media; and to some journalists.

The main body of the report is in four sections. The first section contains an account of the dispute between the United Kingdom and Argentina from 1965 to 1979; the second describes in more detail the sequence of events and the development of policy since the present Government took office; the third contains a detailed account of events from the landing of a party of Argentine scrap merchants on South Georgia on 19 March 1982 to the invasion of the Falkland Islands on 2 April; and the final section sets out the judgments reached. Annex A contains a refutation of some of the more important assertions and allegations that have been made in the press and elsewhere.

In the Committee's review it has taken particular care to avoid the exercise of hindsight in reaching judgments on the development of policy and on the actions of Ministers and officials. It has sought to judge on each important issue whether the views expressed and the action taken by those concerned were reasonable in the light of the information available to them and the circumstances prevailing at the time, and not to substitute its judgment of what might have been done in those circumstances.

It has also borne in mind that its task required its members to focus exclusively on the Government's responsibilities for the Falkland Islands and the Dependencies, whereas those concerned, both Ministers and officials, had to deal with many other major and pressing preoccupations.

AN ACCOUNT OF THE DISPUTE
FROM 1965 TO 1979

This section summarises the principal events from 1965 until the present [Thatcher] Government took office in 1979. The events of 1976 and 1977 are described in more detail than those of other years, since before 1981 this was a time of particular tension between Argentina and the United Kingdom, and parallels have been drawn between these two years and 1982.

1965–1975

In 1963 and 1964 there was a resurgence of Argentine interest in the Falklands and a campaign was mounted in Argentina in support of its claim to the Islands. In addition to various official measures, such as the inauguration of a "Malvinas Day", an Argentine civilian landed a light aircraft at Port Stanley in September 1964, planted an Argentine flag in the ground, handed a proclamation to a bystander, and took off again. The Argentine Government publicly dissociated themselves from this incident.

In 1964 the Argentine Government raised the matter in the United Nations, in a sub-committee of the Special Committee on the situation with regard to the implementation of the Declaration of the Granting of Independence to Colonial Countries and Peoples (The Committee of 24). In reply the British Representative on The Committee of 24 declared that the British Government held that the question of sovereignty over the Islands was not negotiable, but they were willing to discuss the maintenance and development of peaceful relations between the United Kingdom and the Falkland Islands on the one hand and Argentina on the other. Following the Special Committee's report, a Resolution (No. 2065) was passed on 16 December 1965 at the General Assembly. It referred in its preamble to the "cherished aim of bringing to an end everywhere colonialism in all its forms, one of which covers the case of the Falkland Islands (Malvinas)"; invited the Governments of Argentina and of the United Kingdom to proceed without delay with negotiations with a view to finding a peaceful solution to the problem "bearing in mind the provisions and objectives of the Charter of the

United Nations and of Resolution 154(XV) [on colonial-ism] and in the interests of the population of the Falkland Islands (Malvinas)"; and requested the two Governments to report to the Special Committee, and to the General Assembly at its next session.

In March 1965 the Joint Intelligence Committee (see Annex B) had re-assessed the external threat to the Falkland Islands and Dependencies. It considered that it was unlikely that the Argentine Government would launch an assault against the Islands, but that, if an unofficial party of raiders were able to obtain a footing on the Falklands, the attitude of the Argentine Government might change radically and rapidly under pressure of public opinion.

The Argentine claim to the Islands was raised with the Foreign Secretary, Mr Michael Stewart (as he then was), when he visited Buenos Aires in January 1966; and in July a preliminary meeting was held in London, at which the Argentine Ambassador submitted a note formally claiming the "restitution" of the Falkland Islands to Argentina. The British delegation rejected the implication that Britain's occupation of the Islands was illegal, but there was agree-ment that there should be detailed examination at a later date of ways of decreasing friction and of limiting the scale of the dispute.

In September 1966 a further unofficial incident, known as "Operation Condor", took place. An armed group of 20 young Argentines hijacked an Argentine Airlines DC4 and forced it to go to the Falklands, where it landed on the race-course at Port Stanley. As in 1964, the Argentine Government publicly dissociated themselves from the inci-dent, but there were demonstrations throughout Argentina in support of the Argentine claim to the Islands, and shots were fired at the British Embassy in Buenos Aires while the Duke of Edinburgh was on an official visit there. In the light of the Condor incident, the Royal Marine detachment on the Islands, which had been established in 1965 but reduced to one officer and five men in 1966, was restored to platoon strength. Although consideration was subsequently given from time to time to its withdrawal, it was retained at that level thereafter.

Further talks were held in November 1966, and in 1967. In a paper to the Defence and Oversea Policy Committee in preparation for the talks in November 1966, the Foreign and Colonial Secretaries (Mr George Brown and Mr Fred Lee (as they then were)) pointed out that Argentina could easily occupy the Islands by force. At the talks the British side initially proposed a "sovereignty freeze" for a minimum of 30 years, to allow for normalisation of relations between the Islands and Argentina while each side's position on sovereignty was protected. At the end of this period the Islanders would be free to choose between British and Argentine rule. The Argentine Government rejected this proposal, and in March 1967 the British Government for the first time stated formally to Argentina that they would be prepared to cede sovereignty over the Islands under certain conditions, provided that the wishes of the Islanders were respected. Negotiations at official level were directed to agreeing the text, *ad referendum* to Governments, of a "Memorandum of Understanding". Early in 1968 the Governor of the Falkland Islands showed the Islands' Executive Council in confidence the text of an early version of the Memorandum. On 27 February 1968 the unofficial members of the Council sent an open letter to all Members of Parliament stating that negotiations were proceeding between the British and Argentine Governments "which may result at any moment in the handing over of the Falkland Islands to the Argentines".* There were strong protests in Parliament and in the press, and the Foreign and Commonwealth Secretary, Mr Stewart, and other Foreign Office Ministers made clear on several occasions that there would be no cession of sovereignty against the wishes of the Islanders.

Agreement on the text of the Memorandum of Understanding was reached at official level in August 1968. On sovereignty the crucial passage was as follows:

> The Government of the United Kingdom as part of such a final settlement will recognise Argentina's sovereignty over the Islands from a date to be agreed. This date will be agreed as soon as possible after (i) the two governments have resolved the present divergence between them as to the criteria according to which the United Kingdom Government shall consider whether the interests of the Islanders would be secured by the safeguards and guarantees to be offered by the Argentine Government, and (ii) the Government of the United Kingdom are then satisfied that those interests are so secured.

Publication of the Memorandum was to be accompanied by a unilateral statement making it clear that the Government would be willing to proceed to a final settlement with Argentina that involved the transfer of sovereignty, but only if and when they were satisfied that the transfer of sovereignty,

---

* In March 1968 in response to these events the Falkland Islands Emergency Committee, an unofficial body, was formed to bring to notice in the United Kingdom the wishes of the Falkland Islanders regarding their future. In 1973 it was renamed the United Kingdom Falkland Islands Committee. Its membership includes Members of Parliament of the main political parties.

and the basis on which such a transfer should take place, were acceptable to the people of the Islands.

Lord Chalfont, Minister of State at the Foreign and Commonwealth Office, visited the Islands in November 1968 to explain the policy that the Government had been pursuing in their talks with the Argentine Government. On his return the Government made statements in both Houses of Parliament on 3 December 1968 about Lord Chalfont's visit. They received a critical reception and were widely reported in the press. In view of the Parliamentary and press reaction, the Government decided at a Cabinet meeting on 11 December not to continue to attempt to reach a settlement on the basis of the Memorandum of Understanding, since Argentina was not prepared to accept either that the Memorandum should include a statement that any transfer of sovereignty would be subject to the wishes of the Islanders; or that the unilateral statement, enshrining this safeguard, should be specifically linked to the Memorandum. It was recognised, however, that failure to reach an understanding with Argentina carried the risks of increased harassment of the Islanders and the possibility of an attack. The Government therefore decided to endeavour to continue negotiations with Argentina while making clear the British attitude on sovereignty. Mr Stewart made a statement in Parliament later the same day, which announced the decision to continue negotiations and which confirmed that the British Government would continue to insist on the paramountcy of the Islanders' wishes.

In 1969 talks were resumed. They were continued, following the change of Government in June 1970, by Mr Heath's administration, but sovereignty was not discussed. Progress was reported to Parliament annually. The talks were concerned with improving communications between Argentina and the Islands and were held without prejudice to either side's position on sovereignty. (This was known as the "sovereignty umbrella".) In 1971 agreement was reached on a wide range of communications matters, of which the most important was the establishment of air and sea services between the Islands and Argentina, to be provided by Argentina and the United Kingdom respectively. Other matters covered in the Agreements were the provision by Argentina of a travel document (the "white card"), which would guarantee freedom of movement within Argentina for residents of the Islands and serve as the only documentation necessary for Argentine residents travelling to the Islands; certain reciprocal exemptions from duties and taxes; exemption for residents of the Islands from any obligation to Argentine military service; the harmonisation of postal, telegraphic and telephone rates with the rates obtaining in the country of origin; provision of school places and scholarships in Argentina for children in the Islands; and the establishment of a special consultative committee in Buenos Aires, consisting of representatives of the Argentine Ministry of Foreign Affairs and the British Embassy, to deal with questions arising over the setting up and promotion of communications in both directions. The Agreements were set out in a joint statement signed by both Governments, the text of which was reported to the House of Commons in September 1971.

Following the Agreements, the Argentine Government returned to the question of sovereignty, and in January 1972 called for a resumption of the talks held between 1966 and 1968. They said that they would accept further talks on communications only if the British Government accepted later discussions on sovereignty in London.

Nevertheless, in a separate agreement concluded in May 1972, the Argentine authorities undertook to build a temporary airstrip (which came into operation in November 1972) to enable land-based aircraft to replace the amphibian service that they had provided up to then.

Further exchanges followed, in which the Argentine Government pressed strongly for renewed negotiations on sovereignty while the British Government sought to establish that the talks did not constitute negotiations on that issue. In the course of 1973, however, it became clear that an impasse had been reached. Argentina again took the issue to the United Nations, where the Special Committee adopted a resolution, which formed the basis of a further Resolution (3160(XXVIII)) passed by the General Assembly calling on both parties to accelerate negotiations towards a solution of the sovereignty issue. In January 1974 the Defence Committee agreed that, in view of the pressure in the United Nations to reach a settlement and the risks of economic and military action against the Islands, the likely attitude of the Islanders to the possibility of condominium★ as an alternative to a transfer of sovereignty should be discussed with the Governor of the Falkland Islands. The Governor and the British Ambassador in Buenos Aires advised that in their opinion the idea was worth pursuing. Before this could be done, the General Election of March 1974 led to a change of Government. A Labour Government took office, with Mr Wilson (as he then was) as Prime Minister and Mr Callaghan as Foreign and Commonwealth Secretary.

★ Joint control of a state's affairs vested in others.

The new Government, having been presented with a range of options, decided in the Defence Committee to consult the Falkland Islands Executive Council on the possibility of initiating talks with Argentina on condominium. The Council indicated that it would raise no objection to talks on condominium going ahead, provided that there was no Islander participation initially. The subject of condominium was broached with the Argentine Government; but, in the face of the Islanders' continuing refusal to participate, it was decided that there would be no purpose in proceeding without them, and the Argentine Government were so informed in August 1974. Despite this setback, further commercial agreements were concluded in September 1974, the most important being one providing for *Yaciementos Petroliferos*, the Argentine State Oil Company, to supply certain petroleum products on the Islands at mainland prices.

In December 1974 an Argentine newspaper, *Cronica*, mounted a press campaign advocating invasion of the Islands. The Argentine Government publicly dissociated themselves from it, their Minister for Foreign Affairs, Sr Vignes, informing Congress that he preferred negotiation to invasion. Nevertheless, following remarks made by Sr Vignes to the press in March 1975, a few days before the arrival of the new British Ambassador in Buenos Aires, the Ambassador was instructed to warn him that an attack on the Islands would meet with a military response. The British Ambassador delivered this warning to Sr Vignes in April 1975, at his first meeting with him.

Over the period from 1965 to 1975 assessments were made by the Joint Intelligence Committee, usually about once a year but more frequently at times of increased tension. In the earlier years the conclusions were, broadly speaking, that official military action against the Falkland Islands and the Dependencies was unlikely, at least until diplomatic means of settling the dispute had been exhausted, but that there was a continuing risk of unofficial action. In the early 1970s, when the Communications Agreements had led to improved relations with Argentina, the assessments were that direct military action could be discounted and that even the risk of an "adventurist" operation was very slight. Towards the end of 1973 it was thought that Argentine attitudes were hardening, and for the first time there were indications that the Argentine Government (of President Peron) might be preparing contingency plans for an occupation of the Islands. In 1974 the Joint Intelligence Committee assessed that "adventurist" operations were still the main threat, but with less likelihood of the Argentine Government's discouraging them; official military action was thought unlikely, as long as Argentina believed that the British Government were prepared to negotiate on sovereignty, but it was not ruled out.

INCREASED TENSION 1975–1977

The next British initiative was a proposal, approved by the Defence Committee in July 1975, for discussions of joint Anglo-Argentine development of the resources of the South West Atlantic. In response to this proposal Sr Vignes suggested linking such an initiative to the possibility of a transfer of sovereignty followed by simultaneous leaseback for a period of years, as a means of settling the dispute. He also proposed that Argentina should occupy the uninhabited islands of South Georgia and the South Sandwich Islands, and that the occupation should be accepted without condemnation by the British Government. Sr Vignes was warned that any such unilateral action would be quite unacceptable. The Argentine Government rejected the Government's proposal for talks on economic co-operation, which they saw as excluding discussion of the sovereignty issue.

As a result of growing concern about the decline of the Falkland Islands' economy and the Islands' loss of population, the Government commissioned a comprehensive, long-term economic survey, under the leadership of Lord Shackleton, of the possibilities for the development of the Falkland Islands and the Dependencies. The terms of reference for the survey were drawn up in consultation with the Falkland Islands Executive Council and were announced in October 1975. This provoked a very hostile reaction in Argentina. The Argentine Ministry of Foreign Affairs issued a *communiqué* stating that the survey was an unwelcome initiative, to which Argentina had not agreed. The survey went ahead and the Shackleton Report was published in May 1976.

On 8 December 1975 the Argentine Representative at the United Nations made a long speech on the dispute at a plenary session of the General Assembly, in which he said:

> We are prepared to continue our efforts, but the limits of our patience and tolerance should not be underestimated if we should have to face an obstinate and unjustified refusal to negotiate by the other party.

He concluded by saying:

> The Argentine Government reserves its position regarding
> the responsibility which rests with the British Government
> for the breaking-off of negotiations and will not fail to assert
> its rights in the form which it deems most appropriate.

On 2 January 1976 the Argentine Foreign Minister, then
Sr Arauz Castex, sent a reply to messages from
Mr Callaghan about the Shackleton survey. Sr Arauz Castex
described the arrival in the Islands of Lord Shackleton's
team on the anniversary of their "illegal occupation" by
Britain in 1833 as an "unfriendly and unthoughtful"
coincidence; expressed the Argentine Government's understanding that the British Government had unilaterally
broken off negotiations; and referred to the "decidedly negative implications" of the British Government's attitude, and
to their exclusive responsibility for breaking off negotiations. In giving this message to the British Ambassador in
Buenos Aires, Sr Arauz Castex said that, if the British
Government refused to resume negotiations,

> we were rapidly moving towards a head-on collision ... in
> the end he could only see one course open to Argentina
> irrespective of what Government might be in power ...
> Fortified by the support of the entire Argentine nation as
> well as all the other nations of the world assembled in New
> York, his Government could accept no responsibility for
> such a disastrous outcome.

On the same day the Argentine Ministry of Foreign Affairs
issued a press *communiqué* referring to the British
Government's unilateral breaking off of negotiations and
concluding:

> The people of the Republic should take note that its
> Government, together with the armed forces and the other
> institutional organisations which make up the Argentine
> State, share an unbreakable zeal for the defence of the
> dignity and rights of the nation, and that they will act
> without precipitation but with all the persistence, prudence
> and energy which may be necessary to achieve justice.

Mr Callaghan sent a conciliatory reply to Sr Arauz Castex on 12 January, in which he offered to send a senior official to hold confidential discussions. The Argentine reply on 13 January expressed regret at not finding in it any "positive elements" with regard to the reopening of negotiations on sovereignty, and took exception to Mr Callaghan's reference to a "sterile" dispute. It was announced in a press *communiqué* the same day that the Argentine Government had decided not to send their Ambassador back to London and to "suggest" that the British Ambassador in Buenos Aires should be withdrawn.

There was hostile press comment in Argentina in the first weeks of 1976. The British Embassy in Buenos Aires reported that some newspapers had advocated invasion "in veiled terms". Some of the popular newspapers, evidently briefed by the Argentine Ministry of Foreign Affairs, published reports in the middle of the month of a long meeting which the Argentine Foreign Minister had held to consider counter-measures. Unspecified "firm" and "concrete" decisions were promised. But the British Embassy reported on 21 January that, while the Argentine popular press "had been waging their usual campaign over the Islands over the last couple of weeks", there had been no repetition of the invasion campaign run by *Cronica* the previous year. A further report a week later stated that the storm that had

blown up at the beginning of the month had at last begun
to abate; there were indications that the Argentine
Government had not wished to allow the "anti-British
bandwagon" to get out of control; there had been no threats
or demonstrations against the Embassy.

Mr Callaghan made a statement in the Commons on
14 January 1976 in conciliatory terms, concluding that
"given goodwill on both sides, Britain and Argentina
should be able to transform the area of dispute concerning
sovereignty over the Islands into a factor making for co-
operation between the two countries which would be
consonant with the wishes and interests of the Falkland
Islanders".

Intelligence reports and assessments

In November 1975 the Joint Intelligence Committee had
prepared a new assessment on the Falkland Islands. It concluded that a deliberately planned invasion of the
Falkland Islands in the near future still seemed unlikely
but could not be wholly excluded. It followed earlier
assessments in judging that there was a greater possibility
of some kind of "adventurist" operation, particularly if
the Shackleton survey went ahead in the face of continued public Argentine opposition: this opposition might
be expressed by a propaganda campaign and possibly
some practical harassment of the Falkland Islanders; the
suspension of the air service would be an easy measure for
Argentina to take.

In a further assessment on 8 January 1976 the Joint
Intelligence Committee concluded that Argentina was
unlikely to launch a sudden invasion in the near future,
but that the likelihood had increased of the Argentine

Government's intensifying political pressures and taking specific measures, such as the recall of Ambassadors and the suspension of the air service. It concluded that physical aggression remained a remoter prospect, but certainly could not be excluded. On 22 January 1976 a further assessment was prepared of the events leading up to the withdrawal of Ambassadors. It judged that the Army and Navy commanders were against any military action which might help Sra Peron's régime to stay in power; and noted that an Argentine Ministry of Foreign Affairs announcement on 8 January that the Argentine Government were going ahead immediately with the extension of the airstrip suggested that they did not wish, at least for the time being, to interfere with communications. It assessed, however, that, although there might be a short lull, further counter-measures against British interests, in the form of more hostile political and economic pressure, were possible in due course. The likelihood of an "adventurist" operation had increased. The assessment concluded that military operations remained a more remote possibility but, as the sequence of counter-measures proceeded, must be regarded as that much nearer. An intelligence report of 23 January 1976 referring to a meeting in December 1975 indicated that the armed forces commanders had at that stage ruled out invasion.

RRS Shackleton

In December 1975 the British Naval *Attaché* in Buenos Aires had been warned by the Chief of the Argentine Naval Staff that the RRS *Shackleton*, an unarmed research ship engaged on a programme of international scientific research unconnected with Lord Shackleton's mission, would be arrested if she entered "Argentine waters" (i.e. within

200 miles of the Argentine coast or continental shelf, which in Argentina's view included the waters surrounding the Falkland Islands). In February 1976 an Argentine destroyer fired shots at the RRS *Shackleton* when she was 78 miles south of Port Stanley, and attempted, unsuccessfully, to arrest her. Subsequent intelligence indicated that plans for the interception had been in existence for about six weeks; that the decision had been taken by the armed forces, not the Government; and that Admiral Massera, the Commander-in-Chief of the Argentine Navy, had authorised firing into the ship but without causing casualties or sinking it. The Joint Intelligence Committee assessed the purpose of the operation as being an assertion of Argentine sovereignty over the Falkland Islands and their surrounding waters, in order to bring pressure to bear on the British Government to negotiate. It also judged that the armed forces commanders were opposed to military invasion, and concluded that the Argentine Government intended to follow a policy of "continued pin-pricks", which could bring about a progressive deterioration in Anglo-Argentine relations.

On 11 February 1976 Mr Rowlands, Minister of State at the Foreign and Commonwealth Office, went to New York for talks with the new Argentine Foreign Minister, at which he was instructed by Mr Callaghan to ask what proposals the Argentines had about discussions on sovereignty and to make it plain that the British Government "would defend the Islands if the Argentines attempted to use force". Despite the RRS *Shackleton* incident the talks were satisfactory. Mr Rowlands obtained an assurance that the final leg of the RRS *Shackleton's* programme would not be interfered with; and it was agreed in principle that the dialogue on the Falklands dispute should in due course be resumed.

Defence considerations

As explained earlier, a detachment of Royal Marines has been stationed at Port Stanley since 1965. In addition, over the period an ice-patrol vessel was stationed in the area during the Antarctic summer months, which, in addition to her guardship role, undertook hydrographic and other work in the area of the Falkland Islands and the Dependencies. HMS *Endurance* was brought into service in this capacity in 1967, when she replaced HMS *Protector*. She is armed with two 20-mm Oerlikon guns and carries two Wasp (in 1976 Whirlwind) helicopters equipped with air-to-sea missiles. One consequence of the 1974 Defence Review, which resulted in a phased rundown of overseas commitments outside NATO, was a decision to take HMS *Endurance* out of service. Following the RRS *Shackleton* incident, however, the Secretary of State for Defence, Mr Roy Mason, agreed to one further deployment of HMS *Endurance*. Following later representations from successive Foreign and Commonwealth Secretaries she was subsequently retained on an annual basis, until 1978, when the Secretary of State for Defence, then Mr Fred Mulley, agreed to two further deployments, in 1979/80 and 1980/81.

In February 1976, in view of the increasing risk of hostile action by Argentina, Mr Mason agreed to a proposal from Mr Callaghan for the deployment to the area of a frigate with Royal Fleet Auxiliary* support.

In the same month, with a view to discussion in the Defence Committee, Mr Callaghan asked Mr Mason for "a full and up-to-date military assessment on possible military options and limitations" considering the range of possible

---

*A Royal Fleet Auxiliary is a civilian manned Royal Navy support vessel.

deployments in a number of eventualities, including a determined Argentine assault intended to eject the British garrison. A paper on military options to counter possible Argentine actions was approved by the Chiefs of Staff on 19 February 1976 and circulated as an annex to a paper for the Defence Committee.

The Chief of Staffs paper drew attention to the fact that air reinforcement was ruled out by the limitations of the airstrip at Port Stanley; the adverse weather conditions there; its distance from Ascension Island; and the likely unavailability of South American airfields in the event of a conflict. To dislodge Argentine occupation of part of the Falkland Islands or the Dependencies would require an amphibious force with embarked troops. It would not be practicable to provide, transport and support the force necessary in the Islands to ensure that a determined Argentine attempt to eject the British garrison was unsuccessful. To recover the Islands by military means, though far from impossible, would be a major operation at very long range. The least force for this purpose would be of Brigade Group strength, the transport of which would entail the use of all the Navy's amphibious resources, a sizeable Task Force, including HMS *Ark Royal*, and substantial logistic support.

Resumption of negotiations (in confidence)

In the light of the deterioration of relations with Argentina, and the agreement in principle reached between Mr Rowlands and the Argentine Foreign Minister in New York, Mr Callaghan decided to undertake a major review of policy. In March 1976 the Defence Committee and the Cabinet approved his proposals for a fresh dialogue on all aspects of the dispute, both the possibilities of Anglo-Argentine economic co-operation in the South West Atlantic and "the nature of a hypothetical future constitutional relationship".

Once Argentina had been informed that the Government were prepared to resume negotiations, including discussion of sovereignty, the threat of military action receded. Exploratory talks with Argentina were held in confidence at official level in July and August 1976. By then, following a *coup* on 23 March 1976, Argentina was under the rule of a military Junta, which, with changes in membership, remained in power.

In July 1976 the Joint Intelligence Committee assessed the Argentine political situation in the light of events since the military *coup* in March. On the Falklands it concluded that Argentina might have unduly high expectations of the current negotiations. If these were dashed, it could be expected to return to a more aggressive approach, initially in the United Nations. It assessed, however, that it was most unlikely that the Argentine Government would react by taking military action against the Islands. This assessment derived from intelligence that it was the view of President Videla and others that, if it proved impossible to reach a solution through bilateral negotiations, Argentina would be obliged to seek a solution via the United Nations.

In December 1976 the United Nations General Assembly passed another Resolution (31/49 (XXXI)) approving a further report of the Special Committee; expressing "its gratitude for the continuous efforts made by the Government of Argentina ... to facilitate the process of decolonization and to promote the well-being of the population of the Islands"; and requesting the Governments of Argentina and the United Kingdom to expedite the negotiations and to report to the Secretary-General and to the

General Assembly as soon as possible on the results. The Resolution was passed by 102 votes to one (the United Kingdom) with 32 abstentions.

Southern Thule

On 20 December 1976 a helicopter from HMS *Endurance* discovered the existence of an Argentine military presence on Southern Thule in the South Sandwich Islands. An intelligence report indicated that the presence was probably established the previous month with the approval of the naval Commander-in-Chief. On 5 January 1977 the Argentine *Chargé d'Affaires* in London was summoned to the Foreign and Commonwealth Office and asked by the head of the Latin America Department to explain the Argentine presence. At the same time the British *Chargé d'Affaires* in Buenos Aires was instructed to seek an explanation from the Argentine Ministry of Foreign Affairs.

On 14 January 1977 the Argentine Ministry of Foreign Affairs delivered a communication to the British *Chargé d'Affaires* in the form of a *bout de papier* claiming that the purpose of the operation was to establish a station with a view to scientific investigation within the jurisdiction of Argentine sovereignty and expressing the hope that nothing would cloud the "auspicious perspectives" for negotiations. The *bout de papier* also stated that the station's permanency would depend on the practicability of the tasks undertaken, although the official delivering it hinted that it would not be permanent. A formal protest was delivered on 19 January 1977 stating that the British Government considered the establishment of the scientific station, without prior reference to the British authorities, a violation of British sovereignty; pointing out that the British Government were entitled to expect that the Argentine Government would have approached them before taking action; and expressing the hope that they would learn that the scientific programme was being terminated. The British Government took no steps to make public the Argentine presence on Southern Thule, which did not become known in the United Kingdom until May 1978.

It became clear later in the month that the Argentine presence was larger than the *bout de papier* had indicated. On 27 January 1977 intelligence indicated that the original intention had been to announce the existence of the base in mid or late March, when it was too late for British ships to enter South Atlantic waters. The Argentine expectation had been that the British reaction would have been stronger. If the Argentine personnel had been captured, the British Antarctic Survey party on South Georgia would have been taken off as a reprisal. According to further intelligence, there was an Argentine Navy contingency plan for a joint air force and navy invasion of the Falkland Islands combined with a diplomatic initiative at the United Nations.

The Joint Intelligence Committee assessed the situation on 31 January 1977. It thought it unlikely that the establishment of an Argentine presence on Southern Thule could have been mounted without the approval of the Junta and judged that the Argentine Government's intentions were:

(i) to make a physical demonstration of Argentine sovereignty over the Dependencies;
(ii) to probe the British Government's reaction to such a demonstration; and
(iii) to obtain a bargaining counter in the forthcoming discussions.

The assessment concluded that the Argentine Government were unlikely to order withdrawal until it suited them to do so and, depending on the British Government's actions in the situation, could be encouraged to attempt further military action against British interests in the area.

On 7 February 1977 intelligence indicated that the Argentine Navy's contingency plans had been shelved for the time being on the ground that, although an occupation would have had much to commend it for internal political reasons, Argentina could not count on the support of the Third World or the Communist Bloc.

On 14 February 1977 *Ultima Clave*, a Buenos Aires weekly political news-sheet, published an article about the occupation of an "island" (Southern Thule) in the South Sandwich Islands. Argentina maintained a presence there up to the time of the invasion of the Falkland Islands.

Formal resumption of negotiations

On 2 February 1977 in a statement to Parliament the Foreign and Commonwealth Secretary, Mr Crosland, announced the Government's decision that "the time has come to consider both with the Islanders and the Argentine Government whether a climate exists for discussing the broad issues which bear on the future of the Falkland Islands, and the possibilities of co-operation between Britain and Argentina in the region of the South West Atlantic". He made it clear that in any discussions the Government would reserve their position on sovereignty; that any changes which might be proposed must be acceptable to the Islanders; and that there must be full consultation with the Islanders at every stage. In the same statement, Mr Crosland announced the Government's conclusions on the recommendations in the Shackleton Report. He said that a number of further studies would be set up, but the Government were not prepared to accept the more costly recommendations, notably the enlargement of the airport and lengthening of the runway. Mr Crosland reported to the Cabinet the following day that the statement had been received without controversy.

The Defence Committee approved a proposal by Mr Crosland that, following his statement, a Foreign and Commonwealth Office Minister should visit the Islands and have talks in Buenos Aires. Before the visit, which was made by Mr Rowlands, the Joint Intelligence Committee assessed that, if the talks broke down or ended in deadlock, Argentina might decide on military action against British shipping or the Falkland Islands. In the light of this assessment, Foreign and Commonwealth Office and Ministry of Defence officials considered whether any precautionary measures should be taken. Mr Rowlands was advised that a Royal Navy task group of six warships, three support ships and a submarine would be in the Atlantic, sailing from Gibraltar to the Caribbean, at the time of the talks. Mr Rowlands suggested to the Minister of State at the Ministry of Defence that, if, during his discussions with the Argentine Foreign Minister, the Argentines were to threaten the use of force to further their claims in the South West Atlantic, it might be useful for him to let them know that the task group was in Atlantic waters. Mr Mulley agreed to this proposal on condition that he was consulted again before reference was made to it. In the event, Mr Rowlands judged that it was not necessary to refer to the existence of the task group.

Mr Rowlands visited the Islands in February 1977 and held an intensive round of meetings there. The Island

Councils agreed to co-operate in working out terms of reference for formal negotiations covering political relations, including sovereignty, and economic co-operation, provided that the talks were covered by the "sovereignty umbrella" and that the Islanders were fully consulted. Following Mr Rowlands's subsequent talks in Buenos Aires and further exchanges, agreement on the terms of reference was reached with Argentina in April 1977 and announced by the new Foreign and Commonwealth Secretary, Dr Owen, in the House of Commons on 26 April. They were:

> The Governments of the Argentine Republic and the
> United Kingdom of Great Britain and Northern Ireland
> have agreed to hold negotiations from June or July 1977
> which will concern future political relations, including
> sovereignty, with regard to the Falkland Islands, South
> Georgia and South Sandwich Islands, and economic
> co-operation with regard to the said territories, in particular,
> and the South West Atlantic, in general. In these negotiations
> the issues affecting the future of the Islands will be discussed
> and negotiations will be directed to the working out of a
> peaceful solution to the existing dispute on sovereignty
> between the two states, and the establishment of a
> framework for Anglo-Argentine economic co-operation
> which will contribute substantially to the development of
> the Islands, and the region as a whole.
>
> A major objective of the negotiations will be to achieve a
> stable, prosperous and politically durable future for the
> Islands, whose people the Government of the United
> Kingdom will consult during the course of the negotiations.
>
> The agreement to hold these negotiations, and the
> negotiations themselves, are without prejudice to the
> position of either Government with regard to sovereignty
> over the Islands.

The level at which the negotiations will be conducted, and the times and places at which they will be held, will be determined by agreement between the two Governments. If necessary, special Working Groups will be established.

Before the first round of talks Dr Owen presented a paper to the Defence Committee in July 1977, which argued that serious and substantive negotiations were necessary to keep the Argentines in play, since the Islands were militarily indefensible except by a major, costly and unacceptable diversion of current resources. The Committee took the view that it was likely that the Government would be forced back in the end on some variation of a leaseback solution linked with a programme of joint economic co-operation. The aim should be to keep the negotiations with the Argentine Government going so as to allow time for the education of public opinion at home and in the Islands to be carried forward. Broadly speaking, the Government's strategy was to retain sovereignty as long as possible, if necessary making concessions in respect of the Dependencies and the maritime resources in the area, while recognising that ultimately only some form of leaseback arrangement was likely to satisfy Argentina. The talks, which were held at official level, went reasonably well and the options were kept open. The British side put forward the idea that the sovereignty of the uninhabited Dependencies might be looked at separately from the sovereignty of the Falkland Islands themselves.

Threat of Argentine military action

Before the next round of talks, conducted by Mr Rowlands in New York in December 1977, there were several indications that the Argentine position was hardening. In

September intelligence indicated that the Argentine Government and Ministry of Foreign Affairs considered that they should take a hard line in the talks as they thought the British were using pretexts to delay progress. At the end of September and the beginning of October 1977 Argentine naval units arrested seven Soviet and two Bulgarian fishing vessels in Falklands waters. An Argentine vessel fired on one of the Bulgarian ships, wounding a Bulgarian sailor. It was known that Admiral Massera's orders were to sink the vessel if necessary. He had also said that there would be a similar riposte to intrusions by any other flag carrier and at any other place. The Argentine Naval *Attaché* in London (Admiral Anaya, who later became Commander-in-Chief of the Navy and a member of the Junta) drew this statement to the attention of the Foreign and Commonwealth Office. On the diplomatic front, the British *Chargé d'Affaires* in Buenos Aires was said to have been subjected to a "barrage of *aide-mémoires* and *bouts de papier*" urging the immediate establishment of working groups and other evidence of progress. In addition, the Foreign and Commonwealth Office judged that the failure of the Beagle Channel arbitration—Argentina's other principal foreign policy preoccupation—and its failure to make progress with Brazil in its dispute on the River Plate Basin increased the likelihood of its seeking a success on the Falklands issue.

On 11 October 1977 a Joint Intelligence Committee assessment referred to information that another Argentine naval party was due to land on Southern Thule in the middle of the month. It judged that military action was still unlikely pending the negotiations, although Admiral Massera might act unilaterally against a Royal Fleet

Auxiliary vessel going to Southern Thule. A fuller assessment on 1 November 1977 referred to the increasing resentment in the Ministry of Foreign Affairs of what were seen as the British Government's delaying tactics; and to the militancy of the Navy. The assessment concluded that the military Junta as a whole would prefer to achieve its sovereignty objectives by peaceful means and that, as long as it calculated that the British Government were prepared to negotiate seriously on the issue of sovereignty, it was unlikely to resort to force. If negotiations broke down, or if Argentina concluded from them that there was no prospect of real progress towards a negotiated transfer of sovereignty, there would be a high risk of its then resorting to more forceful measures, including direct military action. The assessment judged that in those circumstances action against British shipping would be the most serious risk; another possibility was the establishment of an Argentine presence on one or more of the Dependencies, which might involve a risk to the British Antarctic Survey base on South Georgia. A private "adventurist" operation against the Falklands, which the Junta might feel obliged to support, was always possible. In the Committee's view invasion of the Falkland Islands was unlikely, but could not be discounted.

Consideration of counter-measures

In the light of the deteriorating situation, the Foreign and Commonwealth Office asked the Ministry of Defence at the end of October 1977 for a paper on the defence implications of the Argentine threat. The Ministry of Defence circulated a paper on 4 November, which had been approved by the Chiefs of Staff, on the military options to counter possible Argentine actions as identified in the Joint

Intelligence Committee's assessment. It followed closely the lines of the paper prepared the previous year and, in relation to the main threats, reached broadly similar conclusions.

In the light of the intelligence assessment Ministers decided at a meeting on 21 November 1977 that a military presence in the area of the Falkland Islands should be established by the time the negotiations began in December. The objective would be to buttress the Government's negotiating position by deploying a force of sufficient strength, available if necessary, to convince the Argentines that military action by them would meet resistance. Such a force would not be able to deal with a determined Argentine attack, but it would be able to respond flexibly to limited acts of aggression. The Committee agreed that secrecy should be maintained about the purpose of the force. One nuclear-powered submarine and two frigates were deployed to the area, the submarine to the immediate vicinity of the Islands with the frigates standing off about a thousand miles away. Rules of engagement were drawn up.

Cabinet Committee papers show clearly that it was agreed that the force should remain covert. We have found no evidence that the Argentine Government ever came to know of its existence. In the event the negotiations went reasonably well. The Argentine threat receded, and it was agreed after the talks that the naval force could be withdrawn. Consideration was subsequently given to the possibility of deploying the force again for the next round of negotiations in Lima in February 1978, but Ministers decided not to do so.

CONTINUATION OF NEGOTIATIONS TO SPRING 1979

At the negotiations in New York on 13–15 December 1977 it was agreed, in accordance with an earlier Argentine suggestion, to set up two working groups to prepare detailed reports on sovereignty and economic co-operation. Mr Rowlands was able to avoid proposing leaseback. Following the meeting Mr Rowlands went to Rio de Janerio to brief a delegation of Island Councillors on 18 December on the progress of the talks.

At the talks in Lima in February 1978 the British side proposed an arrangement to provide for British and Argentine scientific activities in the Dependencies, which would have retrospectively legitimised the Argentine presence on Southern Thule. However, little progress was made at the first meeting of the two working groups, when the Argentine side claimed that the Falklands and Dependencies did not generate a continental shelf; and that the shelf rights therefore belonged to Argentina and were outside the scope of the negotiations.

There were no further formal negotiations until, following Argentine agreement to discuss maritime zones and shelf rights within the negotiations, a meeting at ministerial level was held in December 1978 in Geneva. Mr Rowlands led the British delegation. Agreement in principle was reached on a draft co-operation agreement on scientific activities in the Dependencies. The Falkland Islands Councillors, however, when formally consulted about the scheme, rejected it on the ground that, unless restricted to Southern Thule, it would give Argentina a further foothold in the Dependencies, which would start a process leading to eventual loss of sovereignty over the Falkland Islands themselves. It was explained to the Argentine side at the next round of negotiations held in New York in March 1979 at official level, that, owing to the Falkland Islanders' suspicions of the motives of the Argentine Government, it was not possible to sign the agreement. Little progress was made at this round of talks.

SIGNIFICANT THEMES OF THE PERIOD

Without attempting to summarise in any detail the history of the Falkland Islands dispute between 1965 and 1979, the Committee wishes to highlight three points:

(i) Successive British Governments sought a solution to the Falkland Islands dispute by negotiation; and they recognised that any solution negotiated with Argentina had to be acceptable to the Islanders.

(ii) The negotiating options gradually narrowed. The Labour Government made clear in 1977 that sovereignty was an issue for negotiation; but, although transfer of sovereignty combined with leaseback had come to be regarded by the British Government as the most realistic solution, the leaseback proposal was not discussed with Argentina during this period.

(iii) The military threat to the Islands varied in the light of the course of negotiations; it also changed character from "adventurist" operations in the Islands to wider and more aggressive forms of military action by the Argentine Navy.

MAY 1979 TO
19 MARCH 1982

Following the General Election in May 1979 the present Conservative Government took office. Mrs Thatcher became Prime Minister and Lord Carrington Foreign and Commonwealth Secretary. The Foreign and Commonwealth Office presented the new Minister of State, Mr Ridley, with a full range of policy options. These were to break off negotiations and be prepared to maintain and defend the Islands against Argentine harassment or worse ("Fortress

Falklands"); to give up the Islands, offering to resettle the Islanders elsewhere (which, it was suggested, would be politically and morally indefensible); to go through the motions of negotiations; and to continue the negotiations in good faith in search of a solution which might ultimately prove acceptable to the Islands and Parliament. Mr Ridley discussed these options with Lord Carrington, and it was agreed that, before the Government decided on the handling of any formal negotiations, Mr Ridley should visit the Falkland Islands and Argentina to sound out views there at first hand. On 12 June 1979 Mr Ridley had an exploratory meeting with the Argentine Deputy Foreign Minister, Comodoro Cavandoli. While Mr Ridley emphasised the Government's interest in economic co-operation with Argentina, Comodoro Cavandoli indicated that his Government would require sovereignty to be a part of any negotiations.

Mr Ridley visited the Falkland Islands in July 1979. At meetings with the Islanders he discussed the advantages of co-operation with Argentina, but also made clear that the British Government would not conclude an agreement which did not meet the Islanders' wishes. Informal soundings of Islands Councillors' opinion showed a preference for a lengthy "freeze" of the dispute and little enthusiasm for the idea of leaseback. Following his visit to the Islands Mr Ridley had further talks with Comodoro Cavandoli in Buenos Aires, at which agreement was reached on the reinstatement of Ambassadors in Buenos Aires and London. On his departure, however, Mr Ridley was handed a toughly worded communication in the form of an *aide-mémoire* which expressed the Argentine Government's view that negotiations should be resumed "at a more dynamic pace".

The *aide-mémoire* referred to the position adopted by the British side at the New York meeting in March 1979 as "a regrettable step backwards"; expressed the hope that an agreement on scientific co-operation could be carried forward in the terms agreed at Geneva the previous year; and reiterated the Argentine position that, while the interests of the Islanders must be taken fully into account, they could not become a third party in negotiations. Mr Ridley restated the British Government's position that no settlement could be concluded which failed to respect the wishes of the Islanders.

On 20 September 1979 Lord Carrington sent a minute to the Prime Minister and other members of the Defence Committee seeking agreement to a policy towards the Falkland Islands. The minute set out three options: "Fortress Falklands"; protracted negotiations with no concession on sovereignty; and substantive negotiations on sovereignty. Lord Carrington recommended the last option on the ground that it was in the British interest and that of the Islanders themselves to try to find a way forward through negotiation. He suggested that the solution best fitted to meet the Government's objectives and the wishes of the Islanders would be leaseback, which might be acceptable to the Islanders on the right terms. Continued negotiations would make an unpredictable and possibly violent Argentine reaction less likely. There would, however, be difficulties in carrying out this policy and, if negotiations developed positively, it would be necessary to ensure that it had the support of the Islanders and of Parliament. Lord Carrington asked for agreement to this policy before his meeting the following week in New York with the Argentine Foreign Minister, Brigadier Pastor, at which he hoped to suggest the resumption of negotiations later in the year. After discussion with Lord Carrington, and later with Mr Ridley, the Prime Minister concluded that a decision of principle on the Government's approach to the problem could not be rushed but should be discussed at an early meeting of the Defence Committee.

At the meeting with Lord Carrington in New York Brigadier Pastor proposed a programme of work involving weekly contact between Ambassadors, twice yearly meetings of junior Ministers and an annual meeting of the two Foreign Ministers. Brigadier Pastor said he recognised that the Islands were a long way down in British priorities, but they were at the top of the list for Argentina. Lord Carrington replied that he hoped the difficulties were not insoluble, but that he was not yet in a position to put forward a solution while other pressing foreign policy problems remained outstanding.

On 12 October 1979 Lord Carrington circulated a memorandum to the Prime Minister and other members of the Defence Committee with a view to discussion by the Committee at a meeting the following week. The paper restated the options set out in Lord Carrington's minute of 20 September. It pointed out that the "Fortress Falklands" option and the option of continuing talks but without making any concessions on sovereignty both carried a serious threat of invasion. One of the annexes to the memorandum was a paper on the Argentine political and military threat, which assessed that, if Argentina concluded that there was no prospect of real progress towards a negotiated transfer of sovereignty, there would be a high risk of its resorting to more forceful measures including direct military action. It pointed out that Argentina had the capability to capture the Islands. Lord Carrington recommended that talks with Argentina should be resumed at Ministerial level to explore, without commitment and without seeking to rush matters, political and economic solutions.

The Prime Minister decided, however, that discussion of the Falkland Islands by the Defence Committee should be postponed until after the Rhodesian issue had been settled. In November 1979 Mr Ridley declined an invitation from the Argentine Government for a further informal exchange of views.

Also in November 1979 the Joint Intelligence Committee reassessed the Argentine threat to the Falklands. It reviewed developments since the last assessment (in November 1977), since when, as it judged, the Argentine military threat had been diminished by the British Government's decision to negotiate and by Argentina's preoccupation with higher priorities in foreign affairs, notably its dispute with Chile over the Beagle Channel, and with changes in the Argentine Government. It considered, however, that there was no diminution in Argentina's determination to extend its sovereignty to the area of the Falklands, and that the overriding consideration for the Argentine Government remained their perception of the British Government's willingness to negotiate about, and eventually to transfer, sovereignty. It concluded that, while the Argentine Government would prefer to achieve their sovereignty objectives by peaceful means, if negotiations broke down or if for some other reason the Argentine Government calculated that the British Government were not prepared to negotiate seriously on sovereignty, there would be a high risk of their resorting quickly to more forceful measures against British interests; and that in such circumstances direct military action against British shipping or against the Falkland

Islands could not be discounted, although "the risk of such action would not be as high as hitherto".

On 24 January 1980 Lord Carrington sent a minute to the Prime Minister and other members of the Defence Committee in preparation for a meeting the following week. He advised that exploratory talks with the Argentine Government should be started soon since to continue to stall could be risky. The Defence Committee considered Lord Carrington's memorandum of 12 October 1979 on 29 January 1980. The Committee agreed that it was undesirable that talks should be resumed on the basis of the terms of reference announced by the previous Government in April 1977. It invited Lord Carrington to seek written confirmation from the Falkland Islands Council that it was its wish that talks with the Argentine Government should be resumed; and to propose new terms of reference for them. The agreement of the Falkland Islands Councillors was obtained, and it was announced in the House of Commons on 15 April 1980 that talks would take place later that month in New York.

The first round of talks was held in New York in April 1980. The British delegation, led by Mr Ridley, included an Islands Councillor. The talks were exploratory and, although the Argentine delegation restated the Argentine position on sovereignty, it was agreed that this fundamental difference of opinion should not inhibit further discussion of the possibility of co-operation in the development and conservation of the resources of the South West Atlantic.

LEASEBACK

In July 1980 the Defence Committee reviewed the position in the light of these discussions, on the basis of a further memorandum by Lord Carrington. It agreed to attempt to reach a solution of the dispute on the basis of a leaseback arrangement. At a further meeting on 7 November the Committee agreed that Mr Ridley should visit the Islands to discover the level of support there for such an arrangement.

Mr Ridley visited the Falkland Islands again from 22 to 29 November 1980. While in Buenos Aires on his way to the Islands he called on Comodoro Cavandoli. In the Islands Mr Ridley had a full programme of public and private meetings, at which he put forward several possible future policies, including leaseback. On leaseback Islander opinion appeared to be divided, with a substantial minority opposed to it and the majority undecided.

On his return Mr Ridley made a statement in the House of Commons on 2 December. It referred to leaseback as one of the possible bases for seeking a negotiated settlement that had been discussed. Although the statement included an assurance that any eventual settlement would have to be endorsed by the Islanders, and by Parliament, it received a very hostile reception from all sides of the House (see Annex C). Ministers considered the views of the Islanders and the reaction of Parliament at a meeting of the Defence Committee on 3 December 1980, and in Cabinet the following day. The Cabinet noted that this was a highly emotive issue for Parliamentary and public opinion in Britain, where the Islanders' hostility to Mr Ridley's approach seemed to have been exaggerated: it would be tragic if the Islands' chances of escaping from economic blight were to be diminished by the attitude of their champions at Westminster.

On 6 January 1981 the Falkland Islands Joint Councils passed a motion in the following terms:

> While this House does not like any of the ideas put forward
> by Mr Ridley for a possible settlement of the sovereignty
> dispute with Argentina, it agrees that Her Majesty's
> Government should hold further talks with the Argentines
> at which this House should be represented and at which the
> British delegation should seek an agreement to freeze the
> dispute over sovereignty for a specified period of time.

The Defence Committee reviewed the position on 29
January 1981 on the basis of a memorandum by Lord
Carrington. He judged that, in withholding support for
leaseback, the Islands Councils' response was less than had
been hoped for; but they had given a mandate for future
talks, although the idea of a freeze of the dispute was
unlikely to be acceptable to the Argentines. In his view the
aim should be to keep negotiations going; and, while apply-
ing no pressure, to let the Islanders come to see the need to
explore a realistic settlement based on leaseback. Lord
Carrington recommended that the Government should
agree to early talks, for which Argentina was pressing, before
the change of government there in March. The Defence
Committee endorsed Lord Carrington's recommendations.

Talks were held in New York in February 1981: Mr
Ridley led the British side, which included two Falkland
Islands Councillors. Mr Ridley proposed a "freeze" of the
dispute, which was rejected outright by the Argentine side.

On 13 March 1981 Lord Carrington sent a minute to
the Prime Minister and other members of the Defence
Committee reporting the outcome of these talks. He said
that, although the Argentines had rejected the "freeze" proposal, the talks had been helpful education for both the
Islanders attending them and the Argentines, and had narrowed the issues. Lord Carrington saw little point in further

talks until the Islanders had cleared their own minds. He considered that, if in the end the Islanders decided that they would prefer the *status quo*, it would be necessary to prepare for the possibility of a deterioration of relations with Argentina, which might involve supplying the Islands, if Argentina withdrew its services, and perhaps defending them against physical harassment.

Following a press conference given by the Falkland Islands Councillors on their return home from the talks in New York, Foreign and Commonwealth Office officials advised Mr Ridley on 26 March 1981 that there were grounds for cautious optimism about eventually being given a mandate to develop negotiations, but expressed concern that the timetable envisaged by Islands Councillors for reaching a decision would be unacceptable to Argentina. It was unlikely that the Councillors would begin to consider the issues until their elections in the autumn at the earliest. At the beginning of May 1981 the British Ambassador in Buenos Aires wrote to the Foreign and Commonwealth Office strongly urging at least one further round of talks during the year, including discussion of sovereignty, in order to avoid a deterioration of relations with Argentina. The Foreign and Commonwealth Office replied that they were under no illusions about the limits of Argentine patience or the risk of serious confrontation if the British Government appeared unwilling or unable to continue substantive negotiations on sovereignty. However, substantive negotiations without the approval of the Islanders ran up against the Government's public commitment to the principle that the wishes of the Islanders were paramount, on which Parliament had strong views. If Argentina chose to exert pressure, as might be expected, it would be necessary to deal with the situation as it arose, but always with the proviso that Islander wishes were paramount. It was decided to send a senior official (Mr J.B. Ure, the Assistant Under-Secretary of State concerned) to visit the Falkland Islands, in order to encourage an early decision, and to visit Argentina to reassure the Argentine Government of the British Government's wish to make progress towards a solution and to seek to persuade them not to force the pace.

One indication of Argentine impatience at lack of progress in the talks was a speech made on 29 May 1981 (Army Day in Argentina) by General Galtieri, then the Army Commander-in-Chief, in which he said:

> Neither are we prepared to allow those who are discussing with us the return of island territories that are Argentine by historical inheritance and legal right to interfere in the slightest way with the search for and exploitation of the wealth of our continental shelf.
>
> Nobody can or will be able to say that we have not been extremely calm and patient in our handling of international problems, which in no way stem from any appetite for territory on our part. However, after a century and a half they [these problems] are becoming more and more unbearable.

On 15 June 1981 Mr Ridley had a general discussion of the Falklands issue in Paris with the new Argentine Deputy Foreign Minister, Sr Ros. The Argentines appeared to be reconciled to awaiting the results of the Falkland Islands Council elections, but were concerned that the results might foreclose the options; they feared that the generally negative and critical attitude of the Islanders towards Argentine efforts to improve relations by providing air and fuel services might cause domestic opinion in Argentina to conclude that there was no value in positive gestures or even in continuing negotiations.

On 30 June 1981 a major review of policy was undertaken in the Foreign and Commonwealth Office at a meeting chaired by Mr Ridley, which was attended by, among others, Sir Michael Palliser, the Permanent Under-Secretary of State; Mr D. M. Day, the Deputy Under-Secretary of State concerned; Mr A. J. Williams, H M Ambassador in Buenos Aires; Mr R. M. Hunt (as he then was), the Governor of the Falkland Islands; Mr J. B. Ure, the Superintending Assistant Under-Secretary of State for the South America Department; and Mr P. R. Fearn, the Head of the South America Department. The meeting had before it a paper prepared by Mr Ure following his visit to Argentina and the Falkland Islands earlier in the month. In the paper Mr Ure said that he had "found Argentine Foreign Affairs Ministers and officials reasonably relaxed about progress—or lack of progress—on the Falklands negotiations and well disposed towards the leaseback idea". They had warned, however, that the military leaders were "less patient and might require a more 'forward' policy at any time". In the Islands Mr Ure had formed the impression that opinion had not hardened irrevocably against leaseback; but he judged that, in order to secure agreement to it, much more would need to be done to educate Islander and United Kingdom opinion about the danger of inaction and the safeguards on which the Government would insist in any leaseback arrangements. He suggested a number of measures to assist a campaign of public education, including assurances to the Islanders on access to the United Kingdom, a resettlement scheme for those dissatisfied with any arrangements reached, further land distribution schemes, and the initiation of more productive economic schemes for the Islands. He recommended that, if such an approach were considered unacceptable, consideration should be given to preparing fuller contingency plans for the defence and development of the Islands.

In preparation for the meeting the British Ambassador in Buenos Aires had also set out his views, in a telegram on 10 June 1981. He said that ground had been lost since February both because it was less possible to depend on continued Argentine patience and understanding and because Islander opinion of the realities of the situation had been allowed to slide back. If the only practicable outcome was some form of negotiated leaseback, it was apparent that acceptance of that conclusion would not come of itself in the Islands, in Parliament or even in the whole of Government. The Ambassador recommended that the forthcoming meeting should concentrate on the possibility of a "sales campaign", perhaps mainly by bringing home to British opinion the potential cost of any alternative. He warned that the risk of Argentina's using Britain as a scapegoat for its domestic troubles could well be much more threatening by the end of the year. If the Government sponsored more visibly the idea that a negotiated settlement must be envisaged and achieved, it would help to reduce the risk of Argentina's concluding that the Government were simply bamboozling them without any basic intention of reaching a mutually acceptable settlement.

At the meeting on 30 June the situation in Argentina and in the Islands was also discussed in detail. The Governor gave the view from the Islands. He said that the Islanders wished to have nothing whatsoever to do with the Argentines; they did not believe that any terms which could be agreed for a leaseback settlement could ever provide them with the guarantees that they wanted.

The conclusions reached by the meeting were that the immediate aim should be to play for time with Argentina; that the new Falkland Islands Legislative Council, when elected, should be persuaded to allow talks to continue; that a paper for the Defence Committee should be prepared recommending a major public education campaign; and that up-to-date contingency papers, both civil and military, should be prepared as annexes to it.

Intelligence assessment

On 9 July 1981 the Joint Intelligence Committee circulated a new assessment of the likelihood of Argentina's resorting over the next few months to forcible action in the Falkland Islands dispute. It reviewed developments since the last assessment in 1979, including the progress of talks held with Argentina in that period, political and economic developments in Argentina, the progress of its sovereignty dispute with Chile about islands in the Beagle Channel and its improving relations with the United States and Brazil. The assessment reviewed the options open to the Argentine Government if they decided to resort to direct measures in the dispute. It took the view that it was likely that in the first instance Argentina would adopt diplomatic and economic measures. The latter could include the disruption of air and sea communications, of food and oil supplies and of the provision of medical treatment. There was also a possibility that Argentina might occupy one of the uninhabited Dependencies, following up its action in 1976 in establishing a presence on Southern Thule; and a risk that it might establish a military presence in the Falkland Islands themselves, remote from Port Stanley. In the Committee's view harassment or arrest of British shipping would not be likely unless the Argentines felt themselves severely provoked.

As in 1979, the assessment noted that there was no sign of diminution in Argentina's determination eventually to extend its sovereignty over the Falkland Islands area, but that it would prefer to achieve this objective by peaceful means and would turn to forcible action only as a last resort. As before, it judged that the overriding consideration would be Argentina's perception of the Government's willingness to negotiate genuinely about, and eventually to transfer, sovereignty. It recorded evidence of impatience in Argentina at the absence of progress in negotiations and at the attitude of the Islanders. Earlier in the year Argentina had reduced the scheduled flights to the Islands and delayed a supply ship. These actions were seen as evidence that in any escalation of the dispute such measures would be likely to come first. It was thought, however, that relatively small-scale military action could not be ruled out. The final paragraph of the assessment stated that, if Argentina concluded that there was no hope of a peaceful transfer of sovereignty, there would be a high risk of its resorting to more forcible measures against British interests, and that it might act swiftly and without warning. In such circumstances military action against British shipping or a full-scale invasion of the Falkland Islands could not be discounted.

Mr Ridley's report to Lord Carrington
On 20 July Mr Ridley sent a minute to Lord Carrington. He recorded the agreement of his meeting on 30 June that there

was no alternative to the leaseback idea which stood any chance of solving the dispute, while noting that the prospects for negotiating a sovereignty solution with Islander agreement had receded in recent months. The forthcoming general elections in the Islands seemed certain to lead to a new Legislative Council opposed to substantive sovereignty talks with Argentina. While it might be possible to manage one more round of talks without specific sovereignty proposals on the table, it must be expected that Argentine patience would then run out. Mr Ridley warned that, if Argentina concluded, possibly by early 1982, that the Government were unable or unwilling to negotiate seriously, retaliatory action must be expected: in the first instance through the withdrawal of communications, fuel and other facilities which it provided; in the longer run through some form of military action. Mr Ridley then examined the options available. He dismissed that of simply playing for time, except in the very short term, and suggested that there were three possible courses of action: to open negotiations on leaseback with or without Islander concurrence or participation, but with the outcome remaining conditional on the agreement of the Islanders and of Parliament; to embark on a public education campaign to educate Islander and British public opinion about the facts of the situation, the consequences of a failure to negotiate and the corresponding advantages of a sovereignty solution; or to let Argentina conclude that the Government would not discuss sovereignty, and to set in hand contingency action to deal with the consequences. Mr Ridley advised against the first of these on the ground that it would breach the long-held policy of acting only in accordance with the Islanders' wishes; and the third on the ground that it would be difficult and very costly to sustain the Islands and could lead to a military confrontation with Argentina. He recommended adopting the second option, despite the public criticism that it was likely to attract, and suggested that the matter should be discussed in the Defence Committee in September.

On 27 July 1981 a note was delivered to the British Ambassador in Buenos Aires from the Argentine Foreign Minister, Dr Camilion, expressing the Argentine Government's serious concern at the lack of progress at the last round of talks in February 1981. It referred to the fact that ten years had passed since the Communications Agreements and stated that in the Argentine Government's view it was not possible:

> to postpone further a profound and serious discussion of the complex essential constituents of the negotiations— sovereignty and economic co-operation—in a simultaneous and global fashion with the express intention of achieving concrete results shortly. A resolute impetus must therefore be given to the negotiations. The next round of negotiations cannot be another mere exploratory exercise, but must mark the beginning of a decisive stage towards the definitive termination of the dispute.

The Argentine Ministry of Foreign Affairs issued a simultaneous *communiqué* referring to the note, rehearsing Argentina's claim and stating that the Argentine Government considered that "the acceleration of negotiations on the Malvinas, with resolution and with clear objectives in view, had become an unpostponable priority for its foreign policy". The *communiqué* expressed the Argentine Government's determination to continue the negotiations "in an eminently realistic spirit and with the full certainty that there are rational and attainable solutions"; and concluded, "there is a national awareness of the problem, which on the one hand allows for negotiation and which on the other believes that it is not possible to defer this question which affects territorial integrity and national dignity".

Lord Carrington's decision and Argentine reaction

On 7 September 1981 Lord Carrington discussed the position with the Lord Privy Seal (Sir Ian Gilmour), Mr Ridley and officials. A draft Defence Committee paper was prepared for consideration at the meeting. It drew attention to the increasing urgency of finding a solution to the dispute and set out the options in similar terms to Mr Ridley's minute to Lord Carrington, recommending, as he had, a much more public and active campaign to educate Islander and British public opinion.

Lord Carrington did not accept this course of action. As, in accordance with normal Foreign and Commonwealth Office practice, no minutes of the meeting were taken, the reasons for his decision were not recorded at the time. But Lord Carrington told us that, in his view, such a campaign would not have been agreed to by his colleagues and would have been counter-productive. In a personal letter to the British Ambassador in Buenos Aires on 23 September, Mr Fearn, the Head of the South America Department, explained that Ministers had decided that:

> the domestic political constraints must at this stage continue
> to prevent us from taking any steps which might be
> interpreted either as putting pressure on the Islanders or as

overruling their wishes. Specifically that meant that an education campaign in the Islands and the United Kingdom has, at least for the present, been ruled out.

In oral evidence Sir Michael Palliser, the Permanent Under-Secretary of State at the time, told us that, according to his recollection, it was decided that it was not an appropriate time for Ministers to discuss the matter collectively in the Defence Committee, because of, among other things, the absence of any immediate danger of hostile Argentine reactions.

But, although he did not seek a meeting, Lord Carrington sent a minute to the Prime Minister and to other members of the Defence Committee on 14 September 1981, in advance of discussing the dispute with Dr Camilion at the United Nations General Assembly in New York later that month. In it he referred to the Argentine note and *communiqué*, which had been circulated at the United Nations, and expressed his conviction that leaseback still provided the most likely, and perhaps the only, basis for an agreed solution of the dispute. He noted, however, that the prospects for negotiating such a solution with Islander agreement had diminished and, given the Islanders' views, there was little prospect of doing more than keeping some sort of negotiation with Argentina going. Putting pressure on the Islanders to take any decisions against their will could only be counter-productive. Lord Carrington proposed to tell Dr Camilion that the British Government wanted to end the dispute, but that they could act only in accordance with the wishes of the Islanders, and to invite the Argentine Government to put forward constructive proposals of their own. He recognised, however, that this would be unwelcome to the Argentine Government and that, if they concluded that the British Government were unable or unwilling to negotiate seriously, they might see little purpose in trying to maintain a dialogue. This could lead to the withdrawal of the Islands' air service and a significant part of their fuel supply. The risk of ultimately becoming involved in a military confrontation with Argentina could not be discounted. Lord Carrington explained that contingency studies were being undertaken by officials (see below), but that it was clear that supplying and defending the Islands would be both difficult and costly.

On 22 September 1981 Dr Camilion addressed the UN General Assembly. He referred to the "present illegal occupation" of the Islands and expressed his Government's hope that they would be "able to report in due course to the General Assembly that this series of negotiations concerning the Malvinas, South Georgia and South Sandwich Islands, which we hope will begin soon, was the last one".

Lord Carrington met Dr Camilion the following day. The relevant telegram reported that he had told him that the British Government wanted negotiations, but, although they would continue to do their best to persuade the Islanders of the benefits of an accommodation, they could not seek to coerce them. Lord Carrington suggested that it would be preferable if Argentina put forward proposals when talks resumed. Dr Camilion emphasised that the key question was that of sovereignty, which had to be negotiated between the United Kingdom and Argentina. The Islanders could not be allowed to veto the resumption of negotiations.

Argentine press comment after the meeting, based on a press conference that Dr Camilion gave, presented the talks as a most significant development in the Falklands negotiations, with Britain agreeing for the first time with Argentina that the present status of the Islands could not be maintained. Dr Camilion was reported as having emerged visibly satisfied from the talks. He was quoted in the Argentine press as saying that "Lord Carrington advanced to the point of saying that the present *status quo* is difficult to sustain today".

When he was informed of Lord Carrington's decision not to pursue a public education campaign, the British Ambassador in Buenos Aires protested strongly in a letter to Mr Fearn on 2 October 1981. He said that, as he understood it, the decision was to have no strategy at all beyond a general Micawberism. It had to be recognised that the "unguided 'wishes of the Falkland Islanders' were very, very unlikely in any foreseeable future to provide even a grudging acceptance of sovereignty transfer in any form". There was a clear risk that the Argentines would conclude that talking was a waste of time. The Ambassador said that "talks for the sake of talking" were something the Argentines conceded to the British and not *vice versa*; and he was dubious about their being ready to concede them any longer. If it was no longer possible to negotiate meaningfully about sovereignty, it would be better to tell the Argentines frankly and face the consequences.

Dr Camilion discussed his ideas for negotiations with the British Ambassador in Buenos Aires at some length on 14 October 1981. He said that, for serious and constructive negotiations, it was necessary to tackle all the component parts of what was a complex issue. There would be a need to establish a methodology and draw up a catalogue of the subjects to be covered, and then to examine them piece-meal, even if the final settlement had to be concluded globally. Dr Camilion recognised that meaningful negotiations would have to be long and difficult. These remarks were welcomed in the Foreign and Commonwealth Office as indicating Argentine acceptance that no early solution was obtainable and reluctance on their part to move to confrontation. While it was recognised that there was no weakening in the Argentine Government's ultimate and overriding objective of securing a transfer of sovereignty, their position as stated by Dr Camilion was seen as offering scope for a protracted dialogue.

Falkland Islands elections

The elections to the Falkland Islands Legislative Council were completed on 14 October 1981 and, as expected, reflected a hardening of Islanders' attitudes against negotiations on sovereignty. The new Legislative Council agreed, however, to the need to keep a dialogue going, provided that sovereignty was not on the agenda. It supported a proposal to send representatives to further talks with Argentina, which were originally arranged to be held in Geneva on 17 and 18 December 1981. Because of the change of Government in Buenos Aires Argentina asked for the talks to be postponed until January 1982; they were then further postponed until the end of February because of Mr Luce's★ other commitments, in particular in connection with the Canada Bill.

On 2 December 1981 Lord Carrington sent a further minute to the Prime Minister and other members of the Defence Committee, referring to his meeting with Dr

★ Mr Luce had succeeded Mr Ridley as Minister of State in September 1981.

Camilion and the outcome of the Falkland Islands elections. He noted that Argentine and Islander attitudes left little room for manoeuvre at the next round of negotiations, and that it would be left to the Argentine side to make the running. Lord Carrington said that he could not be optimistic on the outcome of the talks, but there was some hope that they would not end in a complete stalemate. The Argentines were likely to press for parallel working groups on economic co-operation and on sovereignty, and in this event the aim would be to seek to persuade the Island Councillors to agree that the establishment of the latter group would not involve any surrender of their rights. Lord Carrington also referred to the possible need to provide alternative services, based on sea rather than air communication, at an initial cost of about £6 million, if Argentina withdrew its services.

CONTINGENCY PLANNING

Early in 1981 the Foreign and Commonwealth Office, which was responsible for initiating civil contingency plans for the Islands, had begun to look at what could be done in the event of Argentina's withdrawing the services it provided. In May 1981 Foreign and Commonwealth Office officials consulted the Overseas Development Administration about the possibility of extending the runway at Port Stanley to accommodate long haul jets; the provision of alternative sea communications; and the cost of providing better medical facilities. The Civil Aviation Authority provided estimates of the cost of extending the runway to different lengths. The Department of Trade was consulted about the feasibility of various forms of sea service. The outcome of these consultations was a note by officials prepared in September 1981 as an annex to the draft paper for the Defence Committee, which was considered at Lord Carrington's meeting on 7 September. The note concluded that an alternative air service was likely to be impracticable. The only country from which such a service could be provided without extension of the runway at Port Stanley was Chile. It would need to be extended to 7,000 feet to accommodate aircraft from Uruguay or Brazil, at an estimated cost of about £11 million at 1981 prices. It was unlikely, however, that South American countries would be prepared to allow the provision of alternative air services, in which case the runway would need to be extended to 10,000–12,000 feet to accommodate long-haul aircraft from South Africa at a cost of about £16 million. A far more sophisticated airport would also be required. Even then there would be difficulties, as Argentina could refuse to allow Argentine airfields to be designated as alternatives to Port Stanley if an aircraft needed to divert. It was likely, therefore, to be possible to provide only a sea service. The cost of a charter would be of the order of about £8,000 a day. Consideration was also given to the need to prepare alternative means of providing the Islands with fuel and of transporting freight and to the effects of Argentina's withdrawing its educational facilities and emergency medical service.

Earlier in the year the Foreign and Commonwealth Office had also asked the Ministry of Defence to update the assessment prepared in 1977 of what could be done to counter military action by Argentina. Some explanation of nomenclature is required here. The former Chief of the Defence Staff (Lord Lewin) explained to us that in military terminology "contingency planning" has a precise meaning. It is a form of planning that leads to the preparation of a Joint Theatre Plan. A Joint Theatre Plan is a detailed plan to meet a specified contingency, usually one requiring air reinforcement. It is prepared on the instructions of the Chiefs of Staff and is regularly reviewed and updated. The papers prepared at various times by the Ministry of Defence at the request of the Foreign and Commonwealth Office were not contingency plans in this sense, but a much broader appreciation of the action that would be necessary to counter various forms of military action by Argentina. They did, however, incorporate a "concept of operations", on which military action could be based.

At a meeting between Ministry of Defence and Foreign and Commonwealth Office officials on 1 May 1981 it was agreed that what was required was a "short politico-military assessment of the United Kingdom's ability to respond militarily to a range of possible Argentine actions, the implications of responding in a particular way and the chances of success, with some indication of the possible cost". (It was also agreed that plans for the evacuation of the Island population in the event of an emergency should not be prepared.) It was envisaged that the paper would form an annex to a paper for the Defence Committee. On completion the paper was formally approved by the Chiefs of Staff on 14 September 1981.

This paper, which was similar in scope to that prepared in 1977, examined the military options identified by the July 1981 Joint Intelligence Committee assessment as open to Argentina and possible responses to them. It noted that Argentina had some of the most efficient armed forces in

South America, and gave a brief account of its naval and air capability. It also drew attention to Britain's very limited military capability in the area, consisting of only the garrison of 42 lightly armed Royal Marines on the Islands, the part-time Falkland Islands' defence force, and HMS *Endurance*, which was due to be withdrawn in March 1982. The paper explained that the length of the runway at Port Stanley, the lack of diversion airfields, the limited airfield facilities and the adverse and unpredictable weather conditions precluded air reinforcement on any significant scale. A British military response would therefore have to be primarily a naval one. Passage time was of the order of 20 days for surface ships, and additional time would be required to assemble and prepare sea reinforcements, which could involve significant penalties to other military commitments.

The paper then examined possible responses to various forms of Argentine action: harassment or arrest of British shipping; military occupation of one or more of the uninhabited islands; arrest of the British Antarctic Survey team on South Georgia; a small-scale military operation against the Islands; and full-scale military invasion of the Islands. On the last option the paper judged that, to deter a full-scale invasion, a large balanced force would be required, comprising an Invincible class carrier with four destroyers or frigates, plus possibly a nuclear-powered submarine, supply ships in attendance and additional manpower up to brigade strength, to reinforce the garrison. Such a deployment would be very expensive and would engage a significant portion of the country's naval resources. There was a danger that its despatch could precipitate the very action it was intended to deter. If then faced with Argentine occupation of the Falkland Islands on arrival, there could be no certainty that such a force could retake them. The paper concluded that to deal with a full-scale invasion would require naval and land forces with organic air support on a very substantial scale, and that the logistic problems of such an operation would be formidable.

In the period that the Chiefs of Staff paper was being prepared there was some anxiety in the Ministry of Defence (Navy Department) about the lack of detailed contingency plans for the protection of the Falkland Islands themselves and of the Royal Marine platoon there. The United Kingdom Commanders-in-Chief's Committee gave further consideration to the matter in February 1982, when the Assistant Chief of the Defence Staff (Operations) reported that, pending consideration of the Chiefs of Staff paper by the Defence Committee, there was no enthusiasm in the Ministry of Defence for detailed contingency planning. Since these discussions at the planning level were not carried to the point of consideration by the Chiefs of Staff at that stage, the Committee does not regard them as significant for its review, particularly in the light of the evidence given by the former Chief of Defence Staff.

HMS *ENDURANCE*

One consequence of the 1981 Defence Review was the decision to withdraw HMS *Endurance* at the end of her 1981–82 deployment. Lord Carrington wrote to the Secretary of State for Defence, Mr Nott, on 5 June 1981 on several aspects of the defence programme, including the withdrawal of HMS *Endurance*. He pressed for her retention on the ground that, until the dispute with Argentina was settled, it was important to maintain the British

Government's normal presence in the area at the current level; any reduction would be interpreted by both the Islanders and Argentina as a reduction in Britain's commitment to the Islands and in its willingness to defend them. Lord Carrington also pointed out that the hydrographic survey tasks HMS *Endurance* undertook and the operation of her helicopters over a wide area of the British Antarctic Territory were an important aspect of the maintenance of the British claim to sovereignty. Although HMS *Endurance* was nearing the end of her normal working life, it was essential that she should be replaced by a vessel of similar type for Antarctic work. This approach was followed up by a meeting of officials on 10 June 1981, following which Foreign and Commonwealth Office officials judged that there was no prospect of the decision being reversed, and so reported to Mr Ridley. The decision to withdraw HMS *Endurance* was confirmed in Parliament on 30 June 1981.

When they were informed of the decision, the Falkland Islands Councils held a joint meeting on 26 June 1981, following which they sent a message to Lord Carrington in the following terms:

> The people of the Falkland Islands deplore in the strongest
> terms the decision to withdraw HMS *Endurance* from
> service. They express extreme concern that Britain appears
> to be abandoning its defence of British interests in the
> South Atlantic and Antarctic at a time when other powers
> are strengthening their position in these areas. They feel that
> such a withdrawal will further weaken British sovereignty in
> this area in the eyes not only of Islanders but of the world.
> They urge that all possible endeavours be made to secure a
> reversal of this decision.

In July 1981 the British Embassy in Buenos Aires reported, in a letter to the Foreign and Commonwealth Office at official level, that several Argentine newspapers had carried prominently versions of a report of an article in *The Daily Telegraph* on the subject. The letter reported that all the newspaper articles highlighted the theme that Britain was "abandoning the protection of the Falkland Islands". An intelligence report in September 1981 quoted an Argentine diplomatic view that the withdrawal of HMS *Endurance* had been construed by the Argentines as a deliberate political gesture; they did not see it as an inevitable economy in Britain's defence budget since the implications for the Islands and for Britain's position in the South Atlantic were fundamental.

Lord Carrington wrote again to Mr Nott on 22 January 1982 referring to the protests that the news of HMS *Endurance's* withdrawal had aroused. He referred to an Early Day Motion in the House of Commons that had been signed by over 150 MPs, and to a debate in the House of Lords on 16 December 1981 that had centred on the decision. Lord Carrington said that the decision was being interpreted as a stage in a deliberate British policy of reducing support for the Falkland Islands; and as demonstrating a lack of commitment to Britain's sovereignty, and to the related economic potential, in Antarctica. He suggested a discussion of the matter. Mr Nott replied on 3 February 1982 declining to reverse the decision. He argued that the Government were on reasonable grounds as regards their commitments in the Falklands as they would be keeping the Royal Marine garrison there at its present strength. Royal naval ships would continue to visit periodically, though less frequently than HMS *Endurance*. In answer to a question in the House of Commons on 9 February 1982 about the future of HMS *Endurance* the Prime Minister said that the decision to withdraw her had been very difficult and that, in view of the competing claims on the defence budget and the defence capability of HMS *Endurance*, the Secretary of State for Defence had decided that other claims on the budget should have greater priority.

Lord Carrington wrote to Mr Nott again on 17 February 1982 expressing his continued concern at the strength of public and Parliamentary opposition to HMS *Endurance's* withdrawal and at the consequence for the Government's position on the Falklands. He said that he did not wish to rule out an approach to the Defence Committee for additional finance, but suggested that it would be better to wait until the outcome of the talks in New York on 26 and 27 February 1982, when Argentine intentions and the defence implications would be clearer.

EVENTS LEADING UP TO THE NEW YORK TALKS IN FEBRUARY 1982

General Galtieri succeeded President Viola as President of Argentina on 22 December 1981. He was in a stronger position than his predecessors since he also retained his position as Commander-in-Chief of the Army, which he was due to hold until the end of 1982. It is also significant, in view of the traditional inter-service rivalry in Argentina, that he is said to have been a personal friend of Admiral Anaya, the Commander-in-Chief of the Navy. The British Ambassador in Buenos Aires reported at the time that the Argentine Navy, traditionally the hardest of the services on the Falklands issue, was playing a decisive role in the change of Government, which it was likely to maintain in the new Junta.

General Galtieri took office at a time of improving relations with the United States. 1981 had been marked by a number of high level visits between the United States and Argentina. President Reagan's personal emissary, General Vernon Walters, had visited Argentina in February and September; the United States Army Commander-in-Chief, General Meyer, in April and the United States Ambassador to the United Nations, Mrs Kirkpatrick, in August. General Viola had visited the United States in March and General Galtieri had himself paid two visits there, in August at the invitation of General Meyer, and in October for the inter-American Conference of Army Commanders-in-Chief.

In the new Government Dr Nicanor Costa Mendez, who had previously been Foreign Minister in the Government of President Ongania from 1966 to 1969 (at the time of negotiations between the United Kingdom and Argentina on the "Memorandum of Understanding"), was appointed Foreign Minister in place of Dr Camilion. The Foreign and Commonwealth Office view of the implications of the new Government for the Falklands dispute was that the basic Argentine position was unlikely to change, but a more forceful approach could be expected. In his inaugural speech to the nation on 23 December 1981 President Galtieri made no mention of the dispute, although he had, as noted earlier, made a reference to it in strong terms in a speech the previous May.

On 1 January 1982 the British Ambassador in Buenos Aires submitted his Annual Review for 1981. He noted that the Ministers chosen by the new President were a great improvement on their predecessors. 1981 had been a difficult year for relations between Britain and Argentina, mainly on account of the Falklands dispute. He said, "We have come through without a bust-up, but certainly with the Argentines and the Islanders more on each other's nerves than a year ago." In submitting to Mr Ure and Mr Luce a draft reply to the Ambassador, Mr Fearn observed that, while they had managed to avoid matters developing into a confrontation, they would be fortunate to do so for a further year unless Islanders' attitudes changed. In his reply to the Ambassador on 28 January 1982 Mr Fearn made the point that, unless the Islanders modified their attitudes, which was unlikely, it was going to be increasingly difficult to persuade the Argentines of the virtues of continuing to seek a solution by negotiation.

On 19 January 1982 the Governor of the Falkland Islands submitted his Annual Review for 1981. He noted that the Islanders' relations with both Britain and Argentina had deteriorated during the year. Islander opinion had hardened against leaseback. Their suspicions of the Government's intentions had been increased by a number of unconnected matters, including the refusal to grant British citizenship to Falkland Islanders in the British Nationality Bill, the announcement of the withdrawal of HMS *Endurance*, and financial cuts in the British Antarctic Survey, especially the threatened closure of its base at Grytviken in South Georgia. A large number of Argentine actions had antagonised the Islanders, in particular the reduction at very short notice in the frequency of the air service and the fact that there had been six overflights by Argentine Air Force aircraft. The elections had led to a Legislative Council on which the elected members were unanimously opposed to leaseback. In consequence the Governor saw no way ahead in future talks, as long as Argentina continued to insist upon sovereignty first and the British Government continued to maintain that

Islander wishes were paramount. He thought that, if talks broke down, the first step that Argentina would take would be to stop the air service, and he discussed various measures that would be necessary to meet that contingency and other action of a similar kind that Argentina might take.

In a detailed analysis of the Review, which he submitted to Mr Ure and Mr Luce, Mr Fearn observed that in 1981 the leaseback initiative had run into the ground and the Islanders had moved to open support of a "Fortress Falklands" policy. Leaseback was now "effectively dead"; its demise meant that "we are left with no alternative way to prevent the dispute moving sooner or later to more open confrontation".

A formal reply, approved by Mr Luce, was sent to the Governor by Mr Ure on 4 March. In it he confirmed the Governor's pessimistic analysis of the future of the dispute and commented that, given Argentine and Islander attitudes, "we are now perilously near the inevitable move from dialogue to confrontation". It was explained to us in evidence that the word "confrontation" was not intended to mean primarily military confrontation, and that the purpose of the letter was in part to serve as a warning to the Islanders, through the Governor, of the consequences of a breakdown in negotiations. The reply pointed out that the range of options open to the Argentines went far wider than a withdrawal of present services. It had to be recognised that for the British Government it would be difficult not only to find the necessary finance but also, in the final analysis, to defend the Islands and the Dependencies in any adequate way. It would be necessary to carry forward the contingency planning already undertaken against a withdrawal of services. It was unlikely to be possible to provide an alternative air service.

While the Islanders should be in no doubt of the strength of the Government's commitment to act only in accordance with their wishes, they should be under no illusion on the difficulties ahead or on the limits on their ability to mitigate the consequences. Unless there was a negotiated settlement, the way forward for the Islanders could only be downhill.

On 27 January 1982 the Argentine Ministry of Foreign Affairs delivered to the British Ambassador in Buenos Aires a communication in the form of a *bout de papier* setting out at length the Argentine position on its claim to sovereignty. It stated that British recognition of Argentine sovereignty over the Malvinas, South Georgia and the South Sandwich Islands remained a *sine qua non* requirement for the solution of the dispute. However much time might pass, Argentina would never abandon its claim nor relax its determination. It called for serious and in-depth negotiations culminating "within a reasonable period of time and without procrastination" in the recognition of Argentine sovereignty over the disputed Islands. It pointed out that so far there had been no concrete progress and the matter had now reached a point which "demands solutions, without further delays or dilatory arguments". It drew attention to the fact that the United Nations Resolutions referred to the "interests" (rather than the wishes) of the Islanders and reaffirmed Argentina's intention of respecting those interests, including the preservation of the way of life and cultural traditions of the Islanders. It claimed that the United Nations Resolutions did not refer to the "wishes" of the Islanders because the dispute was confined to the Argentine and British Governments. It also referred to the need to exploit the natural resources of the area, but stressed that "any idea of making progress in the search for pragmatic formulae for exploration and exploitation which might mean a delay or paralysis of the solution to the sovereignty question is totally unacceptable to Argentina". In order to resolve the dispute "peacefully, definitively and *rapidly*", Argentina proposed the establishment of a permanent negotiating commission, to meet in the first weeks of each month alternately in each capital. The commission would have a duration of one year and would be open to denunciation by either side at any time without prior warning to the other side.

The *bout de papier* was analysed in detail in the Foreign and Commonwealth Office. Although toughly worded, little of the substance of the paper was regarded as new. The greater part of it was seen to be a re-working of the *communiqué* issued in July 1981. The new element was the proposal for a permanent negotiating commission working to a timetable of one year. A note, approved by Ministers, was sent to the British Ambassador in Buenos Aires as the basis on which he should speak to the Argentine Deputy Foreign Minister, Sr Ros. The note reaffirmed that the British Government were in no doubt about British sovereignty over the Falkland Islands and their Dependencies, maritime zones and continental shelves. They could not therefore accept the Argentine assumption that the purpose of the negotiations was the eventual recognition by the British Government of Argentine sovereignty in the area. They would, however, remain ready to continue the negotiating process at the talks to be held in New York later in the month, and would be ready to discuss in detail the proposal to establish working groups to look at particular aspects of the dispute. The note also reaffirmed the British Government's wish to find, by negotiation, "an early and peaceful solution to this dispute which can be accepted by all concerned, namely the British and Argentine Governments and the people of the Falkland Islands". The British Ambassador in Buenos Aires delivered this message on 8 February 1982.

In a letter on 3 February 1982, the British Ambassador in Buenos Aires reported to the Foreign and Commonwealth Office that all the indications were that Admiral Anaya, probably with President Galtieri's full agreement, had "got into the driving seat" in regard to the Malvinas negotiations and had ruled, in effect, that a test period should be allowed to see if negotiation got anywhere. The Ambassador suspected that the period allowed might be up to the 150th anniversary, in January 1983, of the British occupation of the Islands. He expected that the position of Sr Ros, the leader of the Argentine delegation at the talks, would be very circumscribed.

Argentine press comment

The period leading up to the New York talks was marked by widespread comment in the Argentine press. In an article in *La Prensa* on 24 January 1982 (before the *bout de papier* was delivered), Sr Iglesias Rouco, a journalist regarded as usually well informed, predicted that the Argentine Government would shortly present the British Government with a series of conditions for the continuation of negotiations over the Malvinas and that, if they were not accepted, Argentina would immediately break off negotiations. He said that, according to reliable diplomatic sources, the conditions would be "firm and clear" and would set very precise time-limits for the solution of the different aspects of the problem and the final return of the Islands to Argentina. He linked this new initiative with development of Argentine policy towards the Beagle Channel, as part of "an ambitious diplomatic and strategic plan which would assure the country of a relevant role in the South Atlantic". Sr Rouco speculated that Argentina would receive support from the United States for any action leading to the recovery of the Islands, not excluding military action. According to the article, it was believed in both the United States and in Europe that, if the Argentine attempt to clarify the negotiations with London failed, Argentina would recover the Islands by force "this year ... a military attempt to resolve the dispute cannot be ruled out when sovereignty is at stake". In a further article in *La Prensa* on 7 February 1982 Sr Rouco again predicted that the Argentine Foreign Ministry would present a series of deadlines to resolve the various aspects of the problem and a demand for British recognition of Argentine sovereignty over the Islands and of their intention to return them in accordance with United Nations resolutions. He believed that Buenos Aires was not prepared to go on talking indefinitely and that, if the British Government did not agree to bind themselves to a written timetable, would "apparently reserve the right to take other action, which might by no means exclude the recovery of the Islands by military means".

On 9 February 1982 an editorial in the English language *Buenos Aires Herald* drew attention to the apparent willingness of the new Argentine Government to accept the risks any serious attempts to recover the Falkland and the Beagle Channel Islands might entail, and to hints that their Falklands/Malvinas approach would be far tougher than anything seen so far. It referred to talk of the pros and cons of simply invading the Islands and telling the world that justice had been belatedly done, but judged that invasion would be "utterly unnecessary". However, unless the dispute was solved in the only reasonable way, by transferring the Islands to Argentina, it would be solved "in a messy and damaging way".

In a further article on 18 February 1982, Sr Rouco argued that there were three relatively new circumstances which justified taking a military initiative to recover the Malvinas: Argentina's isolation from western strategic policy; the unfavourable results of the Beagle Channel arbitration and Papal mediation; and Soviet penetration of the area. In discussion with British Embassy staff in Buenos Aires, reported by them on 19 February 1982, Sr Rouco insisted that the opinions expressed in his articles were his own. The British Embassy was sceptical of this assertion, and subsequent intelligence, which became available at the end of February and during March 1982, indicated that the articles by Sr Rouco, who had close connections with the Argentine Foreign Ministry and the Navy, together with other press reports, were part of a concerted effort to exert pressure on the British before the New York talks.

There were also articles in other journals. A long article in the magazine *Siete Dias* on 3 February 1982 reported that "unimpeachable sources" indicated that Argentina would adopt a new diplomatic approach in the next round of talks. It considered that the new impetus which the Argentine Foreign Ministry had given to foreign policy, among other things, pointed to 1982 as being the key year for the effective recovery of the Islands. Those advocating a military operation saw occupation as a consequence of British intransigence or indifference in face of a possible Argentine ultimatum to reach a realistic understanding through peaceful negotiations. In the event of an eventual breakdown of the talks "a veritable avalanche of massive and authoritative public opinion would descend in favour of the alternative of force". It considered that, although substantive progress had not so far been achieved, Argentina would persist with "her traditional peaceful negotiating approach, perhaps in the hope that this time the United Kingdom, faced with the real alternative of armed occupation, would take the bull by the horns and press the negotiations to a final conclusion".

The New York talks

On 15 February 1982, in advance of the talks in New York on 26 and 27 February 1982, Lord Carrington sent a minute to the Prime Minister and to other members of the Defence Committee referring to the *bout de papier* and the proposal for a permanent negotiating commission; and to the response that the British Ambassador in Buenos Aires had been instructed to give. Lord Carrington observed that in principle the idea of setting up working groups to look at particular aspects of the dispute had considerable appeal since it was in the Government's interest to keep a dialogue going in order to avoid the difficult and costly consequences of a breakdown. But it would be necessary to resist the unrealistic timetable of work proposed by Argentina. It would also be difficult to carry the Islanders since they would be most reluctant to agree to any discussion of sovereignty with the Argentines, and the Argentines would accept nothing less. The British delegation would make it clear at the outset of the talks that any agreement reached on the future of the negotiations would be strictly *ad referendum*, but the tougher attitude being shown by the new Argentine Government, together with the strong disinclination of the Islanders to envisage any change from the *status quo*, narrowed the options. In the same minute Lord Carrington said that he expected that there would need to be a further discussion of the Falklands in the Defence Committee in March. The Prime Minister commented that it must be made clear to the Argentines that the wishes of the Islanders were paramount.

On 23 February 1982 Lord Buxton, the Chairman of Anglia Television, who has wide experience of matters concerning the South Atlantic, had a private conversation with Dr Costa Mendez when he was in Buenos Aires awaiting passage on HMS *Endurance*. He gave an account of it to the British Embassy in Buenos Aires afterwards and subsequently sent Mr Luce, on 26 March 1982, a detailed account of his interview. The British Embassy reported that Dr Costa Mendez had stressed that sovereignty was crucial for Argentina and some alternative solution to leaseback had to be found; but he had discounted the possibility of invasion. In his later and fuller report Lord Buxton recorded that Dr Costa Mendez had repeatedly said that he was under pressure from public opinion, but Lord Buxton's impression had been that the pressure was coming from the Junta. Dr Costa Mendez said he was willing to renew discussion of leaseback, provided it was presented in a different way. Lord Buxton said that he had received the clear impression that an invasion was unlikely, but that the military might plan unopposed landings, probably in South Georgia; and Dr Costa Mendez had said that incidents such as "Operation Condor" could not necessarily be prevented.

At the talks in New York at the end of February, after each side had set out its position, the British delegation presented a working paper on how it saw the framework within which a permanent negotiating commission would operate. Most of the subsequent discussion was concerned with the detailed arrangements for the commission, but the Argentine delegation pressed for a substantive response to its proposals within a month and for the commission to meet for the first time on 1 April 1982. The talks concluded with agreement of an informal working paper setting out the purpose of the permanent negotiating commission, and of a brief joint *communiqué*.

The purpose of the commission was stated in the working paper to be to accelerate progress towards a peaceful and comprehensive solution of the dispute. It would be presided over by Ministers, who would direct its work and decide on the agenda of, and participation in, meetings. The working paper recognised that the British delegation might include Islanders. The commission's task would be to identify all the elements in the dispute, to consider them in depth and to recommend how they might be resolved within an overall settlement. The period of operation of the commission would be for one year, at the end of which Ministers would review progress and reach conclusions on whether the commission should continue its work. During this period it would be open to either party to propose at any stage the commission's termination. Meetings would be held alternately in the capitals of the two countries, and would be chaired by the Minister of the host Government, although this function could be delegated to a senior official. The work of the commission would be conducted without prejudice to the sovereignty position of either Government. The working paper made no reference to the frequency of meetings.

By agreement, the joint *communiqué*, which was issued on 1 March 1982, gave none of the details of the informal working paper. Its substance was confined to the following:

> The meeting took place in a cordial and positive spirit. The two sides reaffirmed their resolve to find a solution to the sovereignty dispute and considered in detail an Argentine proposal for procedures to make better progress in this sense. They agreed to inform their Governments accordingly.

AFTERMATH OF THE NEW YORK TALKS

On the day that the joint *communiqué* was issued, before the Argentine delegation had returned to Buenos Aires, the Argentine Ministry of Foreign Affairs issued a unilateral *communiqué* which, contrary to what had been agreed in New York, disclosed the full scope of the discussions. It stated:

> At the meeting held in New York on 26 and 27 February, the representatives of Argentina and Great Britain considered an Argentine proposal to establish a system of monthly meetings with a pre-established agenda, pre-arranged meeting place, and led by top-level officials. The aim of such meetings will be genuinely to speed up to the maximum the negotiations in train to achieve recognition of Argentine sovereignty over the Malvinas, South Georgia and the South Sandwich Islands, and by this means to achieve substantial results within a time which at this advanced stage of the discussions will necessarily have to be short.
>
> Argentina has negotiated with Great Britain over the solution of the sovereignty dispute over the Islands with patience, loyalty and good faith for over 15 years, within the

framework indicated by the relevant United Nations Resolutions. The new system constitutes an effective step for the early solution of the dispute. However, should this not occur, Argentina reserves to terminate the working of this mechanism and to choose freely the procedure which best accords with her interests.

This *communiqué* was accompanied by a good deal of press comment in Argentina. *La Nacion* quoted a Government source as saying that parallel plans had been formulated in case the proposed meetings did not produce sufficient progress towards a solution. These included recourse to the United Nations and the breaking off of economic and political relations. The source preferred, however, "at the moment" to discount suggestions of Argentina's using force to resolve the dispute. *La Prensa* speculated, after conversation with Ministry of Foreign Affairs officials, that, if present tactics were unproductive, a first step might be to cut off services to the Islands followed by a progressive cooling of bilateral relations. Sr Rouco quoted sources saying that Britain would have no more than three or four months to acknowledge Argentine sovereignty and agree on an early date for the return of the Islands to Argentina. There would be no flexibility in Argentina's minimum demand for restitution of sovereignty before the 150th anniversary and for the holding of monthly meetings to discuss the handing over of sovereignty and guarantees for the Islanders. Thereafter Argentina would resort to other means if there was no progress. Sr Rouco also discussed the advantages of a direct seizure of the Islands, which he believed would be "understood" by the United States, to whom joint naval facilities in the Islands could be offered. He suggested that such direct action might be taken between the middle and end of the year. The *Buenos Aires Herald* saw the Argentine statement as containing a "veiled threat" and warned Britain that this time Argentina seemed to "mean business". In its view there was no alternative to a British handover.

On 3 March Mr Luce sent a personal message to Sr Ros expressing concern about the unilateral *communiqué*, which contravened the understanding in New York that the proposals would remain confidential until Governments had been consulted. He said the *communiqué* and accompanying press comment created a more difficult and unhelpful climate for continuing the negotiating process. Mr Luce added that he was deeply disturbed by what might be interpreted as threats and that it would be very difficult to make progress unless there was a clear understanding that the issue could only be resolved through peaceful negotiation.

On 4 March the British Ambassador in Buenos Aires saw Sr Ros, who assured him that he had been unaware of the unilateral *communiqué* and accepted that it was unfortunate. He also said that the Ministry of Foreign Affairs accepted no responsibility for remarks ascribed to it unattributably in the press. The following day the British Ambassador saw Dr Costa Mendez, who explained formally and at some length Argentine dissatisfaction with progress, but denied that the Argentine Government wished in any way to threaten. Dr Costa Mendez referred to statements he had made earlier that day in Brazil making it clear that the Argentine Government were not imposing deadlines but setting out a proposed programme which included only recourses contemplated in the United Nations Charter. He repeated the need for a programme of monthly meetings.

Mr Enders's visit to Buenos Aires

Following the New York talks Mr Luce went to Washington to see Mr Thomas Enders, the United States Assistant Secretary of State for Latin American Affairs, before Mr Enders's forthcoming official visit to Buenos Aires. Mr Luce briefed Mr Enders on the British Government's position on the dispute and the progress of negotiations. In view of the danger of confrontation if negotiations broke down, Mr Luce asked him to encourage the Argentines to "keep things cool", which Mr Enders undertook to do.

Following the unilateral *communiqué* on 1 March 1982 the British Ambassador in Washington was also asked to brief Mr Enders on the terms of the British reaction and make it clear that, while the British Government had every wish to find a solution to the dispute, it was politically impossible to negotiate against a background of threats. There was not time, however, for this to be done before Mr Enders left for Buenos Aires, and instead the British Ambassador in Buenos Aires was asked to brief the United States Embassy there in similar terms.

Mr Enders visited Buenos Aires from Sunday 6 to Tuesday 8 March 1982, and met, among others, President Galtieri and Dr Costa Mendez. *La Prensa* reported that he had been given a very full report on the progress of the Falklands negotiations. The British Ambassador in Buenos Aires reported that his information from the American Embassy was that Mr Enders had not taken the opportunity specifically to advise the Argentines to keep the temperature down, but Mr Enders himself subsequently asked that Mr Luce be informed that he had raised the matter both privately with Dr Costa Mendez and publicly, stressing the strategic and human aspects of the problem, both of which had to be resolved for a successful outcome. Although the Argentines had been somewhat non-committal, they had not given him the impression that they were about to do anything drastic.

On 3 March the British Ambassador in Montevideo reported to the British Ambassador in Buenos Aires, and to the Foreign and Commonwealth Office, the views of a leading Uruguayan, who had told her that he had been struck by the much tougher way in which everyone in Buenos Aires was talking about the Falkland Islands. He thought that, if Argentina did not get what it wanted, it might well take some military action.

The Foreign and Commonwealth Office's assessment of the situation

On his return to London Mr Luce answered a Parliamentary Question on 3 March on the discussions he had held in New York. In answer to supplementary questions he stated that there would be no contemplation of any transfer of sovereignty without consulting the wishes of the Islanders, or without the consent of the House. He referred to the *communiqué* issued by the Argentine Ministry of Foreign Affairs as "not helpful to the process that we all wish to see, that will resolve this dispute"; and, when asked for an assurance that all necessary steps were in hand to ensure the protection of the Islands against unexpected attack, said, "we have no doubts about our sovereignty over the Falkland Islands and no doubt about our duties to the Islanders".

At a short meeting on 5 March 1982 Lord Carrington reviewed the situation with Mr Luce, Mr Ure and Mr Fearn. In accordance with normal Foreign Office practice, no minutes of the meeting were taken, but Mr Ure recorded the points for action that had emerged. These were that:

(i) draft messages should be prepared urgently for Mr Luce to send to Sr Ros, and for Lord Carrington to send to Dr Costa Mendez urging him to put the talks back on the rails on the lines agreed in New York;

(ii) a draft personal message should be prepared for Lord Carrington to send to Mr Haig;

(iii) a note should be prepared on United Nations Resolutions on the Falklands; and the Department should consider what initiative might be taken there if the present negotiations broke down; and

(iv) a draft paper should be prepared for a Defence Committee meeting to be held "fairly soon", probably as soon as the Argentine response to the ministerial messages was received.

Mr Ure recorded that the Cabinet Office had said that the Prime Minister would like the next Defence Committee paper on the Falklands to include annexes on both civil and military contingency plans.

Although the fact is not recorded in Mr Ure's note, he also took the opportunity, after consulting the Permanent Under-Secretary of State (who was not present at the meeting) to tell Lord Carrington that, in November 1977, at an earlier period of heightened tension in the dispute, the previous Government had covertly sent a small naval task force to the area. Lord Carrington asked whether the Argentines had known about it and, when told that they had not, he did not pursue the matter. Officials did not recommend to Ministers at the meeting that they should consider a similar naval deployment.

Intelligence reports

In early March 1982 a number of intelligence reports were available indicating the views of Argentine Ministers and officials in the preceding weeks. The general tenor of these reports was that, while it was important for the Argentine Government to make progress in the negotiations, military action was not being contemplated in the immediate future. Reports available immediately prior to the New York talks reflected the views of Argentine officials that there would be no invasion unless the talks broke down; that it would be unrealistic to think of invasion before the next southern summer; and that invasion was not considered a realistic option. A further report at the beginning of March, reflecting an Argentine diplomatic view, was to the effect that Argentina was determined to achieve progress on sovereignty by the end of the year; and, if this was not forthcoming, would take the issue to the General Assembly with a view to obtaining a declaration recognising Argentine sovereignty over the Falklands. There was information that Dr Costa Mendez had decided that, if the talks did not produce results, a campaign would be mounted against Britain in international organisations; if this failed and the talks on the Beagle Channel made no progress, there was likely to be little alternative to the use of force.

On 2 March 1982 the British Defence *Attaché* in Buenos Aires wrote to the Governor of the Falkland Islands, copying his letter to the Ministry of Defence and the Foreign and Commonwealth Office (where it was received on about 9 March) on the Argentine military threat to the Falklands. This followed a private visit that he had made to the Islands on his own initiative in January 1982 to enable him to judge at first hand the military situation there in the event of Argentine action. On his return to Buenos Aires he had briefed the British Ambassador there about his visit, but had not made a formal report in view of its unofficial nature. In the light of later developments, in particular Argentine press comment about the possibility of military measures, the Defence *Attaché* decided to circulate his views more widely. In his letter he commented that, on the worst possible interpretation of developments, an Army President, who had already demonstrated his lack of patience when frustrated over such issues, could give orders to the military to solve the Malvinas problem once and for all in the latter half of the year. He judged that, unless and until the talks broke down, the most likely threat was posed by the Argentine Navy, which could take a number of measures to demonstrate how the Argentine claim to sovereignty could be backed by strength, such as establishing a naval presence on an outlying island or landing marines on one of the islands for a 24-hour exercise. If the Argentines came to believe that a negotiated settlement was no longer possible, a straight seizure of the Islands was an obvious alternative. The Defence *Attaché* pointed out that in Argentina a military *coup* was a fairly well practised art; the Argentine Army studied and admired *coup de main* operations of all sorts. He examined several ways in which Argentina might mount an operation of this kind, and pointed out that the chance of providing early warning from Argentina could be increased if some special arrangements could be made, but that as things were they could not realistically expect to be able to detect any Argentine military moves.

On 10 March an officer in the Defence Intelligence Staff of the Ministry of Defence circulated a minute widely within the Ministry of Defence; it was also copied to the

Foreign and Commonwealth Office. It drew attention to recent intelligence indicating that the belligerent press comment had been inspired by the Argentine Navy in an attempt to achieve an early settlement of the dispute. The intelligence also indicated that, if there was no tangible progress towards a settlement by the end of June, the Argentine Navy would push for a diplomatic offensive in international organisations, a break in relations with Britain and military action against the Islands, but that neither President Galtieri nor the Army was thinking along those lines. Summarising the position, the minute said that all other diplomatic and intelligence reporting in recent weeks confirmed that all elements of the Argentine Government apart from the Navy favoured diplomatic action to solve the dispute and that the military option was not under active consideration at that time. It saw no reason to believe that the Argentine Navy had any prospect of persuading the President or other Government members to adopt its proposed course of action or of going it alone; and did not therefore consider that the Navy's attitude posed any immediate or increased threat to the Falkland Islands beyond that outlined in the most recent Joint Intelligence Committee assessment, prepared in July 1981.

The Prime Minister's reaction to the deteriorating diplomatic situation

On 3 March the British Ambassador in Buenos Aires had reported further comment in the Argentine press on the unilateral *communiqué*. When the Prime Minister saw this telegram, she wrote on it, "we must make contingency plans". Her Private Secretary wrote to the Foreign and Commonwealth Office on 8 March, copying his letter to the Ministry of Defence and the Cabinet Office, recording the Prime Minister's comment and saying that he understood that it might be the intention of Lord Carrington to bring a further paper on the Falkland Islands to the Defence Committee in the fairly near future; and that the Foreign and Commonwealth Office might think that this could helpfully contain an account of contingency planning. No immediate response was made to the letter because, the Committee believes, of the general expectation in Whitehall that it would be included on the agenda of an early meeting of the Defence Committee.

On 8 March the Prime Minister also spoke to Mr Nott and asked him how quickly Royal Naval ships could be deployed to the Falkland Islands, if required. The Ministry of Defence replied on 12 March indicating which ships were then deployed in the West Indies, and on exercise in the Gulf of Mexico and off the eastern seaboard of the United States. The reply pointed out that passage time for a frigate deployed to the Falklands, which would require Royal Fleet Auxiliary support, would be in the order of 20 days.

Diplomatic initiatives

On further consideration of the action agreed at Lord Carrington's meeting on 5 March 1982, it was decided to send only one message to the Argentine Government, from Lord Carrington to Dr Costa Mendez. A draft was sent to the Governor on 8 March for consideration by the Island Councillors. It expressed Lord Carrington's pleasure at the progress that had been made in New York towards setting up new procedures for carrying forward and giving fresh impetus to negotiations about the future of the Islands, which reflected the Government's determination to achieve a peaceful solution to a difficult issue which would be acceptable to both Governments and to the people of the Falkland Islands, while expressing disappointment at the statements which had been made in the press reports in Buenos Aires following the talks. It sought agreement on "two essential points": first, that the negotiating commission would encompass all aspects of possible approaches to a solution of the dispute, without prejudice to either side's position on sovereignty; and, secondly, that the negotiations could not be pursued against a background of threats from either side of retaliatory action if they broke down. At a joint meeting of the Island Councils on 16 March, which had been brought forward from 18 March for this purpose, there was unanimous support for the message as drafted. The Councillors asked the Governor to emphasise that there could be no negotiations on the *transfer of sovereignty*; their aim would be to convince Argentina that Britain had the stronger claim to the Islands and that the Islanders were determined to stay British.

On 18 March a draft telegram to the British Ambassador in Buenos Aires was submitted to Mr Luce and Lord Carrington incorporating the message to Dr Costa Mendez. Officials were not optimistic that Argentina would accept the message as a basis for future negotiations. They took the view that it would be necessary to work on the assumption that the Argentine reply would be negative and that Argentina might resort at an early stage to retaliatory measures. This view was reinforced by recent intelligence indicating that, unless a satisfactory reply meeting Argentine conditions was received by the end of March 1982 at the latest, early action to withdraw Argentine services to the

Islands might be taken. Officials recommended that, in advance of the proposed discussion in the Defence Committee, Lord Carrington should seek Mr Nott's agreement, on a contingency basis, to maintain HMS *Endurance* on station in the area for the time being; and should circulate to members of the Defence Committee the paper by officials seeking political and financial authority to carry forward urgently contingency plans for the replacement of services to the Islands. This paper was submitted to Foreign and Commonwealth Office Ministers on 19 March 1982.

Lord Carrington subsequently decided to circulate the draft of the proposed reply to Dr Costa Mendez to his colleagues with his minute of 24 March 1982 (see below) to the Prime Minister, but it was held up in consequence of events on South Georgia and was never sent.

The second initiative decided on at Lord Carrington's meeting on 5 March was the sending of a personal message to Mr Haig. This was sent to the British Embassy in Washington on 8 March for delivery to Mr Haig. It expressed the British Government's increasing concern about the Argentine Government's attitude, in particular about the threats in the Argentine press, apparently with some measure of Government inspiration, to use force if the negotiations did not soon reach a conclusion on Argentine terms. It said that Mr Haig would realise that it was politically impossible to negotiate against such a background, so that anything that Mr Enders could do while in Buenos Aires to bring the Argentines to a more reasonable and pacific frame of mind would be much appreciated: it was in everyone's interest that the issue should not be allowed to develop into a dangerous source of tension in the region.

Lord Carrington expressed the hope that the Government could count on Mr Haig's help in ensuring that the issue was settled peacefully and in accordance with the democratically expressed wishes of the inhabitants of the Islands. Mr Haig's reply was delivered on 15 March. In it he referred to Mr Enders's visit to Buenos Aires, where he had urged the Argentines to continue negotiations. He said that they had been non-committal but not negative. Mr Haig added that, as opportunities presented themselves, the Americans would continue to urge a constructive approach with due regard for all interests at stake.

Intelligence: mid-March 1982

In mid-March Foreign and Commonwealth Office Ministers received a number of intelligence reports. One reported that Mr Enders had been told that Argentina planned to mount an international diplomatic offensive if there were no immediate signs of British willingness to bring negotiations to a successful conclusion within the next year; the report claimed that Mr Enders had indicated that the US Government would see no problem in this course of action. Another, reflecting Argentine military views, referred to a plan to achieve gradual British withdrawal from the Falklands over 30 years, at the end of which full sovereignty would pass to Argentina; the talk of invasion since the New York talks was said to have been part of a design to put psychological pressure on Britain. A further report indicated that senior Argentine naval officers doubted that Argentina would invade the Falklands, although it would be relatively simple to do so and they thought that Britain would not prevent it.

Other intelligence reports indicated that the Junta had been displeased with the agreement reached in New York and that the unilateral Ministry of Foreign Affairs *communiqué* had been issued on the orders of the President. The view of the Ministry of Foreign Affairs was said to be that the negotiating team in New York had properly carried out its instructions except in failing to obtain British agreement to a date in March 1982 for a meeting to begin the monthly series of talks. This had caused the trouble with the Government. It had been decided that, if no reply were forthcoming from the British side on a date in March 1982, Argentina would retaliate by withdrawing the air or sea services to the Islands. There had been no final decision on the action to be taken if the British agreed to a date after March but there was a disposition in the Ministry of Foreign Affairs to take action to show all concerned that they were serious. Dr Costa Mendez was also concerned to make up for the Argentine failure in the Beagle Channel dispute. An invasion was said not to have been seriously considered but in the last resort it could not be discounted in view of the unpredictability of the President and some senior members of the Armed Forces.

At this stage in the diplomatic exchanges with Argentina, the initiatives directed towards the resumption of negotiations on the basis agreed at the New York talks at the end of February were, in effect, overtaken by the South Georgia incident, with is dealt with next.

19 MARCH TO 2 APRIL 1982

THE SOUTH GEORGIA INCIDENT

Sr Constantino Davidoff, a scrap-metal merchant from Buenos Aires, first approached Christian Salvesen, the Edinburgh-based firm managing the Crown leases for the disused whaling stations on South Georgia, in 1978. The following year he signed a contract giving him an option to purchase equipment and dispose of it. The option was exercised in 1980 under an agreement that any

equipment remaining after March 1983 would revert to
Salvesens. Sr Davidoff was occasionally in contact with the
British Embassy in Buenos Aires in 1980 and 1981.

Sr Davidoff left Buenos Aires on 16 December 1981 on
the Argentine naval ice-breaker, *Almirante Irizar*, to inspect
the scrap on South Georgia and arrived at Leith on 20
December. He notified the British Embassy in Buenos Aires
of the visit in a letter which arrived after he had departed.

On 31 December 1981 the Governor of the Falkland
Islands relayed to the Foreign and Commonwealth Office a
report by the British Antarctic Survey Base Commander at
Grytviken of the unauthorised presence of the *Almirante
Irizar* in Stromness Bay. The Governor pointed out that the
Almirante Irizar was required by the Dependencies' legisla-
tion to obtain entry clearance at Grytviken and that Sr
Davidoff knew this. He recommended instituting proceed-
ings against Sr Davidoff and making a strong protest to the
Argentine Government.

A reply was sent instructing the Governor not to insti-
tute proceedings, which "would risk provoking a most
serious incident which could escalate and have an unforeseeable outcome". He was instructed that, if Sr Davidoff
presented himself at Grytviken and asked for entry clearance, it should be granted; if the Argentine vessel was naval
and clearance for her also was not sought, the Base
Commander should deliver a formal written protest; if
Sr Davidoff attempted to land at Grytviken without proper
clearance, the party should be ordered to depart immediately but without threats being used; and, if it refused to
comply, further instructions should be sought from the
Foreign and Commonwealth Office. The reply also said that
the Foreign and Commonwealth Office would probably

wish in due course to make a protest to the Argentine Government but would first see what transpired at Grytviken.

On 4 January 1982 the Foreign and Commonwealth Office instructed the Ambassador in Buenos Aires to deliver a formal protest in the strongest terms at this violation of British sovereignty and warn against the undesirable consequences which could follow from a repetition. The Ambassador was to say that, if any further attempt were made to land at Grytviken or elsewhere in South Georgia without proper authority, the British Government reserved the right to take whatever action might be necessary, and that it was up to Sr Davidoff to comply with the laws of the Falkland Islands Dependencies. The British Ambassador in Buenos Aires approached the Argentine Ministry of Foreign Affairs on 6 January, but withheld the protest pending an investigation by the Ministry, which denied any knowledge of the incident. Following the receipt of evidence corroborating the visit of the *Almirante Irizar*, the Foreign and Commonwealth Office instructed the British Embassy on 3 February 1982 to lodge a formal protest. The Embassy reported on 9 February that the protest had been delivered, and on 18 February that the Argentine Ministry of Foreign Affairs had rejected it.

On 8 January 1982 Captain Barker, the Captain of HMS *Endurance*, reported that he had spoken by radio to Captain Trombetta, the Officer commanding the Argentine Antarctic Squadron, who was embarked on the *Almirante Irizar*. Captain Trombetta had told him that he was *en route* for the Belgrano base in the Antarctic, but shortly afterwards it had become apparent that he was really making for Southern Thule. Later in the month, on 25 January 1982,

Captain Barker reported that HMS *Endurance* had received a cold reception at the Argentine port of Ushuaia. He had heard that there had been an order not to fraternise with the British. An Argentine pilot had told him on his departure that something was "very wrong" with the Argentine Navy. In contrast to her reception at Ushuaia, HMS *Endurance* was warmly received when she visited another Argentine port, Mar del Plata, shortly afterwards.

The landing on South Georgia on 19 March 1982

The British Ambassador in Buenos Aires reported on 23 February 1982 that Sr Davidoff had called at the Embassy that morning. He had apologised for the problems caused by his visit on the *Almirante Irizar* in December 1981 and said that he intended soon to return to South Georgia with a party to salvage the equipment. He was anxious not to create difficulties and had asked for full instructions on how to proceed. The Ambassador sought advice from the Governor on this point, but did not receive a substantive reply before the party left for South Georgia.

On 9 March Sr Davidoff sent the British Embassy in Buenos Aires formal notification that 41 workmen were going to South Georgia on 11 March on the *Bahia Buen Suceso*, an Argentine naval support vessel, and would remain there for an initial period of four months. He offered to transport supplies to the British Antarctic Survey and to make available to them the services of a doctor and nurse travelling with the party. The British Embassy reported this to the Governor and informed the Foreign and Commonwealth Office, and asked Sr Davidoff for further details of the ship and the workmen. Salvesens reported to the Foreign and Commonwealth Office and to the Governor on 16 March that Sr Davidoff had notified them of the visit and that they had granted his request for an extension of the contract to 31 March 1984.

On 20 March the Governor of the Falkland Islands informed the Foreign and Commonwealth Office of a signal from the Base Commander at Grytviken late the previous day. The British Antarctic Survey had observed the *Bahia Buen Suceso* in Leith Harbour and a sizeable party of civilian and military personnel ashore. Shots had been heard, the Argentine flag had been raised, and a notice warning against unauthorised landings had been defaced. The British Antarctic Survey had informed the Argentines that they should have reported to Grytviken, but was told that permission had been given by the British Embassy in Buenos Aires. The Governor instructed the Base Commander to tell the Argentines again to report to Grytviken and to lower the Argentine flag. The Governor gave his view that the Argentine Navy was using Sr Davidoff as a front to establish an Argentine presence on South Georgia. He suggested that, since this was the second violation by Sr Davidoff, the party should be ordered to leave even if it did report to Grytviken. Having consulted Captain Barker, he also suggested that HMS *Endurance* should sail to South Georgia with marines to enforce the eviction. The Foreign and Commonwealth Office approved the instructions to the Base Commander at Grytviken, but said that Ministers would need to be consulted about the deployment of HMS *Endurance*. The Foreign and Commonwealth Office instructed the British Embassy in Buenos Aires to give a message to the Argentine Ministry of Foreign Affairs that the incident was regarded as serious and that, if the *Bahia Buen Suceso* did not leave forthwith, the British Government would have to take whatever action seemed necessary. The message also indicated that, while both sides were considering how best to continue negotiations on the sovereignty dispute in order to solve it peacefully, it would be hard to understand if the Argentine Government endorsed the incident. The Argentine *Chargé d'Affaires* in London was also summoned and given this message. The British Ambassador in Buenos Aires reported that the Ministry of Foreign Affairs professed to have been unaware of the visit. He confirmed that Sr Davidoff had not been given any permission by the British Embassy. He advised that great restraint should be used, at least until it was clear whether or not the incident was a deliberate challenge authorised at high level. Foreign and Commonwealth Office and Defence Ministers agreed the HMS *Endurance* should sail for South Georgia the next day, with additional marines, unless the Argentines obeyed the Governor's instructions. The Commander-in-Chief, Fleet, sent the necessary instructions to HMS *Endurance* towards midnight on 20 March 1982. The Governor was instructed to report any developments on South Georgia and to keep the destination of HMS *Endurance* confidential, in order to avoid the appearance of escalating the incident.

The following day, Sunday 21 March, the Base Commander at Grytviken, who had arranged an observation party at Leith, reported that the Argentine flag had been lowered, but that there was no indication that the Argentines were preparing to leave. The British Ambassador in Buenos Aires reported the Argentine Government's official response, which, without making an apology, expressed the hope that the significance of the affair would not be exaggerated. It confirmed that the party and the ship would be leaving the same day; that they were in no way official; and that the party included no serving service personnel and was not carrying military arms. The Foreign and Commonwealth Office informed the Governor that HMS *Endurance* would sail for South Georgia unless the Argentine ship and party left, and asked for confirmation that the party was civilian. The Base Commander reported that some of the Argentines were dressed in what appeared to him to be military-style clothing and had behaved in a military way, but had not carried firearms. Between 50 and 60 Argentines had been seen, most of them in civilian clothing. Although no firearms had been seen, further shots had been heard and reindeer had been killed, which was contrary to the provisions of Sr Davidoff's contract.

On Monday 22 March the Base Commander at Grytviken reported that the *Bahia Buen Suceso* had sailed from Leith and that there was no sign of the shore party.

On the same day the Governor telegraphed a personal message to Lord Carrington from Lord Buxton, who said that he had gained the impression from his recent talk with Dr Costa Mendez that open attack was unlikely but that casual unopposed landings were probable. He urged that Sr Davidoff should not be regarded as a casual scrap-dealer and that his contract should be rescinded immediately in view of the deliberate breaches of its terms. He judged that, if the British reaction was placatory, more illegal landings would follow, the next time probably on the Falkland Islands.

The Argentine *Chargé d'Affaires* informed the Foreign and Commonwealth Office that the *Bahia Buen Suceso* had departed from Leith on 21 March, leaving behind equipment, and that he assumed that all the personnel had left with the ship. He stressed that the action taken by Sr Davidoff had been on his own responsibility and in no way reflected any deliberate intention by the Argentine Government to raise the political temperature; the ship was not a warship but a naval transport vessel operating under a commercial charter and without service personnel or weapons on board. The Foreign and Commonwealth Office informed the *Chargé d'Affaires* that the British Government had no wish to build up the incident. HMS *Endurance* was instructed to resume her normal duties unless the Base Commander reported a continued Argentine pressure at Leith.

On 22 March diplomatic exchanges also took place in Buenos Aires, where the Ministry of Foreign Affairs expressed concern at news of an insult to the Argentine flag at the LADE (Argentine Air Force airline) office in Port Stanley. The Governor reported that on the night of 20/21 March the LADE office had been entered, apparently by someone using a key. A Union Flag had been placed over the Argentine flag there and "tit for tat, you buggers" written in toothpaste on a desk. In a later incident, during the night of 22/23 March, "UK OK" was written on two external windows of the LADE office.

Later on 22 March the Base Commander at Grytviken reported that some Argentines were still at Leith, and that a French yacht, the *Cinq Gars Pour*, had ignored his instructions not to go to Leith and was making contact with the Argentines. Captain Barker sent a signal expressing his view that there were indications of collusion between Sr Davidoff and the Argentine Navy. The naval headquarters in Buenos Aires had congratulated the *Bahia Buen Suceso* on a successful operation and directed her to return to Buenos Aires as soon as possible. The Governor strongly recommended that HMS *Endurance* should be instructed to remove the men from Leith.

HMS *Endurance* was ordered to continue towards South Georgia and await further instructions. The same evening, the British Ambassador in Buenos Aires reported that the Ministry of Foreign Affairs had confirmed that some men had been left behind at Leith but had urged that no forceful action should be taken which would irritate public opinion in Argentina.

On 23 March Captain Barker sent a signal suggesting that the events in South Georgia were linked with the misinformation he had been given in January 1982 about the activities of the *Almirante Irizar* and with three recent Argentine Air Force overflights of South Georgia. The signal also noted that the *Bahia Buen Suceso* had observed strict radio silence throughout her stay at South Georgia. In drawing this signal to the attention of Mr Luce, Foreign and Commonwealth Office officials commented that it was evidence that the operation in South Georgia had been undertaken with the full knowledge and probable guidance of the Argentine Navy.

The Base Commander at Grytviken reported that there were an estimated ten Argentines left at Leith. Ministerial approval was given for HMS *Endurance* and the Royal Marines aboard her to be used to remove them.

That afternoon Mr Luce made the following statement to the House of Commons:

> We were informed on 20 March by the commander of the British Antarctic survey base at Grytviken on South Georgia

that a party of Argentines had landed at Leith harbour nearby. The base commander informed the Argentine party that its presence was illegal as it had not obtained his prior authority for the landing. We immediately took the matter up with the Argentine authorities in Buenos Aires and the Argentine embassy in London and, following our approach, the ship and most of the personnel left on 21 March. However, the base commander has reported that a small number of men and some equipment remain. We are therefore making arrangements to ensure their early departure.

In reply to questions expressing concern, Mr Luce referred to the presence in the area of HMS *Endurance*, which was in a position to help if necessary. He also said that it was the duty of any British Government to defend the Islands to the best of their ability but that the deployment of a defence force was a matter for the Defence Secretary.

The British Ambassador in Buenos Aires was informed by the Foreign and Commonwealth Office that Ministers had decided that HMS *Endurance* should continue to South Georgia in order to remove the remaining Argentines. He was instructed to tell the Ministry of Foreign Affairs that the continued presence of the Argentines, contrary to previous assurances, left no option but to take this action, which was the regrettable result of Sr Davidoff's own irresponsibility. The intention was to conduct the operation correctly, peacefully and in as low a key as possible.

On the same day (23 March) the British Ambassador in Buenos Aires reported that he had been summoned to see Sr Ros, who had asked him to account for the incident in the LADE office at Port Stanley and sought an assurance that the matter would be investigated and any breach of the peace duly punished. Sr Ros had also asked for co-operation to reduce the landing at Leith to more realistic proportions since the men left were simple workmen. The British Ambassador told Sr Ros that the British Government shared his wish to avoid exaggeration.

Later in the day the British Ambassador was summoned to see Dr Costa Mendez, who expressed surprise that the British Government were proceeding so rapidly to such very grave action, without exhausting the diplomatic options. Dr Costa Mendez gave a solemn warning that, if action to remove the party on South Georgia was not postponed, those like himself and Sr Ros who were trying to deal with the Falklands in a moderate way, would lose control of events. Harsh action would precipitate a harsh response, but he could not predict what it would be, nor could he undertake to keep it within bounds. Dr Costa Mendez agreed to look at the British Ambassador's suggestion that the *Bahia Buen Suceso* might return to remove the men and urged that in the meantime HMS *Endurance* should not take any action. He added that the incident illustrated the need to get on with the main negotiations and suggested that it might be held over as a first subject for discussion by the negotiating commission.

In reporting this conversation to the Foreign and Commonwealth Office, the British Ambassador warned that, seen from Buenos Aires, the British Government's reaction to Sr Davidoff's "trivial and low-level misbehaviour" could do lasting damage to the whole structure of bilateral relations.

Foreign and Commonwealth Office Ministers decided to make a further attempt to resolve the problem without provocation. HMS *Endurance* was ordered to wait at Grytviken instead of proceeding to Leith. The British Ambassador in Buenos Aires was instructed to pass on a personal message from Lord Carrington to Dr Costa Mendez agreeing to the removal of the men by the *Bahia Buen Suceso*; but making it clear that it was essential that they should be removed without delay. Failing this, they would be removed by other means. The message also said that it was essential not to lose sight of the overriding need to ensure the right political climate for mutual efforts to resolve the Falklands dispute peacefully through negotiations.

In the evening of 23 March Dr Costa Mendez told the British Ambassador in Buenos Aires that he welcomed Lord Carrington's message. He had discussed the issue with the Junta. Dr Costa Mendez said that he assumed it would be possible for another Argentine ship to remove the men, and was about to discuss this with the military. In reporting this conversation to the Foreign and Commonwealth Office, the British Ambassador commented that he thought Dr Costa Mendez was trying to be helpful and sensible, but he was on a short rein with public opinion and the military.

On 24 March the British Ambassador reported that Dr Costa Mendez had told him that he was hopeful of arranging the removal of the men by another vessel but that the decision would be made at a meeting of the Commanders-in-Chief.

On the same day Lord Carrington sent a minute to the Prime Minister and other members of the Defence Committee about the Falkland Islands dispute generally. He said that, since he had last reported, on 15 February 1982, the dispute had developed to a point where an early confrontation with Argentina might need to be faced. He referred to the difficult and demanding proposal that Argentina had put forward at the New York talks; to the subsequent Ministry of Foreign Affairs *communiqué* and bellicose press comment; and to the South Georgia incident. He circulated with his minute the draft message to Dr Costa Mendez (prepared after his meeting on 5 March but never sent). The message was as follows:

I was pleased to hear from Richard Luce about the progress which the Argentine and British delegations (with the assistance of the Falkland Islands Councillors) made in New York on 26 and 27 February towards setting up new procedures for carrying forward and giving fresh impetus to negotiations about the future of the Islands. This reflected our determination to achieve a peaceful solution to this difficult issue, which would be acceptable to your Government, to the British Government and to the people of the Falkland Islands. You must also know of our subsequent disappointment (which Richard Luce has made clear to Sr Ros) at the statements which have been made, and the press reports which have been appearing, in Buenos Aires since the conclusion of those talks.

I therefore think it would be helpful, if we are to be able to proceed further along the lines discussed in New York, that we should confirm our respective Governments' agreement on two essential points. Firstly, it is understood that the work of the proposed Negotiating Commission will encompass all aspects of and possible approaches to a solution of the dispute without prejudice to either side's position on sovereignty. These talks must be genuine negotiations and cannot be based on any predetermined assumptions on what the outcome might be. Secondly, these negotiations cannot be pursued against a background of threats from either side of retaliatory action if they break

down. We would welcome your assurance that the
Argentine Government intends to further the negotiations
on this basis.

In the spirit of the recent meeting in New York, and so
that there may be no misunderstanding, I would intend,
once you have replied, to publish this message and, with
your permission, your reply.

Lord Carrington said in his minute that the draft message
had been agreed by the Falkland Islands Councillors, but
that it would require amendment before issue to take
account of developments over the illegal landing on South
Georgia. Once the Argentines replied, he intended to publish the text of his message in order to demonstrate to both
British and international opinion the importance the
British Government attached to achieving a solution of the
dispute through peaceful and genuine negotiations. He
could not, however, be confident that the message would be
acceptable to the Argentines. Argentina had built up a dangerous head of steam on the issue and Argentine public
opinion had been led to expect rapid progress only on
Argentine terms and with the sole objective of arranging an
early transfer of sovereignty. It was therefore necessary to
recognise that negotiations might be at an end and that the
Argentines would turn to other forms of pressure: international action at the United Nations, diplomatic and
commercial reprisals, and, in the final analysis, military
action against the Islands. Lord Carrington recommended
an early meeting of the Defence Committee to consider the
full implications and the action it might be necessary to take
in response. He also sought approval for officials to carry
forward civil contingency plans to replace air and sea services to the Falklands and financial approval to meet such

costs from the Contingency Reserve. The Chief Secretary to the Treasury replied to Lord Carrington on 29 March saying that he could not agree to meeting the cost from the Contingency Reserve.

Also on 24 March Lord Carrington wrote separately to Mr Nott seeking agreement to HMS *Endurance's* remaining on station for the time being and suggesting that, in advance of the next Defence Committee meeting to discuss the Falklands, the Ministry of Defence should circulate a paper on military contingency planning.

Intelligence was also circulated indicating that Admiral Anaya, the Argentine naval Commander-in-Chief, was behind the hardening Argentine position on South Georgia and that the Navy was planning to do something if the Argentine proposal made at the New York talks did not produce tangible progress towards the transfer of sovereignty within the next few months. It was said that Admiral Anaya had been responsible for the deliberate raising of the temperature since the beginning of the year in order to prepare public opinion; but that there was no central co-ordination of policy, which was conducted from several quarters, including the Ministry of Foreign Affairs and the Navy.

Late on 24 March the British Ambassador in Buenos Aires was summoned by Dr Costa Mendez, who told him that he was having great difficulty, particularly with Admiral Anaya, in taking any action under the threat of force implied in the deployment of HMS *Endurance*. Dr Costa Mendez said that he had been reassured to learn that HMS *Endurance* had sailed to Grytviken rather than Leith and undertook to see whether Sr Davidoff could be persuaded to arrange for the removal of the party, perhaps on a scientific ship, but he was doubtful whether he would succeed.

Also on 24 March, the British Defence *Attaché* in Buenos Aires sent the Ministry of Defence a telegram bringing up to date his earlier assessment of the Argentine military threat to the Falklands. He judged that any attempt at forcible removal of the Argentines from Leith would be met by force, either from a warship at sea or by a "rescue operation" at Port Stanley if the workmen were taken there. The latter could escalate into an occupation of the Falkland Islands. Escalation would suit the hawks in the Argentine Government, who were pressing the leadership to take advantage of the incident. The Defence *Attaché* advised that, before HMS *Endurance* was committed, it would be necessary to take into account the increase in the threat to Port Stanley.

THE DAYS LEADING UP TO THE INVASION

Thursday 25 March

On 25 March information was received in London of the despatch of Argentine warships to prevent HMS *Endurance* from evacuating the Argentines from Leith and of the deployment of further ships to intercept HMS *Endurance*, if required, between South Georgia and the Falkland Islands. Later in the day HMS *Endurance* reported that a second Argentine ship, the *Bahia Paraiso*, had arrived at Leith and was working cargo. In the evening HMS *Endurance* reported three landing craft and a military helicopter between the *Bahia Paraiso* and the jetty at Leith. She also reported that the *Bahia Paraiso* was flying the pennant of the Argentine Navy's Senior Officer, Antarctic Squadron. At that stage the Foreign and Commonwealth Office believed that the *Bahia Paraiso*, although an Argentine naval vessel, was an unarmed, scientific ship.

That morning Lord Carrington reported to Cabinet on the situation in South Georgia. He said that HMS *Endurance* was then at Grytviken and could remove the remaining Argentines from Leith, but that public opinion in Argentina was in a highly charged state over the incident and there was a real risk that, if HMS *Endurance* took this action, Argentine warships in the area might either intercept HMS *Endurance* on her way back to Port Stanley, or carry out some counter-action against the Falkland Islands themselves. Efforts were therefore continuing to persuade the Argentine Government to evacuate the men. There seemed certain to be an adverse effect on negotiations over the Falkland Islands, in which event the Islands' air link might be cut. If the Argentines thereafter threatened military action, Britain would face an almost impossible task in seeking to defend the Islands at such long range. The Cabinet noted that the withdrawal from service of HMS *Endurance* might need to be reconsidered by Mr Nott on his return. (Mr Nott was attending a NATO meeting in Colorado Springs, from which he returned the following day.)

During the day there were further diplomatic exchanges with Argentina, both in London with the Argentine *Chargé d'Affaires*, Sr Molteni, and in Buenos Aires. Foreign and Commonwealth Office officials briefed Lord Carrington and Mr Luce on Dr Costa Mendez's unhelpful response to the request for the Argentine Government to remove urgently the remaining personnel from South Georgia and on the report about the deployment of Argentine warships to prevent their evacuation by HMS *Endurance*. They told them that the Ministry of Defence was urgently assessing the defence implications but that, unless the problem could be resolved by diplomatic action, there was a real risk of military confrontation, which Britain was in no position to win. Lord Carrington agreed that the British Ambassador in Buenos Aires should be instructed to urge Dr Costa Mendez strongly to persuade his colleagues to find a way out of the impasse, and to say that the British Government did not wish to escalate the situation but that the Argentine Government should be in no doubt that "we are committed to the defence of British sovereignty in South Georgia as elsewhere". The British Ambassador in Buenos Aires was also asked to sound out Dr Costa Mendez on whether a personal message from the Prime Minister to President Galtieri or the visit of a special representative of Lord Carrington would help.

These points were also made by the Foreign and Commonwealth Office to the Argentine *Chargé d'Affaires* in London, who made the personal suggestion that it might help if the British Government were to send a positive response to the proposal made at the New York talks for a permanent negotiating commission. Foreign and Commonwealth Office officials advised Ministers that sending Lord Carrington's proposed message to Dr Costa Mendez at that stage might only exacerbate the difficulties and that it would be better to leave the Argentines with the impression that a reply on negotiations depended on clearing up the impasse on South Georgia.

In the afternoon the Foreign and Commonwealth Office briefed the British Ambassador in Washington on the situation by telegram. It explained that there was a grave danger of any conflict spreading more widely and that action against the Falklands could not be discounted. The telegram also said that, while everything was being done to defuse the potentially dangerous situation, "in the final analysis we cannot acquiesce in this infringement of British sovereignty and are bound to take action to restore the *status quo*". At the same time Foreign and Commonwealth Office officials briefed the United States *Chargé d'Affaires* in London, Mr Streator, who undertook to report the British concern to Washington immediately.

The British Ambassador in Buenos Aires reported that afternoon that he had carried out his instructions at meetings with both Sr Ros and Dr Costa Mendez. They had both referred to articles in the British press about HMS *Endurance's* having been sent to South Georgia to take off the Argentine party there and had said that there now seemed to be no way in which the Argentines could remove the men, even if they had agreed to do so, without appearing to have responded to threats. Dr Costa Mendez had also rejected the offers of a message from the Prime Minister and of a special representative. He had, however, asked whether the expulsion order could be revoked if Sr Davidoff ordered his men to complete the necessary landing formalities by having their "white cards"★ stamped at Grytviken. The British Ambassador recommended this course of action in view of the risk of military confrontation. Commenting on the British Ambassador's report, the Governor pointed out that the Dependencies were not included in the 1971 Communications Agreement (and were therefore outside the "white card" régime) and that, if the Ministry of Foreign Affairs had issued "white cards", this indicated its involvement in Sr Davidoff's plans. But he agreed (in a telegram

---

★ The "white card" was a document issued by the Argentine Government for travel between Argentina and the Falkland Islands agreed as part of the 1971 Communications Agreement.

the following day) that this was the most sensible course of action, although it would be unpopular with the Islanders, provided that it was on the basis of stamping the Argentines' passports rather than their "white cards". A reply approved by Ministers was sent to the British Ambassador informing him that the British Government were publicly committed to the Argentines' leaving Leith. He was instructed to tell Dr Costa Mendez that as an ultimate effort of goodwill, if the Argentine party went to Grytviken, documentation would be issued to enable it to return to Leith. The British Ambassador saw Dr Costa Mendez in the evening. Dr Costa Mendez told him that he could not comment on the proposal without consulting the President, which he would do and report back to the Ambassador, if possible the same evening.

The Ministry of Defence reported on the situation to the Chief of Defence Staff, who was abroad. It informed him that the Argentine Ministry of Foreign Affairs appeared to be trying to cool the situation, but that the Argentine Navy were taking a hard line. Two Argentine frigates, with Exocet missiles, had been deployed between South Georgia and the Falklands. The Foreign and Commonwealth Office was informed by the Prime Minister's office of her agreement to Lord Carrington's proposal that officials should urgently take forward civil contingency planning for a sea service.

Reports were received during the day indicating that the Argentine forces were being kept informed about the Royal Marines on the Falkland Islands, about the movements of HMS *Endurance* and other Royal Navy ships, and also about the latest diplomatic situation. The reports indicated that it had been decided that the civilians should remain on South Georgia.

Friday 26 March

On 26 March the Governor informed the Foreign and Commonwealth Office that HMS *Endurance* had reported that the *Bahia Paraiso* had left Leith, but it was not yet possible to tell whether it had taken the party off. HMS *Endurance* later signalled that the Argentines were still ashore at Leith and, from the large quantity of stores visible, appeared to be established for a long stay. Captain Barker added that in his view the operation must have been planned for some time as the *Bahia Paraiso* had arrived from Antarctica, not from Argentina.

The British Ambassador in Buenos Aires reported that he had been told that President Galtieri wished to discuss South Georgia with the Argentine Commanders-in-Chief and that a response to the British proposal would probably not be made until the evening. In the meantime, Foreign and Commonwealth Office officials made a submission to Mr Luce about the options, on the assumptions that the Argentines had no intention of departing and that the proposal to complete the arrangements at Grytviken was rejected. The submission said that the present evidence was that the Argentines were consolidating the landing at Leith but there was still no evidence of an Argentine military capability there. The option of preparing a task force to support HMS *Endurance* was mentioned—but not recommended at that stage—with the comment that the Ministry of Defence would not be in favour of it.

On Mr Luce's advice Lord Carrington decided over the weekend that HMS *Endurance* should evacuate the Argentines but should offer to transfer them to an Argentine vessel if challenged; and that a message should be sent to Mr Haig seeking the good offices of the United

States as a mediator. Foreign and Commonwealth Office Ministers also agreed to take advantage of the arrival of a new party of Royal Marines to double-bank the garrison at Port Stanley pending the outcome of events in South Georgia.

Ministry of Defence officials briefed Mr Wiggin, the Parliamentary Under-Secretary of State, Armed Forces, about the possible retention of HMS *Endurance* and about the situation in South Georgia. After consulting Mr Nott by telephone, Mr Wiggin wrote to Lord Carrington agreeing to the retention on station of HMS *Endurance* for the time being and informing him that arrangements were also being made to sail a support vessel on 29 March to resupply her. Mr Wiggin said that there was an urgent need to decide HMS *Endurance's* long-term future. While he accepted that she had great symbolic importance as a demonstration of commitment to the Falklands, if the Argentines were to bring to bear the sizeable naval forces they had available, HMS *Endurance* could make only a very limited contribution to the defence of the Falklands. The Ministry of Defence could not justify paying for her retention. Mr Wiggin added that for these reasons there was everything to be said for a very early discussion by the Defence Committee, hopefully before Easter. Mr Wiggin separately notified Mr Luce of his agreement to the double-banking of the Port Stanley garrison.

The Ministry of Defence also sent to the Prime Minister's office a revised version of the note approved by the Chiefs of Staff in September 1981 on the defence implications of Argentine action against the Falkland Islands. The only significant changes from the earlier version were the removal of the cost estimates and of a concluding summary paragraph, and the addition of a passage discussing the possibility, at the outset of a period of rising tension with the prospect of Argentine military action against the Falklands, of deploying a nuclear-powered submarine to the region, either covertly or overtly as a deterrent pending the arrival of further naval reinforcements. On the response to an Argentine invasion of the Falkland Islands, the conclusion was unchanged: if faced with Argentine occupation of the Islands on arrival, there could be no certainty that the large balanced force required to deter a full-scale invasion could retake them.

Intelligence reports were circulated—and seen by Mr Luce—indicating that on 23 March there was still no serious intention of invasion by the Argentine Government as a whole, although there was a more hawkish attitude in Navy quarters, and that the Ministry of Foreign Affairs believed that a negotiated solution would be preferable. The reports also indicated that the Argentine Government would try to raise the temperature but would stop short of bloodshed. The British Embassy in Buenos Aires reported, on the basis of information from another Embassy, that all the submarines at the naval base of Mar del Plata had recently put to sea but that this might not be sinister since a joint naval exercise was taking place, probably in the River Plate area, with the Uruguayan Navy.

Saturday 27 March

On Saturday 27 March the British Ambassador in Buenos Aires reported his fears that Dr Costa Mendez had been less than honest with him and that the Argentines had been "playing us along". He took this view because after the Commanders-in-Chief's meeting the previous evening Dr

Costa Mendez did not summon him, as they had agreed, but instead made a public statement that a firm decision had been taken to give the men on South Georgia all necessary protection, which, in view of the presence of the *Bahia Paraiso*, would not be only diplomatic. The British Ambassador reported that he was seeking an urgent interview with Dr Costa Mendez to discuss this statement and to clarify the status of the *Bahia Paraiso*. He later saw Sr Ros and pressed for information about the position of the *Bahia Paraiso* and about suggestions in the press that there were armed marines on board. Sr Ros was unable to answer these questions and said that, following the Commanders-in-Chief's meeting the previous evening, revised instructions had been given to the Ministry of Foreign Affairs, which would be put into a message to the British Government and delivered that day. The British Ambassador in Buenos Aires commented later in the day that he suspected that Argentine intentions were still a subject for debate within the Junta, the Navy being the most, and the Army and the President the least, hawkish. He said that there was still a possibility that action to remove the party from Leith would be taken as a trigger for armed action by the Argentines.

The British Naval *Attaché* in Buenos Aires reported Argentine press reports the previous day of a joint Argentine/Uruguayan anti-submarine exercise and the sailing of a destroyer and corvette from Mar del Plata. He had been aware of the exercise and thought that it was probably genuine. He also reported press articles that day about intense naval activity at Puerto Belgrano, the sailing of various ships, including a submarine, and the embarkation of marines. HMS *Endurance* confirmed that the *Bahia Paraiso* had sailed from Leith, but reported Argentine activity there and the continued presence of a French yacht, whose crew appeared to be working with the Argentines.

Sunday 28 March

On 28 March the British Ambassador in Buenos Aires reported Dr Costa Mendez's reply, which was as follows:

> The events which have taken place on St Peter's Island in the South Georgias are being followed by my Government with close attention. I am convinced that both the British Government and Your Excellency share our concern and this is why I am sending this message with the object of dispelling any misunderstanding about my Government's motives.
>
> The activities of the group of workers disembarked at Leith are of a private and peaceful character based on the undisputed fact that they were known in advance by Her Britannic Majesty's Government and in any case on the fact that they are being carried out on territory subject to the special regime agreed in 1971 between the Argentine and Great Britain. It is moreover within Your Excellency's knowledge that these territories are considered by the Argentine Republic as her own and that the sovereignty dispute about them had been recognised by the United Nations in its relevant Resolutions. Your Excellency's Government has accepted the existence of the sovereignty dispute.
>
> However the British Government has reacted in terms which constitute a virtual ultimatum backed by the threat of military action in the form of the despatch of the naval warship *Endurance* and a requirement for the peremptorily immediate evacuation of the Argentine workers from the Island. These actions have been taken without regard to the special characteristics mentioned above. The reaction to which I refer thus constitutes a disproportionate and provocative response aggravated for having received wide

diffusion in the press which has had a negative effect on developments and which is not the responsibility of the Argentine Government. In this connection I cannot but refer to the comments published in the British press many of which have had an aggravating effect and in any case do not contribute to the maintenance of the desirable climate for the conduct of negotiations.

In the light of this attitude my Government can only adopt those measures which prudence and its rights demand. In this context the Argentine workers in South Georgia must remain there since they have been given the necessary documentation to do so.

I feel I must point out to Your Excellency that the present situation is the direct result of the persistent lack of recognition by the United Kingdom of the titles to sovereignty which my country has over the Malvinas, South Georgia and the South Sandwich Islands. This is confirmed by the negative attitude of Your Excellency's Government throughout many years of negotiations in which Argentina has given adequate evidence of its wish to resolve the dispute by peaceful means with imagination and patience which today have lasted for over fifteen years.

To resolve the present situation I consider it necessary that Your Excellency's Government should display, as does the Argentine Government, the political will to negotiate not only the current problem which concerns us but also the sovereignty dispute bearing in mind that so long as this continues our relations will be open to similar disturbances and crises.

Your Excellency can be sure of counting upon the co-operation and goodwill of my Government to achieve a satisfactory solution.

The British Ambassador commented that the message did not suggest any constructive way of proceeding and withdrew Dr Costa Mendez's proposal for the completion of formalities at Grytviken. He concluded that the Argentines intended no move to resolve the dispute, but to let matters ride while they built up their naval strength in the area. The Governor pointed out that the message contained some inaccuracies, which indicated that the Argentines either misunderstood or were flouting the 1971 Communications Agreement. He thought that the message confirmed the Argentine Government's complicity with Sr Davidoff.

HMS *Endurance* reported that the *Bahia Paraiso* was stationed 15 miles off the north coast of South Georgia and that there appeared to be more than a dozen, possibly 18, Argentines at Leith.

In the evening, Lord Carrington sent Mr Haig the message referred to earlier. It said that it was the British Government's firm wish to resolve the problem peacefully, but that the continued presence of the Argentines was an infringement of British sovereignty "in which we could not acquiesce". It asked Mr Haig to consider taking the matter up with the Argentines and suggested that the matter could be resolved either by the Argentines' seeking permission at Grytviken to regularise their position or by their evacuation by a third-country ship.

Later that evening the Prime Minister, prompted by the most recent telegrams, telephoned Lord Carrington expressing her concern that the Government should respond effectively to the critical situation on South Georgia and worsening relations with the Argentine Government. Lord Carrington said that a message had been sent to Mr Haig, and that Mr Luce was to hold a meeting with officials the next morning and would report to them at midday in Brussels, where they were due to attend a European Community meeting.

Monday 29 March

On the morning of Monday 29 March the Prime Minister and Lord Carrington discussed the matter on their way to Brussels. They decided that a nuclear-powered submarine should be sent to support HMS *Endurance*, and this was notified to the Ministry of Defence. In reply Mr Nott sent a telegram to the Prime Minister in Brussels confirming that contingency plans had been set in hand over the weekend in the context of developments on South Georgia, as a result of which a number of steps had been taken. As HMS *Endurance* might be required to remain at South Georgia for the foreseeable future and would begin to run short of food and other supplies in three weeks, the RFA *Fort Austin* had that day sailed from Gibraltar to replenish HMS *Endurance*. She would also be capable of providing support to other ships should they have to be sent to the area. In addition, a nuclear-powered submarine would be sent covertly to reach the Falklands by 13 April, and a second submarine would be prepared. Mr Nott advised that it would be possible to deploy a fleet of seven destroyers and frigates then on exercise off Gibraltar which could reach the Falklands in two to three weeks, but that this would not in itself constitute a viable full-strength task force. Such a force would take about a week to assemble, which would immediately become public knowledge, and a further three weeks to reach the Falklands. As stated in his subsequent despatch, on 29 March the Commander-in-Chief Fleet ordered the Flag Officer First Flotilla, Rear Admiral Sir John Woodward, to prepare to detach a suitable group of ships from Gibraltar and to be ready to proceed to the South Atlantic if required.

At midday on 29 March Mr Luce reported to Lord Carrington by telegram on his meeting that morning. He recorded the general Foreign and Commonwealth Office view that it would be premature to propose a resumption of the broader Falklands negotiations, or to send a special emissary to Buenos Aires, before a further diplomatic effort had been made to resolve the problem of South Georgia. Mr Luce advised that any resumption of wider talks in New York or Buenos Aires would look too much as if the Government were negotiating under duress, even if the solution of the South Georgia problem were made the first item on any agenda. Later in the day Lord Carrington was also sent drafts of a reply to Dr Costa Mendez, a statement to Parliament and a further message to Mr Haig.

The British Ambassador in Buenos Aires reported on Argentine press treatment of the South Georgia affair, which included reports that five Argentine warships had been despatched towards South Georgia and that all naval leave had been cancelled. He expressed his concern that the Argentine Government would not only gain in popularity by taking a jingoistic stance but would be accepted as doing the right thing in taking even the most extreme measures. Although the relationship between the United States and Argentine Governments had become important, it was questionable whether it would carry the weight of suggesting an Argentine climb-down.

That evening the British Ambassador in Washington reported that he had called on Mr Stoessel, the Deputy Secretary of State at the State Department, who relayed Mr Haig's concern that there should be restraint on both sides and insistence that the United States would not take sides. The British Ambassador had replied that the Americans could surely not be neutral in a case of illegal occupation of sovereign British territory and left Mr

Stoessel in no doubt that, while the British Government remained anxious to keep the temperature down, they could not allow Argentina to assert a claim in this way to a British possession. Mr Stoessel had said that, while the Americans did not have a role to play in resolving the underlying dispute over the Falkland Islands, they were nonetheless willing to use their good offices to bring about a solution to the immediate problem on South Georgia.

In the afternoon the Argentine *Chargé d'Affaires*, Sr Molteni, called on Mr Fearn to obtain reactions to Dr Costa Mendez's message. He said that in his view the solution of regularising the position of the Argentines at Grytviken had been foreclosed since the despatch of HMS *Endurance* to the area and the consequent escalation of the issue. He referred to pressure from "die-hards" in Argentina to capitalise on the South Georgia situation in order to resolve the whole Falklands issue by force. He thought the only probable way out of the impasse would be a positive response from the British Government to the procedural proposals for future negotiations put forward at New York. Sr Molteni was told that this suggestion would be difficult for the British Government to accept.

Intelligence was received which reflected the view of Argentine officials that some form of military action stopping short of a full-scale invasion would take place in the near future and that military action was planned in April, but in the form of occupation of one of the outlying islands, not an invasion of the main islands. It indicated that the Argentine Ministry of Foreign Affairs was making an assessment of the likely reactions of members of the United Nations Security Council to Argentine occupation of the

Falkland Islands. It was also learned that a beach on the Falkland Islands was to be reconnoitred by the Argentines and that an amphibious task force was being prepared.

Tuesday 30 March

On the morning of 30 March Lord Carrington held a meeting with Mr Luce and officials at the Foreign and Commonwealth Office, at which the terms of a Parliamentary statement and of a reply to Dr Costa Mendez's message of 28 March were agreed. It was decided that the reply should propose the visit of a Foreign and Commonwealth Office official as an emissary on behalf of Lord Carrington and the resumption of negotiations on the Falklands once the South Georgia incident had been defused. The message was sent that evening.

In the afternoon Lord Carrington made a statement in the House of Lords summarising developments in the dispute and announcing that HMS *Endurance* would remain on station for as long as was necessary.

Mr Luce repeated the statement in the House of Commons. In reply to questions Mr Luce said that the Islands would be defended if necessary and that the Islanders' wishes were paramount.

Lord Carrington summoned Mr Streator, the United States *Chargé d'Affaires*, to express his displeasure at the message from Mr Haig conveyed through Mr Stoessel the previous day, which had put the British position on the same footing as Argentina's.

The British Naval *Attaché* in Buenos Aires reported to the Ministry of Defence that five Argentine warships including a submarine were sailing to South Georgia; that another four warships had sailed from Puerto Belgrano; and that travel restrictions had been imposed on personnel there. One Argentine newspaper had reported that the four warships were part of a routine training exercise, but another had stated that there had been a rush to put missiles aboard one of them.

Later in the afternoon of 30 March the Ministry of Defence convened a meeting of the Defence Operations Executive, which acts, when the need arises, as the executive agency on behalf of the Chiefs of Staff for the central direction of military operations. The Executive noted the position of Argentine naval ships near South Georgia and of a naval task force, comprising an aircraft carrier, four destroyers and an amphibious landing ship on exercise 800–900 miles north of the Falklands, which was unusual for that time of year. It also noted that there had been no noticeable change in Argentine Air Force readiness and that the Argentine air service to Port Stanley was continuing normally. The Foreign and Commonwealth Office advice at the meeting was that there was an indication that the Argentines planned to occupy at least one island in the Falklands some time in April. They favoured sending one or more nuclear-powered submarines. As a result of the meeting a submission was made to Mr Nott recommending against the deployment of surface ships, which was likely to prove provocative and would require a carrier to provide air support, and against sending a third nuclear-powered submarine. It pointed out that to maintain a presence in the Falklands area for a prolonged period would make enormous demands on military resources, which would have a very serious effect on the ability to meet other commitments worldwide and would incur substantial operating costs. It also noted that the approach of winter in the area would limit the ability effectively to re-inforce the Falklands.

Lord Carrington and Mr Blaker, the Minister of State, Armed Forces, sent a joint minute to the Prime Minister outlining the precautionary steps which had been taken to reinforce the British naval presence in the Falklands area and what else might be done. They reported that, in addition to doubling the Royal Marine garrison at Port Stanley, sending the RFA *Fort Austin* to resupply HMS *Endurance* and sailing a nuclear-powered submarine, it had been decided that morning to confirm the order to send a second submarine. Consideration had been given to sending a third submarine. This action was favoured by Lord Carrington, and a submarine had been earmarked. But it had not yet been given orders to sail since the Ministry of Defence took the view that there would be significant operational penalties elsewhere. The minute also recorded that the possibility of sending the group of seven warships exercising off Gibraltar had been considered but was not thought advisable. The despatch of the force would become known, which would complicate the diplomatic efforts to defuse the situation, and there were military reservations about the adequacy of such a force, which could be easily matched by the Argentines. A credible force would need to be much larger; it would take about 24 days to muster and arrive in the area and would be difficult and expensive to maintain. Its preparation, which could not be concealed, would be highly provocative and escalatory unless the Argentines were preparing to invade the Falklands, of which there was no sign. It was suggested that these matters should be discussed at the meeting of the Defence Committee arranged for Thursday 1 April.

In the evening of 30 March the British Ambassador was instructed to deliver a message from Lord Carrington to Dr Costa Mendez about South Georgia. The message said that the potentially dangerous situation which had now developed had not been of the British Government's seeking. The British objective throughout had been to seek a solution acceptable to both Governments. A confrontation, which could have far reaching consequences and which could seriously prejudice attempts to resolve the whole Falklands issue through peaceful negotiation, was in the interests of neither Government. The message proposed sending a senior Foreign and Commonwealth Office official (Mr Ure) as a personal emissary on his behalf to Buenos Aires with constructive proposals for a solution allowing the salvage contract on South Georgia to be carried out. It said that Lord Carrington would view the defusing of the South Georgia incident as preparing the way for a resumption of the dialogue on the broader issues discussed between Mr Luce and Sr Ros in New York in February.

The same evening the British Ambassador in Buenos Aires reported the United States' Ambassador's account of Dr Costa Mendez's wholly negative reaction to the approach he had made on the instructions of Mr Stoessel, the Deputy Secretary of State at the State Department. Dr Costa Mendez had said that the United States' good offices, while welcome on the underlying dispute, were not required on the current incident and that the compromises suggested by them were not acceptable. There would be no confrontation, provided the British did nothing to disturb the Argentine workmen. The solution of the problem of the incident could be found in starting without delay on negotiation of the main dispute. The British Ambassador noted that this uncompromising stand was taken a few hours before major demonstrations in Buenos Aires by labour unions against the Government's austerity measures. It was generally believed there that the Government had been hoping that the recent jingoist fervour would decide the unions to put off the demonstrations or at least steal the headlines. It also seemed to show Dr Costa Mendez repeating a formula given him in advance to use without discretion. It seemed that the Argentine Government had their tails up and believed that they had found a way of bullying Britain into conceding sovereignty. However, that mood might not last for long. Commenting on his instructions from Lord Carrington, the British Ambassador advised against sending a special emissary and against passing on the message to Dr Costa Mendez at that stage, on the grounds that it had so far been possible for him to maintain civil relations with the Argentines without conceding ground, and a conciliatory gesture and message at that time might serve to convince the Argentines that they had the British Government on the run, not only over South Georgia but over conceding sovereignty. He suggested holding up the message for a day or two while considering the United States' reaction to the report of their Ambassador in Buenos Aires.

Later that evening, the Foreign and Commonwealth Office sent a telegram to Lord Carrington, who was then in Israel, about two intelligence reports received since his departure reflecting Argentine service views. One indicated that a peaceful settlement of the South Georgia incident was possible but that, if any Argentines were killed, Argentina would initiate military action against the

Falkland Islands themselves. The Argentine Government had not provoked the South Georgia incident but, now that it had happened, would take advantage of it to press forward Argentina's claim to sovereignty over all the islands. The Argentine assessment was that, while Britain might send naval reinforcements to the area, this was unlikely. The other report indicated that the Argentine Government could take military action against the Falklands in April, not through a complete invasion, but by occupying one of the outlying islands. A further report indicated that the Argentine Navy was keeping under review British naval dispositions worldwide.

Wednesday 31 March

On the morning of Wednesday 31 March Lord Carrington sent a telegram from Tel Aviv accepting the advice of the British Ambassador in Buenos Aires to delay the message to Dr Costa Mendez. Later in the day, however, Lord Carrington decided that the message should be delivered, in view both of the intelligence reports and of a British press report that day about the sailing of a nuclear-powered submarine, which might give the Argentines the impression that the British were seeking a naval rather than a diplomatic solution. The British Ambassador in Buenos Aires was instructed accordingly, and he delivered the message that evening.

An immediate assessment headed "Falkland Islands— the incident on South Georgia" was prepared and circulated by the Latin America Current Intelligence Group. It assessed that the landing on South Georgia had not been contrived by the Argentine Government, but that the Junta was taking full advantage of the incident to speed up negotiations on the transfer of sovereignty. Despite Sr Davidoff's close contacts with some senior Argentine naval officers, the unauthorised landing was not considered to be part of the Navy's plans. There was no central co-ordination of Argentine policy and the Junta's intentions were not known, but it had a wide range of options open to it. Argentina had overwhelming superiority in the area. There was a possibility that, both because of the strength of Argentine public feeling on the issue and because of imperfect co-ordination and the confused counsel given by various Argentine officials and service advisers, the Junta might take some unexpected action. The assessment concluded that the Argentine Junta's main aim in its handling of the Falkland Islands dispute was to persuade the British Government to negotiate the transfer of sovereignty, and it was likely to try to use the incident on South Georgia to obtain the early opening of talks on the basis discussed in New York in February. This would tend to constrain it from adopting extreme options, but the possibility could not be ruled out that it might in future choose to escalate the situation by landing a military force on another Dependency or on one of the Falkland Islands. But it was believed that at that time the Argentine Government did not wish to be the first to adopt forcible measures. There was, however, a high risk of the Argentine Government's resorting to the use of force to rescue their nationals if the Argentine civilians on South Georgia were arrested or removed from the island. The Argentine Government would see such action by the British authorities as highly provocative and might use it as a pretext for an invasion of the Falkland Islands.

The British Naval *Attaché* in Buenos Aires reported to the Ministry of Defence that, according to the United

States Naval *Attaché*, virtually all the Argentine fleet was at sea, but without the fleet commanders, and that this was well in advance of the next exercises planned for after Easter.

The British Ambassador in Buenos Aires reported Argentine press comment on the dispute, which had been overshadowed by violent demonstrations in Buenos Aires against the Government's economic policies. Lord Carrington's statement had been reported, but the popular press had given greater prominence to the despatch of a nuclear-powered submarine. There were also reports of the despatch of a British destroyer and a Royal Fleet Auxiliary vessel. Dr Costa Mendez was widely quoted as telling reporters that Argentina would not give way to threats of force and that the group on South Georgia was on Argentine soil.

In the early evening of 31 March Mr Nott was briefed by Ministry of Defence officials on intelligence which had been received that day that a time in the early morning of 2 April had been set by the Argentines as the time and day for action. It was considered that, taken with earlier intelligence reports, this provided a positive indication of an Argentine intention to invade the Falkland Islands. These reports were also seen by the Foreign and Commonwealth Office and the Joint Intelligence Organisation.

Mr Nott sought, and obtained, an urgent meeting with the Prime Minister, which took place in her room at the House of Commons. It was also attended by Mr Atkins, Mr Luce, and Foreign and Commonwealth Office and Ministry of Defence officials. The Chief of Naval Staff was also present, having gone to the House of Commons to brief Mr Nott.

At the meeting a message from the Prime Minister to President Reagan was drafted and sent just before 9.00 p. m. In it the Prime Minister referred to intelligence indicating that an Argentine invasion of the Falklands might be imminent and said that the British Government could not acquiesce in any Argentine occupation. She asked President Reagan to talk urgently to President Galtieri and ask for an immediate assurance that he would not authorise any landing, let alone hostilities; she said that he could tell President Galtieri that the British Government would not escalate the dispute or start fighting. The British Ambassador in Washington was asked to speak to Mr Haig to ensure a rapid reaction from the White House. The Chief of Naval Staff advised on the size and composition of a task force likely to be capable of re-taking the Islands and was instructed to prepare such a force without commitment to a final decision as to whether or not it should sail.

The Foreign and Commonwealth Office immediately informed the British Ambassador in Buenos Aires and the Governor of the Falklands of a possible invasion. The Governor was instructed to pass this on only to the garrison commander. HMS *Endurance* was ordered back to Port Stanley.

At 10.30 p.m. the British Ambassador in Buenos Aires delivered the message to Dr Costa Mendez, who said that he would communicate the message to his President and report back. Dr Costa Mendez added, however, that the message was not what he had hoped for. He agreed on the need to avoid confrontation, but said that the statements in Parliament and the press reports of warship movements did not encourage hope for a quick solution.

Intelligence indicated that the Argentine Ministry of Foreign Affairs thought that the minimum acceptable reply from the British Government would be an agreement to enter into immediate negotiations on sovereignty and that Argentina would not now give up its presence on South Georgia. It also indicated that Dr Costa Mendez was being used by the Junta as nothing more than an adviser over South Georgia; and that the Argentine Navy had asked for a forecast of voting in the United Nations Security Council in the event of a military initiative against the Falklands. Dr Costa Mendez was said to have advised the Junta on 26 March that there would be a balance of votes against Argentina. There was also a report of preparations for the disembarkation of a marine infantry brigade.

Thursday 1 April

The British Ambassador in Washington reported having seen Mr Haig. He had outlined to him the intelligence reports of Argentine intentions, the significance of which Mr Haig had been unaware.

At 9.30 a.m. the Cabinet met. In Lord Carrington's absence, Mr Atkins reported the latest developments on South Georgia, the diplomatic efforts being made, and the deployment of Argentine naval forces. He advised that, while certain precautionary measures had been taken, it would not be an easy task to defend the Falklands. Summing up the discussion, the Prime Minister said that the best hope of avoiding confrontation lay in the influence that the United States Government could bring to bear on the Argentine Government.

At the same time an assessment prepared by the Latin America Current Intelligence Group was circulated updating the information about Argentine military dispositions, which would enable Argentina to launch an assault on

2 April. The destination, although not known for certain, appeared to be Port Stanley. The assessment said that, despite these military preparations, there was no intelligence suggesting that the Argentine Junta had taken a decision to invade the Falkland Islands. The evidence of unusual co-operation between the three Argentine military services and their active involvement in the amphibious task force was disturbing. The report judged that the assembled Argentine force now had the capability and logistic support necessary for an invasion of part of the Falkland Islands and that it would be in a position from which it could launch an assault by about the middle of the day on Friday 2 April.

Later in the morning of 1 April the Defence Committee met to consider the precautionary military deployments in hand for the Falkland Islands. The Prime Minister informed the Committee that an Argentine task force could reach Port Stanley during the morning of 2 April, but that the Argentine Government's precise intentions were not known. A diplomatic solution had to be found if possible, and the United States Government would be making representations at the highest level. As it was far from clear that Argentina would be willing to agree to a diplomatic solution, preparations had to be made against the possibilities that it would cut off services to the Islands or that some kind of military invasion might occur. In discussion, the British naval deployments already made were noted, and attention was drawn to the fact that a very large naval task force of surface ships would be required to deal with the Argentine force. The size of the Argentine force, the distances involved, and the importance of avoiding any action which would endanger the Islanders meant that there was no alternative for the moment to seeking to resolve the problem by diplomatic means. The Committee agreed that every effort should continue to be made to resolve the current dispute with Argentina by diplomatic means. The United States Government had been assured that the British Government would not take any early action amounting to an escalation of the situation. The Committee also agreed that HMS *Endurance* should not be withdrawn as earlier planned, but for the time being should remain on station in the South Atlantic. Officials were authorised urgently to make contingency plans for alternative services to those provided by Argentina, including the replacement of the weekly air service between Argentina and the Falkland Islands, probably by a sea service direct to the United Kingdom. The Committee also agreed not to send troops to reinforce the garrison at Port Stanley since they would not arrive in time or in sufficient strength to resist an invasion and their despatch might trigger an immediate Argentine landing.

Mr Streator, the United States *Chargé d'Affaires*, delivered a message from Mr Haig to Lord Carrington undertaking that the United States Government would do all it could to help. Mr Haig said that the United States Ambassador in Buenos Aires had been instructed to urge Dr Costa Mendez to take no steps which would aggravate the crisis. Mr Haig added that he thought that the United States would have a greater chance of influencing Argentine behaviour if they appeared not to favour one side or the other. Later in the day Mr Streator delivered a message to the Prime Minister from President Reagan saying that his Government shared British concern about apparent moves against the Falkland Islands and would contact the Argentine Government at the highest levels to urge them not to take military action.

In the afternoon of 1 April, the British Ambassador in Buenos Aires reported his interview with Dr Costa Mendez, who had told him that the Argentine Government regarded the South Georgia incident as closed. The British Ambassador asked for a written statement of the Argentine position, which was given to him in the following terms:

> Since the problem raised is disregard of Argentine sovereignty—I judge pointless the despatch of a person to examine the events in the Georgias since Argentina considers this incident resolved. In fact the workers there are carrying out their tasks under normal lawful conditions without any breach of the agreement previously reached between our two countries.
>
> —bearing in mind the antecedents and course of the negotiations undertaken from 1964 to today we would have accepted the despatch of the representative proposed by Great Britain if his task had been to negotiate the modalities of transferring sovereignty over the Malvinas Islands and their dependencies to the Argentine Republic which is essentially the central cause of the present difficulties.
>
> I cannot omit to draw attention to the unusual British naval deployment towards our waters reported in the international press which can only be interpreted as an unacceptable threat of the use of military force. This obliges us to refer to the UN organisation where Argentina will circulate a note on the antecedents of this case.

The British Defence *Attaché* in Buenos Aires reported Argentine press statements that Air Force transport aircraft were being prepared to lift troops to the south of the country. The British Ambassador later reported further press statements about the mobilisation of ships and troops and about intentions to widen the scope of the South Georgia incident.

In the early evening of 1 April the British Ambassador to the United Nations, who had been in close touch with the Foreign and Commonwealth Office, reported the success of an initiative, which had led to the Secretary-General's summoning both the Argentine and British Ambassadors to express his concern about rising tension. The Secretary-General would be making a public appeal to both sides to settle their differences through diplomatic means. The British Ambassador prepared a draft statement to the Security Council calling on it to take immediate action to prevent an invasion, and a draft Resolution calling on the Argentine Government to exercise the utmost restraint and to refrain from the use or threat of force in the South Atlantic. It was later agreed with the President of the Council that, instead of the Resolution, he would make a Presidential statement. The British Ambassador subsequently reported that he thought as much action as possible by the Security Council had been achieved. There had been two appeals by the Secretary-General and a firm Presidential statement, and Britain had the sympathy of the majority of the Council. The Argentine Ambassador to the United Nations had, however, ignored his appeal to join Britain in a positive response to the Council's call for restraint.

The Foreign and Commonwealth Office informed the Governor of the Falkland Islands and the British Ambassadors in Washington, New York and Buenos Aires that there was reliable information that an Argentine naval task force would be assembling off Port Stanley the next morning.

The British Ambassador in Washington informed the Foreign and Commonwealth Office that the United States

Ambassador in Buenos Aires had spoken to Dr Costa
Mendez that morning; that Dr Costa Mendez had been
non-committal; and that the United States Ambassador had
arranged to see President Galtieri in the afternoon to
deliver a message from Mr Haig with President Reagan's
authority. The British Ambassador later reported that, at the
meeting with the United States Ambassador, President
Galtieri would not say what Argentina was going to do, but
had talked about the need for the British to discuss surren-
dering sovereignty. The United States Ambassador had
concluded that Argentina would go through with its
military operation. The State Department would now ask
President Reagan to talk personally to President Galtieri.

The Governor reported on the arrangements made for
the deployment of the Royal Marines, and consulted the
Foreign and Commonwealth Office about informing the civilian population and rounding up local Argentines. The Foreign
and Commonwealth Office pointed out that, while the evidence of Argentine intentions to attack the next day was
highly suggestive, it was not yet entirely conclusive and
diplomatic action was being taken to prevent an attack.

Intelligence received on 1 April indicated that at the
end of March the military leaders in Argentina were close
to using the military option to solve the dispute with
Britain and had decided to invade the Falklands if no constructive proposal was forthcoming from the British
Government by the end of the week. The constructive proposal would have to involve a concrete agreement to talk
about the transfer of sovereignty within a set period. The
military option could be put into action on 3 or 4 April.

At a meeting later in the evening of 1 April between
the Prime Minister, Lord Carrington and Mr Nott, it was

decided that troops should be put on immediate notice for deployment to the South Atlantic. They noted that the naval task force assembling in British ports was at four hours' notice to sail within the next 48 hours, and that the ships exercising off Gibraltar were moving south; they would not act independently but would form up with the force assembling in British ports if it sailed.

Friday 2 April

In the early hours of Friday 2 April Mr Haig informed Lord Carrington that President Galtieri had refused to receive President Reagan's telephone call. The President's message was, however, being sent to Buenos Aires immediately and would be delivered within the hour. Mr Haig was trying to reach Dr Costa Mendez on the telephone and the Argentine Ambassador in Washington was being summoned. The Vatican had also been contacted and was trying to get a message to President Galtieri.

At about the same time intelligence was received that orders had been issued on 1 April for the Argentine occupation of the Falklands and Grytviken.

Eventually President Reagan succeeded in speaking to President Galtieri. At 2.45 a.m. he sent the Prime Minister a message reporting on his telephone conversation, in which he said that President Galtieri had spoken in terms of ultimatums and had left him with the clear impression that he was embarked on a course of armed conflict.

A fuller account of President Reagan's initiative was received later on 2 April. Early the previous evening the United States President had tried to telephone the Argentine President, who initially refused to take the call. When President Reagan eventually spoke to him, he had urged in forceful terms that Argentina should not take action against the Falklands, which he said the British would regard as a *casus belli*. He had left President Galtieri in no doubt of the consequences of such action on relations between Argentina and the United States. President Galtieri emphatically rejected President Reagan's offer to send Vice-President Bush immediately to Buenos Aires to assist in a solution.

At 9.45 a.m. the Prime Minister informed the Cabinet that an Argentine invasion appeared imminent. Mr Nott reported that a large amphibious task force had been put on immediate alert. Lord Carrington reported the continuing diplomatic initiatives. It was agreed that a decision to instruct the task force to sail should be considered later.

At midday RRS *Bransfield*, a British Antarctic Survey ship, reported interruptions of local Falkland Islands radio broadcasts confirming that Argentines had landed. There were also reports of invasion from the State Department, from the British Antarctic Survey station at Grytviken and from the Cable and Wireless operator in Port Stanley.

At 7.30 p. m. the Cabinet met and agreed that the task force should sail.

On Saturday 3 April, the Prime Minister announced in the House of Commons that Argentina's armed forces had attacked the Falkland Islands the previous day and established military control of the Islands.

THE GOVERNMENT'S DISCHARGE
OF THEIR RESPONSIBILITIES

In this section the Committee addresses the central issue of their terms of reference: the way in which the responsibilities of Government in relation to the Falkland Islands and the Falkland Islands Dependencies were discharged in the period leading up to the invasion. It has had to consider many questions, but two are crucial. First, could the Government have foreseen the invasion on 2 April? Secondly, could the Government have prevented that invasion? The Committee deals with the first question next. The second question is more complex and in the Committee's view cannot be answered until it has examined how the dispute became critical and how it was handled at various stages by the present Government. The Committee considers the answer to this question at the end of this section.

COULD THE INVASION OF 2 APRIL HAVE BEEN FORESEEN?

The Committee considers first the question whether before 31 March the Government had warning of the invasion of the Falkland Islands on 2 April. It has described in detail in the previous section the events of the days leading up to the invasion and all the information available at the time, including all relevant reports from the intelligence agencies. The Committee believes that its account demonstrates conclusively that the Government had no reason to believe before 31 March that an invasion of the Falkland Islands would take place at the beginning of April.

All the information, including intelligence reports, that has come to light since the invasion suggests that the decision to invade was taken by the Junta at a very late date.

Argentine naval forces were at sea between about 23 and 28 March, in the course of annual naval exercises, which included a joint anti-submarine exercise with Uruguay (press accounts of which the British Naval *Attaché* in Buenos Aires reported on 27 March). The Argentine news agency reported on 2 April that the fleet had sailed south from Puerto Belgrano on 28 March with a marine infantry battalion, an amphibious command section and troops embarked. The actual order to invade was probably not given until at least 31 March, and possibly as late as 1 April. Dr Costa Mendez was subsequently reported as saying that the Junta did not finally decide on the invasion until 10.00 p. m. (7.00 p. m. local time) on 1 April. It is probable that the decision to invade was taken in the light of the development of the South Georgia situation; but it seems that the violent demonstrations in Buenos Aires on the night of 30/31 March were also a factor in the Junta's decision.

It may be thought that, although the Government could not have had earlier warning of the invasion, they must have had fuller and more significant information of Argentine military movements. The fact is that there was no coverage of these movements and no evidence available to the Government from satellite photographs. The Committee discusses these matters further below in the context of the arrangements made for gathering intelligence.

The Committee specifically asked all those who gave evidence—Ministers and officials, the British Ambassador in Buenos Aires and other Embassy staff, the Governor of the Falkland Islands, Falkland Islanders and persons outside Government with special knowledge of and interest in the area—whether at any time up to the end of March they thought an invasion of the Falklands was likely at the beginning of April. They all stated categorically that they did not.

In the light of this evidence, the Committee is satisfied that the Government did not have warning of the decision to invade. The evidence of the timing of the decision taken by the Junta shows that the Government not only did not, but could not, have had earlier warning. The invasion of the Falkland Islands on 2 April could not have been foreseen.

HOW DID THE DISPUTE BECOME CRITICAL?

Before considering the present Government's handling of the dispute, the Committee needs to examine the question: how did the dispute develop into such a critical state that a sudden and unforeseeable invasion took place? To answer it, it is necessary to look back at the main features of the dispute and the positions of the parties to it over a longer period.

From 1965 the positions of the three main parties to the dispute—the Argentine Government, the British Government and the Islanders—remained constant.

First, for all Argentine Governments repossession of the "Malvinas" was always a major issue of policy and a national issue. The dispute has not held the same place in the attention of British Governments or of the British people. Although it pressed its claims with greater force on some occasions than on others, Argentina never wavered in its commitment to recover the Islands. Whatever other issues were proposed for discussion, such as economic co-operation on fisheries or oil exploration, its overriding concern was with sovereignty. In only one instance, namely the talks leading to the Communications Agreements in 1971, did Argentina take part in negotiations that were not in part concerned with some form of transfer of sovereignty. It did so in the hope that, by improving communications between the Islands and the mainland and showing its goodwill, it would persuade the Islanders of the benefits of a closer relationship between them, leading in time to constitutional changes; and it followed up the Agreements by pressing for a resumption of negotiations on sovereignty.

Secondly, all British Governments asserted British sovereignty over the Islands and the Dependencies, without reservation as to their title, coupled with an unchanging commitment to the defence of their territorial integrity. Although at the time of the first United Nations Resolution in 1965 the Government stated that sovereignty was not negotiable, from 1966 all British Governments were prepared to negotiate about sovereignty over the Islands, and to reach a settlement, provided that certain conditions were fulfilled and that it was capable of being carried in Parliament. The most important condition has always been that any settlement must be acceptable to the Islanders, and Ministers of successive of Governments have made unequivocal statements to Parliament to this effect. This was also always made plain to the Argentine Government.

Thirdly, the Islanders always made it clear that they wished to remain British and consistently resisted any change in their constitutional relationship with the United Kingdom. On occasion they acquiesced in negotiations and later took part in negotiations; but they never approved any proposals for a settlement of the sovereignty issue going beyond a lengthy freeze of the dispute. They were not prepared to agree even to the proposed scheme of joint scientific activity in the Dependencies worked out with Argentina in 1979, which they saw as a threat to British sovereignty in the area.

While the positions of the three sides in the dispute remained constant, circumstances in Argentina changed and British Government policy developed in several important respects.

Developments in Argentina

In Argentina itself the military takeover in 1976 was an important factor. The *coup* placed decision-making in the hands of a small group at the head of the armed services, and increased the influence of the Navy, which had always been the most hawkish of the services on the Falklands issue. It introduced a repressive régime, whose appalling human rights record understandably increased the Islanders' reluctance to contemplate any form of closer association with Argentina. There was also a danger that the Junta might at any time seek to divert attention from domestic problems, particularly as economic difficulties grew, by appealing to Argentine nationalism to support an initiative on the Malvinas.

The other main issue in Argentine foreign policy over the period was its sovereignty dispute with Chile over three islands in the Beagle Channel. Argentina's concern is less with the islands themselves, which are occupied by Chile, than with their territorial waters and continental shelves, as it is strongly opposed to any extension of Chilean sovereignty into the South Atlantic. The relevance of this issue to the Falkland Islands dispute was that, if Argentina were preoccupied with the Beagle Channel dispute, it would divert its attention from the Falkland Islands; whereas, if that dispute were going in favour of Chile or reached deadlock, Argentina was more likely to seek a compensatory success in the Falklands.

In 1977 an International Court of Arbitration awarded the islands to Chile, but did not pronounce on the seaward extension of either side's claims. Argentina refused to accept the award, despite earlier agreement to adhere to the Court's findings, and the following year the two countries came to the brink of war on the issue. A Papal mediator was appointed, whose proposals again favoured Chile. Argentina delayed its response to his proposals, and early in 1982 announced its intention of abrogating a treaty with Chile, the effect of which would be to prevent the dispute being referred to the International Court of Justice. From Argentina's point of view the dispute had reached an impasse adverse to the Junta, and this was likely to focus its attention more closely on the Falklands.

A further development in Argentine foreign policy was its rapprochement with the United States from the time President Reagan's administration took office. The Committee referred earlier to evidence of improved relations between the two countries, in particular the visits that General Galtieri made to the United States in 1981, when he was Commander-in-Chief of the Army. It seems likely that the Argentine Government came to believe that the United States Government were sympathetic to their claim to the Falkland Islands and, while not supporting forcible action in furtherance of it, would not actively oppose it. When initially asked to intervene, the United States did adopt an "even-handed" approach, while using their good offices to attempt to find a solution.

Given the relative closeness of the Falkland Islands to Argentina, their distance from Britain and the absence of a substantial British deterrent force in the area, Argentina always had the capability successfully to mount a sudden operation against the Islands. Moreover, in recent years there was a substantial increase in Argentina's military strength in all three of its armed services, which must have increased its confidence in its ability to occupy the Islands and retain them.

Developments in British policy

Argentina's growing military power coincided with an increasing concentration on the part of the United Kingdom on its NATO role and the progressive restriction of its other defence commitments. Even before the Defence Review published in 1966 the South Atlantic had not been a major area of deployment, but the decisions taken in 1967 to withdraw the Commander-in-Chief, South Atlantic, and the frigate on station in the area, and in 1974 to terminate the Simonstown agreements, marked the lower priority attached to a British defence capability in the area. As the Argentine threat grew, in deciding to maintain only a token presence in the area, in the form of a small detachment of Royal Marines and in the summer months HMS *Endurance*, successive Governments had to accept that the Islands could not be defended against sudden invasion. These decisions were taken in the light of wider strategic interests, but it is likely that they were seen by Argentina as evidence of a decreasing British commitment to the defence of the Islands, however strongly that commitment was publicly asserted.

Nor were these the only signals that could be read by Argentina as evidence of diminishing British interest in protecting its sovereignty in the area. Argentina no doubt always had in mind that what it saw as the weakness of Britain's response to the establishment of an Argentine presence on Southern Thule in 1976 was an indication that it might be able to mount similar operations, at least in the uninhabited islands, without provoking serious retaliatory action.

There were other British Government policies which may have served to cast doubt on British commitment to the Islands and their defence. These included the

Government's preparedness, subject to certain restrictions, to continue arms sales to Argentina (and to provide training facilities in the United Kingdom for Argentine military personnel); the decision not to implement some of the recommendations of Lord Shackleton's 1976 report, notably that relating to the extension of the airfield; and the failure in the British Nationality Act to extend British citizenship to those inhabitants of the Islands who either were not themselves patrial or did not have a United Kingdom-born grandparent.

Finally, the 1981 Defence Review may have provided further reassurance to Argentina, in view of the planned reductions in the surface fleet, the sale of HMS *Invincible* and, more particularly, the decision, although it was never implemented, to withdraw HMS *Endurance*. In short, as Argentine military power increased, the British capability to respond to it became more restricted.

The course of negotiations over the years was also itself an important factor limiting the Government's freedom of manoeuvre. As successive initiatives had been tried and failed, and with no signs of softening of either Argentine or Islander attitudes, the picture that the history of the dispute presents is one in which the negotiating options were progressively eliminated until only one—leaseback—was left that might eventually satisfy the aspirations of Argentina on the one hand and the wishes of the Islanders on the other.

It is against that background that the Committee examines the present Government's handling of the dispute. What stands out is the dilemma to which successive Governments were exposed by their policy of seeking to resolve, or at least contain, the dispute by diplomatic negotiation on the one hand and their commitment to the defence of the Falkland Islands on the other. This dilemma sharpened as the policy options diminished. The Islands were always at risk, and increasingly so as Argentina's military capability grew stronger; but a British decision to deploy to the area any additional warships, whose secrecy could not always be assured, also carried a risk, dependent on its timing, of frustrating the prospect of negotiation. This dilemma underlined the importance of the token defence presence, which is examined next.

Did Foreign and Commonwealth Office officials pursue a policy of their own?

Before coming to that, however, the Committee first deals with the allegation that over the years Foreign and Commonwealth Office officials pursued a policy aimed at getting rid of the Islands, irrespective of the views of Ministers. In the Committee's examination of the papers it has found no evidence to support this damaging allegation, and it believes it to be totally without foundation. On every occasion that a new government—or new Ministers—came into office a full range of policy options was put before them. In every case Ministers made a decision of policy and chose to seek a negotiated settlement that would be acceptable to Argentina and to the Islanders. Without exception they rejected the alternative of "Fortress Falklands", which would have involved the isolation of the Islands from Argentina and probably from the rest of Latin America.

HOW DID THE PRESENT GOVERNMENT HANDLE THE DISPUTE?

A chief responsibility of British Governments in relation to the Falkland Islands and the Falkland Islands Dependencies, as for any other part of British territory, is for their defence and security. As already explained, the policy of successive Governments on the defence of the Islands has been to maintain a token presence on the Falklands in the form of a small detachment of Royal Marines. This force was adequate to deal with sudden "adventurist" incursions, which up to about 1975 were regarded as the main threat.

Although from that time the Argentine threat of military action increased, no Government was prepared to establish a garrison on the Falklands large enough to repel a full-scale Argentine invasion, or to provide an extended runway for the airfield, with supporting facilities. A larger airfield, if it could have been afforded within Government defence priorities, might have enhanced Britain's deterrent capacity in the area; but it would not in itself have ensured rapid reinforcement by air in a crisis since, in view of the distances involved and the uncertainties of the South Atlantic weather, landing on the Falklands could not be guaranteed and, at a time of confrontation with Argentina, diversion airfields in South America were unlikely to be available. Before the invasion air reinforcement from Ascension Island, 3500 miles away, was believed to be impracticable because of the distance involved, the lack of a diversion airfield and the refuelling techniques required.

Throughout the period, in addition to the detachment of Royal Marines, a Royal Naval ice-patrol vessel, first HMS *Protector* and subsequently HMS *Endurance*, was kept

on station in the area in the summer months. The decision
to withdraw HMS *Endurance* and the subsequent appeals by
Lord Carrington to Mr Nott to reverse it were described
earlier. The Committee recognises the limited military value
of this vessel; but, as the only regular Royal Naval presence
in the area, her symbolic role was important in relation to
Argentina. With the exception of the occasions in 1976 and
1977 when the Government buttressed negotiations by
undisclosed naval deployments, successive Governments
relied on their negotiating policy and on diplomatic means
to prevent a confrontation with Argentina; and the role of
HMS *Endurance*, as a token of the Government's commitment to the defence of the Falkland Islands and
Dependencies, was a valuable complement to that. That was
clearly borne out by the press and intelligence reports of
Argentine reactions to the decision to pay her off.

The Committee concludes, in view of these factors,
that it was inadvisable for the Government to announce a
decision to withdraw HMS *Endurance* and that, in the light
of the developing situation in the second half of 1981, they
should have rescinded their decision to pay off HMS
Endurance at the end of her 1981/82 tour.

The decisions of September 1981

As 1981 wore on, one of the most significant developments
in the situation was the receding prospect of negotiating a
leaseback solution. Mr Ridley's meeting on 30 June 1981
was held against the background of a general belief that
time was running out and that Argentine impatience was
growing. It reviewed the policy options and concluded that
the only feasible option was leaseback preceded by an education campaign both in the Falkland Islands and at home.

At his meeting on 7 September, however, Lord Carrington decided not to pursue that course of action, but to discuss the whole matter with Dr Camilion in New York later in the month and to suggest to him that it would help if the Argentines were able to make constructive proposals for resolving the dispute. Lord Carrington told the Committee that, in his view, there was no prospect of "selling" leaseback at that stage. It did not have support in the Islands, in the House of Commons or amongst his own Ministerial colleagues in Government. So he saw this approach to Dr Camilion as the best diplomatic tactic in the circumstances. The Government was thenceforth left with no resort other than attempting to keep negotiations going by some means or other, and they were in the position of having nothing to offer Argentina other than what the wishes of the Islanders dictated. Lord Carrington himself recognised this in his minute of 14 September 1981, in which he said that, unless and until the Islanders modified their views, there was "little we can do beyond trying to keep some sort of negotiation going".

The Committee concludes that the Government were in a position of weakness, and that the effect of Lord Carrington's decision was to pass the initiative to the Argentine Government.

Lord Carrington also decided on 7 September not to present a paper for collective Ministerial discussion in the Defence Committee. Instead he circulated a minute to his Defence Committee colleagues on 14 September. This was one of a series of minutes (he circulated others on 2 December 1981, 15 February 1982 and 24 March 1982) by which he kept the Prime Minister and Defence Committee colleagues informed of progress in the dispute up to the time of the invasion. The Committee recognises that Cabinet Committees, such as the Defence Committee, usually meet to take decisions at the invitation of the Minister with proposals to put forward; and it has noted that, in September 1981, the prospect of further negotiations still existed on the basis of agreed Government policy. Nevertheless, it was also evident at the time that the policy road ahead, last endorsed by Ministers in January 1981, could well be blocked, with serious political repercussions. Officials in both the Foreign and Commonwealth Office and the Ministry of Defence were looking to Ministers to review the outcome of the contingency planning they had done in view of a potentially more aggressive posture by Argentina. In the event, Government policy towards Argentina and the Falkland Islands was never formally discussed outside the Foreign and Commonwealth Office after January 1981. Thereafter, the time was never judged to be ripe although the Committee was told in oral evidence that, subject to the availability of Ministers, a Defence Committee meeting could have been held at any time, if necessary at short notice. There was no meeting of the Defence Committee to discuss the Falklands until 1 April 1982; and there was no reference to the Falklands in Cabinet, even after the New York talks of 26 and 27 February, until Lord Carrington reported on events in South Georgia on 25 March 1982.

The Committee cannot say what the outcome of a meeting of the Defence Committee might have been, or whether the course of events would have been altered if it had met in September 1981; but, in its view, it could have been advantageous, and fully in line with Whitehall practice, for Ministers to have reviewed collectively at that time, or in the months immediately ahead, the current negotiating position; the implications of the conflict between the attitudes of the Islanders and the aims of the Junta; and the longer-term policy options in relation to the dispute.

The view at the beginning of 1982

At the beginning of 1982 there was evidence from several sources that Argentina, and particularly the new government of President Galtieri, was committed to achieving success in its Malvinas policy in a much shorter timescale than most previous Argentine Governments had envisaged. It was clear that it attached particular significance to achieving a solution of the dispute on its terms, in which the sovereignty issue was the overriding consideration, by January 1983, the 150th anniversary of British occupation. These indications included General Galtieri's remarks in his speech in May 1981, intelligence about the attitude of different elements in the Argentine Government, the press comment at the beginning of the year and, definitively, the terms of the *bout de papier* at the end of January 1982, which called for serious negotiations with a timescale of one year, culminating in the recognition of Argentine sovereignty.

The Foreign and Commonwealth Office recognised clearly that the situation was moving towards confrontation, as is shown by the advice they gave their Ministers at the beginning of the year, notably in connection with the Annual Report of the Governor of the Falkland Islands. They believed, however—and their belief was supported by evidence—first, that Argentina would not move to confrontation until negotiations broke down; secondly, that there would be a progression of measures starting with the withdrawal of Argentine services to the Islands and increased diplomatic pressure, including further action at the United Nations; and thirdly—and the intelligence bore this out—that no action, let alone invasion of the Islands, would take place before the second half of the year.

Nevertheless, in recognition of the deteriorating situation, the Foreign and Commonwealth Office had set in hand in 1981 contingency plans to provide alternative services for the Islands, and, at its request, the Ministry of Defence prepared a paper on the military options available in response to possible aggressive action by Argentina. A paper on civil contingency planning was also prepared in September 1981 in expectation of a meeting of the Defence Committee, at which Ministerial authority might have been obtained to take the plans further. Chartering ships would have required appropriate financial provision and also Ministerial agreement to acknowledge such measures publicly, and this could have been seen as a form of pressure on the Islanders. As it turned out, the inability to give more substance to these civil plans did not matter, as Argentina did not escalate the dispute in the way expected. On the military side the absence of detailed contingency plans for responding to aggressive action by Argentina did not inhibit a very swift response once it was clear that an invasion was imminent, as can be seen from the remarkable speed with which the task force was prepared and sailed. The Committee discusses below the separate question whether earlier military steps should have been taken to deter an Argentine attack.

Judgment on how the dispute would develop

The Committee believes that the view taken by Foreign and Commonwealth Office Ministers and officials early in

1982 of how the dispute would develop was one which could reasonably be taken in the light of all the circumstances at that time. In the event it proved to be a misjudgment, but not one in the Committee's view for which blame should be attached to any individual. There were, the Committee believes, three important factors in the misjudgment: first, in underestimating the importance that Argentina attached to its timetable for resolving the dispute by the end of the year; secondly, in being unduly influenced—understandably and perhaps inevitably—by the long history of the dispute, in which Argentina had previously made threatening noises, accompanied by bellicose press comment, and indeed backed up its threats with aggressive actions, without the dispute developing into a serious confrontation; and, thirdly, in believing, on the basis of evidence, that Argentina would follow an orderly progression in escalating the dispute, starting with economic and diplomatic measures. Sufficient allowance was not made for the possibility of Argentina's military Government, subject to internal political and economic pressures, acting unpredictably if at any time they became frustrated at the course of negotiations. The July 1981 intelligence assessment had warned that in those circumstances there was a high risk that Argentina would resort to more forcible measures swiftly and without warning.

Response to events after the New York talks

The Committee acknowledges the skill with which Mr Luce and Foreign and Commonwealth Office officials handled the formal talks between the Argentine and British Governments in New York on 26 and 27 February. The agenda for the talks was provided by the Argentine *bout de papier* issued on 27 January. They were held in a cordial atmosphere, and the general view of the British side was that they had gone somewhat better than they feared. A joint *communiqué* was agreed, and in the draft working paper on the negotiating commission reference to the frequency of meetings—an important element in the Argentine proposals—was avoided. At the same time, it had been clear even at the talks that the Argentine side's ability to manoeuvre was strictly limited. The Argentine Government were committed to the establishment of the commission, with negotiations being conducted at high level, at a much faster pace than in the past, and with a strict deadline of a year. They pressed strongly for a formal reply from the British Government to their proposal within a month, with a view to the first round of talks being held at the beginning of April.

The unilateral *communiqué* of 1 March instigated by the Junta marked an important change of attitude on the part of the Argentine Government. It in effect denounced the joint *communiqué* by making public the details of the informal working paper, and commended the proposals in the *bout de papier* for a programme of monthly meetings with the aim of achieving recognition of Argentine sovereignty within a short time; and, if those proposals were not effective, claimed the right to choose "the procedure which best accords with [Argentine] interests". Although Sr Ros expressed regret about the *communiqué* and accompanying press comment, and Dr Costa Mendez assured the British Ambassador in Buenos Aires that no threat was intended, it indicated a hardening attitude on the part of the Argentine Government, and a commitment to the negotiating commission proposals and the timetable for its work.

The increased seriousness of the situation was recognised by Foreign and Commonwealth Office officials. They discussed it with Lord Carrington at a short meeting on 5 March, at which several diplomatic initiatives were set in hand.

This was also the occasion when they mentioned to him the previous Government's decision in November 1977 to deploy ships to the area covertly, though without recommending similar action at that stage. As it happens, 5 March was about the last moment at which, given that the invasion took place on 2 April, it would have been possible to sail a deterrent force to be in place in time. It would have taken nuclear-powered submarines approximately two weeks and surface ships approximately three weeks to reach the Falkland Islands. The evidence received by the Committee suggested that Foreign and Commonwealth Office officials did not press Ministers to consider deterrent rather than diplomatic counter-measures or prompt the Joint Intelligence Organisation urgently to update its July 1981 assessment because they believed that Argentina would not resort to military action before initiating diplomatic and economic measures.

Officials were also looking for an early meeting of the Defence Committee, which Lord Carrington had envisaged taking place after the February talks, and it was expected that the meeting would take place on 16 March. No paper was tabled for that meeting, however, because Lord Carrington thought it right to await the Argentine Government's reaction to the message he was proposing to send to Dr Costa Mendez.

The Committee believes that Foreign and Commonwealth Office officials did not attach sufficient weight at this time to the changing Argentine attitude at and following the February talks and did not give sufficient importance to the new and threatening elements in the Argentine Government's position. It concludes that they should have drawn Ministers' attention more effectively to the changed situation.

The Committee notes that the Prime Minister reacted to the telegrams from the British Ambassador in Buenos Aires on 3 March reporting aggressive Argentine press comment following the New York talks, and called for contingency plans. The Committee regrets that the Prime Minister's enquiries did not receive a prompt response. She also enquired of Mr Nott on 8 March about the timing of possible warship movements to the South Atlantic.

The Joint Intelligence Organisation

The reports by the intelligence agencies and the assessments made by the Joint Intelligence Committee were a key factor in the judgments made by Ministers and officials in the period leading up to the invasion, which have been reviewed above. A description of the structure and role of the Joint Intelligence Organisation is contained in Annex B. For many years Argentina and the Falkland Islands were regarded as a priority for intelligence collection but were in a relatively low category.

From 1965 the Argentine threat to the Falkland Islands was regularly assessed by the Joint Intelligence Committee, the frequency of assessment increasing at times of heightened tension between Britain and Argentina in the dispute on sovereignty, in the light of the internal political situation in Argentina and information about Argentine intentions. The timing of assessments was often related to the rounds of formal negotiations between the British and Argentine Governments. In the period of the present Government a full assessment was prepared in November 1979.

A further full assessment, the last before the invasion, was prepared in July 1981. This assessment was particularly important because, as was apparent from the oral evidence, it had considerable influence on the thinking of Ministers and officials.

Review of the 1981 assessment

The Committee was told in evidence that the Latin America Current Intelligence Group met 18 times between July 1981 and March 1982, but did not discuss the Falkland Islands on those occasions. They were, however, discussed on two occasions in that period at the weekly meetings held by the Head of the assessments staff; and on at least four separate occasions consideration was given by those concerned, who were in close touch with the Foreign and Commonwealth Office on this matter, to the need to update the assessment made in July 1981. These occasions were in November 1981, in preparation for the next round of talks, which were then scheduled for the following month; in December 1981; in January 1982, in the light of the proposals that it was known that Argentina would put forward before the February talks in New York; and in March 1982. On each occasion up to March it was decided that there was no need to revise the assessment.

The Committee was told that the four principal factors that the assessments staff considered in assessing the Argentine threat were: the progress of Argentina's dispute with Chile over the Beagle Channel; the political and eco-nomic situation in Argentina; the state of inter-service rivalry there; and, most importantly, Argentina's perception of the prospects of making progress by negotiation. The information they received after July 1981 was not thought to indicate any significant change in these factors which would have justified a new assessment. The conclusions reached in July 1981 about Argentine intentions and the options open to them were regarded as consistent with more recent intelligence and therefore still valid.

In March 1982 it was agreed that a new assessment should be prepared, and work was started on it. It was thought, however, that it could most usefully be presented to Ministers in the context of a more general consideration of Falkland Islands policy, which they were expected to discuss at a meeting of the Defence Committee on 16 March. In the event, that meeting did not take place, and the new assessment was never completed.

The next assessment was made at very short notice in the morning of 31 March and was concerned with events on South Georgia. In its conclusion it expressed the view that, while the possibility that Argentina might choose to escalate the situation by landing a military force on another Dependency or on the Falkland Islands could not be ruled out, the Argentine Government did not wish to be the first to adopt forcible measures.

The intelligence agencies

This assessment on the eve of the invasion relied chiefly on the information available from the intelligence agencies, whose role and relationship with Government Departments and the Joint Intelligence Organisation are described in Annex B. Throughout the period leading up to the invasion secret intelligence was collected, in accordance with the priority accorded to this target, on Argentina's attitude to and intentions in the dispute, in particular the views of its armed forces and Ministry of Foreign Affairs; on relevant internal factors in Argentina; and on its general military capability. In October 1981, following a general review of intelligence requirements in Central and South America and the Caribbean, the Joint Intelligence Committee notified the collecting agencies that, in view of the increasing difficulty of maintaining negotiations with Argentina over the future of the Falkland Islands, the requirement had increased for intelligence on Argentine intentions and policies on the issue. But additional resources were not allocated for this purpose. The Committee was told in evidence that, for operational reasons which were explained to them, the deployment of additional resources would not necessarily have secured earlier or better intelligence of the intentions of the very small circle at the head of the Argentine Government where decisions were taken.

If, as the Committee believes, the decision to invade was taken by the Junta at a very late stage, the intelligence agencies could not have been expected to provide earlier warning of the actual invasion on 2 April. It might have been possible to give some warning of the military preparations preceding the invasion, if there had been direct coverage of military movements within Argentina in addition to coverage of its general military capability. But it would have been difficult to provide comprehensive coverage of these movements in view of, among other things, Argentina's very long coastline and the distance of the southern Argentine ports from Buenos Aires. The British Defence *Attaché* in Buenos Aires told the Committee that his section at the Embassy had neither the remit nor the capacity to obtain detailed information of this kind. By the time the diplomatic situation deteriorated at the beginning of March it would have been difficult to evaluate such information because of the absence of knowledge about the normal pattern of Argentine military activity.

There was no coverage of Argentine military movements within Argentina, and no advance information was therefore available by these means about the composition and assembly of the Argentine naval force that eventually invaded the Falklands. There was no intelligence from American sources or otherwise to show that the force at sea before the invasion was intended other than for normal naval exercises. No satellite photography was available on the disposition of the Argentine forces. The British Naval *Attaché* in Buenos Aires reported the naval exercises when he became aware of them, mainly on the basis of Argentine press reports.

The Committee has no reason to question the reliability of the intelligence that was regularly received from a variety of sources.

As to assessments, however, the Committee was surprised that events in the first three months of 1982, in particular the Argentine *bout de papier* on 27 January, the unilateral *communiqué* on 1 March and the Prime Minister's comments on the telegram of 3 March reporting Argentine press comment, did not prompt the Joint Intelligence Organisation to assess the situation afresh. As already explained, the assessments staff considered the need for a new assessment on several occasions in this period. Work was started on one early in March, but not completed because of the intention to link it to a meeting of the Defence Committee. It was decided not to prepare a new assessment before the beginning of March because of the view in the Joint Intelligence Organisation that the conclusions of a new assessment were unlikely to be significantly different from those of the July 1981 assessment. The assessment of 31 March 1982, although focused on the South Georgia incident, tends to support this view.

The Committee does not regard the view taken by those concerned of the need for a new assessment as unreasonable in the light of the information available to them at the time. But in consideration of the evidence the Committee remains doubtful about two aspects of the work of the Joint Intelligence Organisation. First, it is not sure that at all important times the assessments staff were fully aware of the weight of the Argentine press campaign in 1982. As a result it seems to the Committee that they may have attached greater significance to the secret intelligence, which at that time was reassuring about the prospects of an early move to confrontation. For instance, certain intelligence pointed out that the press campaign was probably designed to exert pressure on the United Kingdom in the negotiations. The second doubt is whether the Joint Intelligence Organisation attached sufficient weight to the possible effects on Argentine thinking of the various actions of the British Government. The changes in the Argentine position were, the Committee believes, more evident on the diplomatic front and in the associated press campaign than in the intelligence reports.

The Committee does not seek to attach any blame to the individuals involved. But it believes that these factors point to the need for a clearer understanding of the relative roles of the assessments staff, the Foreign and

Commonwealth Office and the Ministry of Defence, and for closer liaison between them. The aim should be to ensure that the assessments staff are able to take fully into account both relevant diplomatic and political developments and foreign press treatment of sensitive foreign policy issues.

The Committee is concerned here with defects in the Joint Intelligence machinery as it has seen it working in an area of low priority. As it has seen only the papers relevant to the subject of the review, it is not able to judge how the assessment machinery deals with areas of higher priority, but it believes that, in dealing with Argentina and the Falkland Islands, it was too passive in operation to respond quickly and critically to a rapidly changing situation which demanded urgent attention.

The Committee considers that the assessment machinery should be reviewed. It cannot say what the scope of such a review should be in respect of the machinery's wider preoccupations, but it thinks that it should look at two aspects in particular. The first, to which it has already referred, is the arrangements for bringing to the Joint Intelligence Organisation's attention information other than intelligence reports. The second is the composition of the Joint Intelligence Committee. On this, consideration should be given to the position of the Chairman of the Committee: to the desirability that he or she should be full-time, with a more critical and independent role; and, in recognition of the Committee's independence in operation from the Government Departments principally constituting it, to the Chairman's being appointed by the Prime Minister and being a member of the Cabinet Office.

The suggestions made about the Joint Intelligence Organisation derive only from consideration of the

Falkland Islands issue. The Committee puts these suggestions forward as a guide for the future. Any view of the
effect they might have had on the period studied would be
hypothetical and speculative.

Impact of the South Georgia incident

If the Joint Intelligence Committee machinery had operated differently, the Committee has no reason to believe
that it would have increased the intelligence available to the
Government about the operations of Sr Davidoff, which led
to the South Georgia incident preceding the invasion.
There are still uncertainties about the full scope and character of those operations. The visits to South Georgia, by Sr
Davidoff himself in December 1981 and by his party in
March 1982, were both made on Argentine naval vessels,
and the Argentine Navy was no doubt aware of them. But
there was no evidence at the time, and none has come to
light since, suggesting that the whole operation was planned
either by the Argentine Government or by the Navy as a
follow-up to the occupation of Southern Thule. The intelligence available indicates that, when the incident grew
more serious it was seized on to escalate the situation until
the Junta finally decided to invade the Falkland Islands.

The Committee recognises that the response of
Ministers had to take account of conflicting pressures at
home, especially from Parliament, and from Argentina. The
initial reports of the incident appeared alarming—shots having been fired and the Argentine flag run up—and it was a
reasonable reaction to order HMS *Endurance* to sail to South
Georgia to take the men off. Thereafter the Government
went to great lengths to avoid exacerbating the situation and
made every effort to offer constructive ways of enabling the

Argentine party to regularise its position. These were all rejected by the Argentine Government, which by then were clearly intent on raising the temperature.

Nevertheless the Committee believes that, if Sr Davidoff's operations had been more closely monitored from December 1981 onwards and there had been better liaison between the Foreign and Commonwealth Office, the British Embassy in Buenos Aires and the Governor in preparation for the second visit in March 1982, Ministers would have been better able to deal with the landing on South Georgia when it occurred.

The possibility of earlier deterrent action

The Committee next examines whether the Government should have taken earlier military action to deter Argentina. It has considered two possible actions that the Government might have taken: the earlier despatch of a task force on a sufficient scale to defend, or if necessary retake, the Islands; and the deployment of a much smaller force in the form of a nuclear-powered submarine, either on its own or supported by surface ships.

The Committee believes that it would not have been appropriate to prepare a large task force with the capacity to retake the Falkland Islands before there was clear evidence of an invasion. As already explained, this was not perceived to be imminent until 31 March. Sending such a force would have been a disproportionate, and indeed provocative, response to the events on South Georgia, and would have been inconsistent with the attempts being made to resolve the problems there by diplomatic means.

A smaller force might have been deployed, either overtly as a deterrent measure or covertly as a precautionary measure, whose existence could have been declared if circumstances required. There were three occasions when such a force might reasonably have been deployed: before the New York talks at the end of February; at the beginning of March in the light of evidence of increased Argentine impatience at lack of progress; or later in March, as events on South Georgia moved towards confrontation.

In this connection parallels have been drawn with the action taken by the previous Government in November 1977, when two frigates and a nuclear-powered submarine were deployed to the area. On that occasion the deployment was made covertly to buttress negotiations. The closest parallel is therefore with the talks in New York in February 1982. At that time there were signs of growing Argentine impatience, in the form of the *bout de papier* and the accompanying hostile press comment in Argentina, but in other respects the circumstances were different from those obtaining at the time of the 1977 talks. 1977 was a tense period in Anglo-Argentine relations and there was a sharper risk of Argentine military action. Ambassadors had been withdrawn at the beginning of the previous year; there had been a much more recent infringement of British sovereignty in the form of the establishment of an Argentine presence on Southern Thule; and there had been physical acts of aggression by Argentina against foreign shipping. Before the talks in 1977 the Joint Intelligence Committee assessed that, if negotiations broke down, there would be a high risk of Argentina's resorting to more forceful measures; in those circumstances action against British shipping was seen as the most serious risk.

It was believed that the round of talks in December 1977 could lead to a breakdown of negotiations. The circumstances leading up to the February 1982 talks were different, and the Committee considers that they did not warrant a similar naval deployment.

There was a stronger case for considering action of this nature early in March 1982, in the light of evidence of increasing Argentine impatience, culminating in the threatening *communiqué* issued on 1 March by the Argentine Ministry of Foreign Affairs and the accompanying bellicose Argentine press comment. As already explained, Lord Carrington was informed of the action taken in 1977 at the end of a short meeting on 5 March. Lord Carrington told the Committee in oral evidence that the matter was mentioned only briefly. He asked whether the Argentines knew about the naval deployment, and, when told that they did not, he took the view that this reduced its relevance to the situation he faced. Lord Carrington also told the Committee more generally that, although the situation had become more difficult, he did not believe that the prospect of continuing negotiations at that time was hopeless. In his view nothing had happened to trigger the sending of a deterrent force. He was concerned that, if ships were sent, the fact would have become known. This would have jeopardised the prospect of keeping negotiations going, which was his objective. With hindsight he wished he had sought to deploy a nuclear-powered submarine to the area at an earlier stage, but on 5 March it did not seem to him that the situation had changed in such a way as to justify such action.

The Committee does not think that this was an unreasonable view to take at the time, but it believes that there would have been advantage in the Government's giving wider consideration at this stage to the question whether the potentially more threatening attitude by Argentina required some form of deterrent action in addition to the diplomatic initiatives and the contingency planning already in hand.

Finally, the Committee considers whether earlier action should have been taken to deploy ships to the area in response to the developing crisis on South Georgia. In Lord Carrington's judgment a deployment involving surface ships was likely to carry too great a risk of becoming known at a time when the Government were concerned to avoid any action that might have appeared provocative. That could have provoked escalatory action by Argentina against the Falkland Islands themselves, which the Government had no means of resisting effectively. This objection would not have applied so strongly to sailing a nuclear-powered submarine, since there would have been more chance of keeping its deployment covert. The decision to sail the first nuclear-powered submarine was taken early on Monday 29 March.

The Committee considers that there was a case for taking this action at the end of the previous week in the light of the telegram of 24 March from the Defence *Attaché* in Buenos Aires and the report of 25 March that Argentine ships had been sailed for a possible interception of HMS *Endurance*. It would have expected a quicker reaction in the Ministry of Defence to these two reports, which were the first indications of hostile activity by the Argentine Government.

Final warnings to Argentina

The British Government took several opportunities in the weeks leading up to the invasion to state publicly their commitment to the defence of the Falkland Islands and the Dependencies. In the House of Commons on

23 March Mr Luce stated that it was the "duty of this Government and of any British Government to defend and support the Islanders to the best of their ability". On 25 March the British Ambassador in Buenos Aires, on instructions, warned Dr Costa Mendez that Britain was committed to the defence of its sovereignty in South Georgia as elsewhere. As soon as a threat to the Falkland Islands themselves was perceived, the Prime Minister contacted President Reagan on 31 March and asked him to make it clear to the Argentine Government that the Government could not acquiesce in action against the Falkland Islands. As the Prime Minister explained in evidence, without the collective advice of the Chiefs of Staff on whether an operation to retake the Islands was feasible and the approval of Cabinet, it was not possible for her to go further. In the event, when speaking personally to General Galtieri, President Reagan stated forcefully that action against the Falklands would be regarded by the British as a *casus belli*.

The Committee concludes that warnings by the British Government of the consequences of invading the Falkland Islands were conveyed to the Argentine Government.

COULD THE PRESENT GOVERNMENT HAVE PREVENTED THE INVASION?

Finally the Committee turns to the more complex question posed earlier. Could the present Government have prevented the invasion of 2 April 1982?

It is a question that has to be considered in the context of the period of 17 years covered by this Report: there is no simple answer to it. A detailed factual account of the period has been given, attaching special importance to the account of events immediately preceding the invasion. It is essential that the Committee's Report should be read as a whole—and to recognise, as the Committee does, that there were deep roots to Argentina's attitude towards the "Malvinas", and that the present Government had to deal with that within the political constraints accepted by successive British Governments.

As to the Argentine Government—and this is quite apart from the influence on the Argentine Government of actions of the British Government—the Junta was confronted at the end of March 1982 with a rapidly deteriorating economic situation and strong political pressures at a moment when it was able to exploit to its advantage the developments in South Georgia. It has already been stated at the beginning of this section the reasons why the Committee is convinced that the invasion on 2 April 1982 could not have been foreseen.

The British Government, on the other hand, had to act within the constraints imposed by the wishes of the Falkland Islanders, which had a moral force of their own as well as the political support of an influential body of Parliamentary opinion; and also by strategic and military priorities which reflected national defence and economic policies: Britain's room for policy manoeuvre was limited.

Against this background the Committee has pointed out in this section where different decisions might have been taken, where fuller consideration of alternative courses of action might, in their opinion, have been advantageous, and where the machinery of Government could have been better used. But, if the British Government had acted differently in the ways the Committee has indicated, it is impossible to judge what the impact on the Argentine Government or the implications for the course of events might have been. There is no reasonable basis for any suggestion—which would be purely hypothetical—that the invasion would have been prevented if the Government had acted in the ways indicated in this report. Taking account of these considerations, and of all the evidence the Committee has received, the Committee concludes that it would not be justified in attaching any criticism or blame to the present Government for the Argentine Junta's decision to commit its act of unprovoked aggression in the invasion of the Falkland Islands on 2 April 1982.

FRANKS, *Chairman*
BARBER
LEVER
PATRICK NAIRNE
MERLYN REES
WATKINSON

A. R. RAWSTHORNE, *Secretary*
P. G. MOULSON, *Assistant Secretary*

31 *December* 1982

ANNEX A: COMMENTS ON SOME SPECIFIC ASSERTIONS

There has understandably been much speculation about the causes of the Falkland Islands conflict and about whether it could have been foreseen and prevented. The truth of these matters is less simple than some commentators have asserted, and for an accurate and comprehensive account of the facts our Report needs to be read in full. In the detailed narrative of events and our comments on them we have answered explicitly or by implication many of the mistaken or misleading statements that have been made, but we think it right also to state for the record our view of some of the more important specific assertions which have been made, in order to clear up damaging misunderstandings.

1. *Assertion*: Ministers and officials secretly told Argentina that Britain was prepared to give up the Falkland Islands against the wishes of the Islanders.

   Comment: We have found no evidence to support this allegation. On the contrary, Ministers and officials made clear to Argentina on numerous occasions that the wishes of the Falkland Islanders were paramount, and that any proposals to resolve the dispute would be subject to approval by Parliament.

2. *Assertion*: Clear warnings of the invasion from American intelligence sources were circulating more than a week beforehand.

   Comment: No intelligence about the invasion was received from American sources, before it took place, by satellite or otherwise.

3. *Assertion*: On or around 24 March 1982 the British Embassy in Buenos Aires passed on definite information to London about an invasion and predicted the exact day.

   Comment: This assertion derives from newspaper interviews after the invasion. We have investigated these interviews. It is not our task to come to any conclusion about what was or was not said to the journalists concerned or whether or not what was said was correctly interpreted. It is our task, however, to ascertain beyond doubt whether any such communication from the

British Embassy in Buenos Aires predicting the invasion was in fact made. We have examined all the relevant telegrams and intelligence reports and interviewed the individuals concerned. We are satisfied that no such communication was in fact made.

4. *Assertions*: (i) Two weeks before the invasion the Cabinet's Defence Committee rejected a proposal by Lord Carrington to send submarines to the area. (ii) The Government rejected advice from the Commander-in-Chief, Fleet, to send submarines soon after the landing on South Georgia on 19 March.

   Comment: These assertions are untrue. We have described in detail the events of the weeks leading up to the invasion. The Defence Committee did not meet at that time. The first discussion between Ministers about sending nuclear-powered submarines took place on Monday 29 March 1982 when the Prime Minister and Lord Carrington decided that a nuclear-powered submarine should be sent to support HMS *Endurance*. No earlier military advice recommending the dispatch of submarines was given to Ministers.

5. *Assertion*: Argentina was informed by the British Government of their decision to send a task force in 1977.

   Comment: The facts relating to the deployment of ships to the area in November 1977 are set out in our Report. We have had no evidence that the Argentine Government became aware of this deployment.

6. *Assertions*: (i) Captain Barker, the Captain of HMS *Endurance*, sent warnings that an invasion was imminent

which were ignored by the Foreign and Commonwealth Office and the Ministry of Defence. (ii) The Secretary of State for Defence saw Captain Barker and ignored his advice.

Comment: These assertions are untrue. Captain Barker reported his concern about events within his knowledge, but none of his reports warned of an imminent invasion. Both the Ministry of Defence and the Foreign and Commonwealth Office saw his reports and took them into account along with other intelligence material. Captain Barker confirmed to us that he never met Mr Nott.

7. *Assertion*: On 11 March 1982 an Argentine military plane landed at Port Stanley to reconnoitre the runway. The incident was reported by the Governor as suspicious.

   Comment: The emergency landing on 7 March of an Argentine Air Force Hercules transport aircraft was reported factually by the Governor to the Foreign and Commonwealth Office on 12 March but not as suspicious. He has subsequently confirmed that the landing was preceded by a "May Day" call and that, after the aircraft landed, fuel was seen leaking from it. The Argentine Air Force would already have had detailed knowledge of the strength of the runway in consequence of its responsibility for operating the flights between Port Stanley and Argentina and of authorised landings by Argentine Hercules aircraft at Port Stanley during 1981.

8. *Assertion*: The Argentine Government made a bulk purchase of maps of the Falkland Islands in Britain before the invasion.

Comment: An investigation by the Foreign and Commonwealth Office found that no such bulk purchase was made. This has been confirmed by the agents for the sale of the hydrographic charts produced by the Royal Navy. It has also been confirmed by the agents for the sale of the 1966 map of the Falkland Islands published by the Directorate of Overseas Surveys, copies of which were left on the Islands by the Argentine forces.

9. *Assertion*: There were massive withdrawals of Argentine funds from London banks shortly before the invasion, of which the Government must have been aware.

   Comment: We are satisfied that the Government had no information about such a movement of funds. The deposit liabilities of United Kingdom banks to overseas countries are reported to the Bank of England on a quarterly basis. The reporting date relevant to the period before the invasion was 31 March 1982, but, because of the complexity of the figures, they normally take several weeks to collect. Withdrawals by Argentine banks in March would therefore not have normally been reported until May. After the invasion the Bank of England asked banks for a special report, and this showed that around $½ billion of the original $1½ billion of Argentine funds were moved out of London just before the invasion, much of it on 1 and 2 April. Since the withdrawals were in dollars, there would have been no effect on the sterling exchange rate to alert the Bank of England.

10. *Assertion*: On 29 March 1982 the Uruguayan Government offered the British Government facilities

for Falkland Islanders who wished to leave the Islands before the Argentine invasion.

Comment: Neither the Foreign and Commonwealth Office nor the British Embassy in Montevideo had knowledge at the time or thereafter of any such offer. The Uruguayan Government have also described this allegation as completely without foundation. They have confirmed that neither they nor their Navy had any foreknowledge of the Argentine invasion of the Falkland Islands.

ANNEX B: ASPECTS OF THE MACHINERY OF GOVERNMENT IN RELATION TO THE FALKLAND ISLANDS

In this Annex we describe briefly the main aspects of the machinery of Government relevant to their responsibilities for the Falkland Islands and the Falkland Islands Dependencies.

THE MACHINERY FOR COLLECTIVE MINISTERIAL CONSIDERATION AND DECISION

Collective Ministerial decisions are taken by the Cabinet and Cabinet Committees. The standing committee of the Cabinet for discussing and deciding foreign policy and defence issues is the Defence and Oversea Policy Committee (to which, for the sake of brevity, we refer as the "Defence Committee"). The Defence Committee is chaired by the Prime Minister. Its membership includes the Secretaries of State for Foreign and Commonwealth Affairs and for Defence and the Chancellor of the Exchequer. The Chiefs of Staff are in attendance as required, to tender professional military advice. The timing and agenda of meetings of the Defence Committee are ultimately a matter for the Prime Minister, advised by the Secretary of the Cabinet and the Cabinet Secretariat. Meetings are arranged as required.

FOREIGN AND COMMONWEALTH OFFICE

The Ministerial head of the Foreign and Commonwealth Office is the Secretary of State for Foreign and Commonwealth Affairs. Lord Carrington was the Foreign and Commonwealth Secretary from the time the present Government took office in May 1979 until his resignation on 5 April 1982. The Foreign and Commonwealth Secretary is assisted by a team of Ministers, to whom he assigns responsibility under his overall direction for specific subjects and matters relating to different parts of the world. While Lord Carrington was Foreign and Commonwealth

Secretary, the second most senior Minister in the Foreign and Commonwealth Office was the Lord Privy Seal, who was also a member of the Cabinet. Sir Ian Gilmour, MP was Lord Privy Seal from May 1979 to September 1981 and Mr Humphrey Atkins, MP from September 1981 until his resignation on 5 April 1982. In addition to his other responsibilities, which did not include matters relating to Argentina or the Falkland Islands, Mr Atkins had a particular responsibility for matters with a significant Parliamentary aspect. Matters relating to Argentina and the Falkland Islands, among many other areas in the world, were the responsibility of one of the Ministers of State, from May 1979 to September 1981 Mr Nicholas Ridley, MP and from September 1981 to his resignation on 5 April 1982 Mr Richard Luce, MP. Formal negotiations at Ministerial level with the Argentine Government about the Falkland Islands were generally conducted by the Minister of State.

The permanent head of the Foreign and Commonwealth Office and Head of the Diplomatic Service is the Permanent Under-Secretary of State, from 1975 until his retirement in April 1982 Sir Michael Palliser. The Office has departments principally organised on a geographical basis, each department being headed by an official of Counsellor rank (equivalent to an Assistant Secretary in the Home Civil Service). At the time of the invasion the relevant department for Falkland Islands matters was the South America Department, which was also responsible for relations with all the countries in South America. It had been headed since November 1979 by Mr P. R. Fearn. The work of this Department was under the supervision of a Superintending Assistant Under-Secretary of State, from January 1981 Mr J. B. Ure, who also supervised the North

America, the West Indian and Atlantic, the Mexico and Central America and (in part) the Hong Kong and General Departments. He in turn was responsible to the Permanent Under-Secretary of State through a Deputy Under-Secretary of State, from February 1980 until February 1982 Mr D. M. Day, and from March 1982 Mr S. Giffard.

In Argentina, the British Government were represented by the British Ambassador in Buenos Aires and his staff. Mr A. J. Williams was British Ambassador from February 1980 until April 1982. The Defence *Attaché* in Buenos Aires was Colonel S. Love and the Naval *Attaché* Captain J. J. Mitchell, RN. The *Attachés* were seconded to the British Embassy from the Ministry of Defence.

GOVERNMENT OF THE FALKLAND ISLANDS AND DEPENDENCIES

Her Majesty's Government are responsible for the government and defence of the Falkland Islands and for external relations in respect of them. The Falkland Islands have a constitution, granted by the British Government, under which they have their own government and legislature.

In the period before the invasion, under the constitution, the Governor of the Falkland Islands, from February 1979 Mr R. M. Hunt (now Sir Rex Hunt), was subject to the directions of the Crown given through the Secretary of State. The Governor had full reserve executive and legislative powers, but in practice these powers were very rarely exercised. He was also Commander-in-Chief.

The Governor was assisted in the administration of Government by an Executive Council composed of two elected members, two *ex officio* members (the Chief Secretary and the Financial Secretary) and two members nominated by the Governor. The Legislative Council was composed of six elected and two *ex officio* members (the Chief Secretary and the Financial Secretary).

The Falkland Islands Dependencies are not part of the colony of the Falkland Islands, but constitute a separate colony. The Governor of the Falkland Islands and the Executive Council were also the Governor and Executive Council of the Dependencies.

MINISTRY OF DEFENCE

The Ministerial head of the Ministry of Defence is the Secretary of State for Defence, from January 1981 Mr John Nott, MP. He is assisted by two Ministers of State, one for the Armed Forces and one for Defence Procurement, and two Parliamentary Under-Secretaries of State. The Minister of State and the Parliamentary Under-Secretary of State for the Armed Forces at the time of the invasion were Mr Peter Blaker, MP and Mr Jerry Wiggin, MP respectively.

The principal military adviser to the Government is the Chief of the Defence Staff, who is Chairman of the Chiefs of Staff Committee. The Chief of the Defence Staff has a right of direct access to the Prime Minister. The Service Chiefs of Staff (the Chief of the Naval Staff, the Chief of the General Staff and the Chief of the Air Staff) are the senior military advisers to the Government on matters concerning their own Services. They have a right of direct access to the Prime Minister on these matters. At the time of the invasion Admiral Sir Terence Lewin (now Lord Lewin) was Chief of the Defence Staff, Admiral Sir Henry Leach Chief of the Naval Staff, General Sir

Edwin Bramall Chief of the General Staff, and Air Chief Marshal Sir Michael Beetham Chief of the Air Staff.

The principal adviser to the Defence Secretary on political, financial and administrative matters is the Permanent Under-Secretary of State, from March 1976 Sir Frank Cooper. The Defence Secretariat is responsible for advising him, and through him the Defence Secretary, on the Defence programme and budget and the political background associated with Defence policy, including overseas matters, in consultation with the Foreign and Commonwealth Office.

JOINT INTELLIGENCE ORGANISATION

The Joint Intelligence Organisation is an organisation based in the Cabinet Office which is responsible for making assessments for Ministers and officials of a wide range of external situations and developments. It draws for its assessments on all relevant information: diplomatic reports and telegrams, the views of Government departments and publicly available information, as well as secret intelligence reports. It also has a co-ordinating role in respect of the work of the security and intelligence agencies.

Assessments are normally considered before circulation by the Joint Intelligence Committee. The Joint Intelligence Committee is normally chaired by a Deputy Under-Secretary of State in the Foreign and Commonwealth Office. Its members include representatives of the security and intelligence agencies, the Foreign and Commonwealth Office, the Ministry of Defence and the Treasury.

Assessments are prepared for consideration by the Joint Intelligence Committee by Current Intelligence Groups, which are serviced by the Assessments Staff, who are civil servants and serving officers seconded to the Cabinet Office from their own Departments, principally the Foreign and Commonwealth Office and the Ministry of Defence. The Current Intelligence Groups are organised on a geographical basis. There is one for Latin America. Their membership is drawn from those in the relevant Departments with special knowledge of the area. They are chaired by members of the Assessments Staff. Assessments are prepared at the instigation of Ministers, of Departments or of the Joint Intelligence Organisation itself.

SECURITY AND INTELLIGENCE AGENCIES

The collection, but not the assessment, of secret intelligence is the responsibility of the security and intelligence agencies. On operational matters relevant to the subject of our review the agencies report to the Foreign and Commonwealth Office, but they serve the Government as a whole and their heads have a right of direct access to the Prime Minister. Their reports are circulated to, among others, the Foreign and Commonwealth Office and the Ministry of Defence as well as to the Joint Intelligence Organisation.

ANNEX C: EXTRACT FROM THE OFFICIAL REPORT, HOUSE OF COMMONS, 2 DECEMBER 1980

The Minister of State, Foreign and Commonwealth Office (Mr Nicholas Ridley): With permission, Mr Speaker, I wish to make a statement on the Falkland Islands.

We have no doubt about our sovereignty over the islands. The Argentines, however, continue to press their claim. The dispute is causing continuing uncertainty, emigration and economic stagnation in the islands. Following my exploratory talks with the Argentines in April, the Government have been considering possible ways of achieving a solution which would be acceptable to all the parties. In this the essential is that we should be guided by the wishes of the islanders themselves.

I therefore visited the islands between 22 and 29 November in order to consult island councillors and subsequently, at their express request, all islanders, on how we should proceed. Various possible bases for seeking a negotiated settlement were discussed. These included both a way of freezing the dispute for a period or exchanging the title of sovereignty against a long lease of the islands back to Her Majesty's Government.

The essential elements of any solution would be that it should preserve British administration, law and way of life for the islanders while releasing the potential of the islands' economy and of their maritime resources, at present blighted by the dispute.

It is for the islanders to advise on which, if any, option should be explored in negotiations with the Argentines. I have asked them to let me have their views in due course. Any eventual settlement would have to be endorsed by the islanders, and by this House.

Mr Peter Shore (Stepney and Poplar): This is a worrying statement.

Will the Minister confirm that involved here are the rights and future of 1,800 people of British descent in a territory which was originally uninhabited—people who, above all, wish to preserve their present relationship with the United Kingdom? Will he reaffirm that there is no question of proceeding with any proposal contrary to the wishes of the Falkland Islanders? Their wishes are surely not just "guidance" to the British Government. Surely they must be of paramount importance. Has he made that absolutely clear to the Argentine Government?

Is not the Minister aware that proposals for a leasing arrangement represent a major weakening of our long-held position on sovereignty in the Falkland Islands, and that to make them in so specific and public a manner is likely only to harden Argentine policy and to undermine the confidence of the Falkland Islanders? Will he therefore make it clear that we shall uphold the rights of the islanders to continue to make a genuinely free choice about their future, that we shall not abandon them and that, in spite of all the logistic difficulties, we shall continue to support and sustain them?

Mr Ridley: The answer to all the right hon. Gentleman's question is "Yes". There are about 1,800 islanders. I make it clear, as I did in my statement, that we shall do nothing which was not "endorsed" by the islanders. I used that word as well as the word "wishes". I agree that that is the predominant consideration in this matter. I am sure that equally the right hon. Gentleman will agree that nothing that he might feel, think or do should be allowed to interfere with what the islanders themselves decide. I confirm that our long-standing commitment to their security and economic well-being remains, and I said that in the islands.

Sir Bernard Braine (Essex, South-East): Does not my right hon. Friend agree that the option of yielding on sovereignty and leasing back undermines a perfectly valid title in international law?

Secondly, does not he realise that the precedent of Hong Kong, which was taken from China by force, is an insult to Falkland Islanders whose ancestors went there more than a century ago and settled peaceably in an uninhabited land?

Thirdly, did my hon. Friend discuss with representatives of the Falkland Islands alternative means of communications, which are perfectly feasible, in order to reduce the islands' total dependence upon the Argentine? Lastly, in view of the fresh anxieties that these talks have caused about the future of the islanders, and bearing in mind that the islanders are wholly British in blood and sentiment, will he give an assurance that the Government will include the Falkland Islanders as an exception in the forthcoming British nationality law?

Mr Ridley: I agree with my hon. Friend that we have a perfectly valid title. There is no question about that in our mind. The question is whether the islanders would prefer to have the dead hand of the dispute removed so that they can not only continue their British way of life but have reasonable prospects of economic expansion. I suggest that that is something upon which they have every right to give their views before we all give ours.

I consulted the islanders on the question of communications, but, of course, in the event of a dispute between ourselves and Argentina becoming more tense, my hon. Friend should realise that it is unlikely that communications could be established with neighbouring countries in South America. The question of British nationality is a matter for my right hon. Friend the Home Secretary.

Mr Russell Johnston (Inverness): Is the Minister aware that his reception in the Falkland Islands left the islanders' views in no doubt, although it left a considerable doubt about his good intentions? Is he further aware that there is no support at all in the Falkland Islands or in this House for the shameful schemes for getting rid of these islands which have been festering in the Foreign Office for years? Will he take this opportunity to end speculation once and for all by declaring quite clearly that he disowns these schemes and that he will work to improve the economic and political links between the United Kingdom and the Falkland Islands? Surely that is the way to end the emigration about which he talked earlier.

Mr Ridley: Perhaps I am more aware of the reception that I received in the islands than the hon. Gentleman is. I hope that even those who did not like what I had to say were at least agreed upon my good intentions. I can assure the hon. Gentleman that a large number of people felt that it was right that something should be done to settle the dispute. Some of them liked some of the ideas, and some did not. The islanders must be allowed to make up their own minds. The hon. Gentleman is rushing it a bit in trying to anticipate what they may eventually decide.

Mr Peter Tapsell (Horncastle): Will my hon. Friend bear in mind that some of us who have interested ourselves in the future of the Falkland Islands over the years have considerable doubts about the tactical wisdom of placing the leasing point on the negotiating table? We therefore particularly welcome that part of his statement which said that no settlement would be pursued which did not have the support of the Falkland Islanders.

Mr Ridley: No offer has been made to the Argentine Government to negotiate on anything. This was a visit to consult the islanders about what they would like to see in any future negotiation or, in the case of a negative answer, if there were to be no future negotiation. There is no question about this being a negotiating offer on the table. This is something which the islanders will discuss among themselves in order to decide whether they wish it to be pursued.

Mr Frank Hooley (Sheffield, Heeley): Is not the Government's argument that the interests of 1,800 Falkland Islanders take precedence over the interests of 55 million people in the United Kingdom?

Mr Ridley: There need be no conflict between the two, especially if a peaceful resolution of the dispute can be achieved.

Mr Julian Amery (Brighton, Pavilion): Is my hon. Friend aware that his statement is profoundly disturbing? Is he also aware, certainly the Falkland Islanders are, that for years— and here I speak from some experience—his Department has wanted to get rid of this commitment? Is he further aware that it is almost always a great mistake to get rid of real estate for nothing, that the Falkland Islands may have an important part to play in the future of the South Atlantic and that, admitting that the interests of the inhabitants and their wishes must be paramount, there is also a considerable British interest in maintaining this commitment, which is probably much cheaper to maintain than it is to lose? Will my hon. Friend look back at the cost to us in terms of oil prices of the surrender of Aden and the Persian Gulf?

Mr Ridley: I think my right hon. Friend knows me well enough to realise that I do not embrace schemes which are thrust upon me by my Department. The Government as a whole have taken the decision to take this initiative. It is of a political nature, and it is not the job of the Foreign Office to devise such an initiative. There is a great deal in what my right hon. Friend said about the need to watch the strategic and other interests in the South Atlantic. It is in order to ensure that these may be peacefully pursued, including the possibilities of oil around the Falklands, that there is a premium on trying to solve the dispute.

Mr Donald Stewart (Western Isles): In order to allay the fears and doubts which his statement will have aroused among islanders, and in order to preserve the honour of the Government in the affair, will the Minister now advise the Argentine Government that the matter is closed unless and until the islanders wish to reopen it?

Mr Ridley: I repeat that I was in the islands more recently than the right hon. Gentleman. It is not for him to say what the islanders do or do not want. I have asked them directly, and I do not need his services to anticipate what they may say.

Mr Kenneth Warren (Hastings): I recognise that the Falkland Islands have severe current economic problems, but does my hon. Friend agree that the potential in terms of fisheries and offshore oil in the Falkland Islands is sufficient to sustain them economically in the not too distant future and that we should give the islanders every support that we can in their economic bargaining?

Mr Ridley: My hon. Friend is right, but he will also know that it has not proved possible under the Governments of either party to exploit those resources, either of fish or oil, because of the dead hand of the dispute with Argentina. We are seeking to find a solution in order to make that possible.

Mr Tom McNally (Stockport, South): Is the Minister aware that his Department's policy over many years has been the major cause of the uncertainty affecting the islands? Instead of making these humiliating excursions to the Argentine, would it not be better for the hon. Gentleman simply to say that whatever the Government, and whatever the majority, there will never be a majority in this House to give this historically separate people and separate islands to the Argentine?

Mr Ridley: The hon. Gentleman speaks as if he knows more about the position than the Foreign Office and the islanders; he seems to speak for the whole House. He may find that he is sometimes wrong.

Viscount Cranborne (Dorset, South): Is my hon. Friend aware that his statement today has caused grave disquiet throughout his own supporters and that merely by entertaining the possibility of the surrender of sovereignty he is encouraging the islanders to think that they do not enjoy the support that they deserve from their home country? Is he also aware that his attitude reminds me of the attitude of the Church of England over the old Prayer Book—

Mr Deputy Speaker: Order.

Mr Ridley: I was happy to be able to assure the islanders that they had our support, whatever course they chose to take. Of course, whether the position remains as it is at present or whether there is a leaseback, the Government are obligated to defend their territories all round the world.

Mr Douglas Jay (Battersea, North): It is clear that the islanders, whatever else they may think, have no wish for a change of sovereignty. Why cannot the Foreign Office leave the matter alone?

Mr Ridley: The right hon. Gentleman should have accompanied me on my visit; it would have been very pleasant. He may then have heard the views of the islanders, a large number of whom believe that it would be to their advantage to settle the dispute. He must listen to the views in the islands instead of preaching what he has always believed to be the case.

Several Hon. Members rose—

Mr Deputy Speaker: Order. I must protect the business on the Order Paper. I propose to take three more questions from either side of the House.

Mr Robin Maxwell-Hyslop (Tiverton): Did my hon. Friend discuss with the islanders the question of their right of access to the United Kingdom in any proposed change of the nationality laws, or did he tell them that a Home Office Minister would be visiting the Falkland Islands to do so? In other words, is it only to the House of Commons that my hon. Member will not answer questions about that, or will a Home Office Minister do so?

What is the position concerning Falkland Islands trade with Southern Chile? There was some experimental trade in lamb. What opportunities are there for further economic links between Southern Chile and the Falkland Islands rather than that the Falkland Islands should be totally reliant on Argentina?

Mr Ridley: The islanders certainly discussed the question of nationality with me, and I said that I would discuss the matter with my right hon. Friend the Home Secretary when I returned home. I am sure that my right hon. Friend will discuss the matter with me at some stage.

The question of trade with Chile is open. There is no reason why the islanders should not trade with Chile, or with any other country. There has been one delivery of sheep to Chile, and we hope that there will be further trade between the two countries.

Mr James Johnson (Kingston upon Hull, West): The House will welcome, and has welcomed, the Minister's unequivocal statement that the islanders will be the arbiters and sole judges of their destiny, but what is he doing to ameliorate their conditions? The islands are 10,000 miles away with a diminishing population, and young people are leaving them. Argentina will not go away, so the Government's duty is to ameliorate conditions between the islands and the mainland. What are the Government doing about fishing ventures, or any other commercial exploitations?

Mr Ridley: I am taking an initiative to see, with the islanders, whether there is a way or solving the dispute. That is the way to unlock the economic potential that the islanders so badly need.

Mr Matthew Parris (Derbyshire, West): Will my hon. Friend explain why the continuing dispute with Argentina precludes help from the United Kingdom Government to the islanders in developing their territory?

Mr Ridley: The possibility of declaring a 200-mile zone round the islands is remote without the agreement of the Argentine, because of the difficulty of enforcing the licensing of fishing or oil exploration. Successive Governments found that that was not possible in the absence of an agreement. There is also considerable difficulty relating to investment and the extension of credit to the islands because of the fear of investors that the dispute may frustrate their investment.

Mr John Home Robertson (Berwick and East Lothian): Will the Minister tell the House more about the leasing proposals? Is it his idea to sell the freehold to Argentina and to lease it back as part of the Government's attempt to reduce the public sector borrowing requirement?

Mr Ridley: The details of any leaseback arrangement would first have to be considered by the islanders, and then it would be the subject of negotiation with the Argentine and then the subject of endorsement by the islanders and this House. It is impossible to go into detail with any accuracy, but it is not envisaged that any money would change hands, either in the transfer or in the lease.

Mr William Shelton (Streatham): I congratulate my hon. Friend on taking the views of the islanders, which is right and proper. Will he confirm that should those views be for a maintenance of the status quo he will accept that? Will he also say whether he has contingency plans to help the islanders, despite the lack of resolution of the problem?

Mr Ridley: We shall have to wait for the answer. That is a hypothetical question, and we must consider the matter when we hear from the islanders.

Mr David Lambie (Central Ayrshire): As one of the few Members to have visited the Falkland Islands, may I ask the Minister whether he is aware of the deeply felt suspicion of the islanders of previous British Governments and British politicians, especially those representing the Foreign Office? Is he further aware that there was no need for today's statement, which will further heighten those suspicions? Is this a further example of the Government reneging on previous promises that were given to those people?

Mr Ridley: As one of the few hon. Members to have visited the Falkland Islands—I have visited them twice—I beg to differ with the hon. Gentleman. My welcome was friendly, and the islanders were kind and listened to me with great attention. They were grateful for the frank discussions that we had.

Mr Shore: The Minister was asked a few moments ago whether, if the islanders were to opt for the status quo, that would then be the Government's view on the matter and they would sustain it. He did not give a clear reply to that.

If the Government are to honour their commitment that the views and wishes of the Falkland Islands are to be paramount, which is the word which has been used hitherto, he must assure the House and the Falkland Islanders that that principle of paramountcy of their wishes about their future will be sustained by the British Government.

Mr Ridley: I have said that anything that was proposed would have to be endorsed by the islanders. There is no need to repeat that. However, I cannot answer a hypothetical question about what might happen in certain circumstances just as I am sure that the right hon. Gentleman would not be prepared to say that, if the islanders endorsed a solution, he could make his whole party vote for it.

Mr Farr: On a point of order, Mr Deputy Speaker. Is it possible to give notice after a ministerial statement that one would wish to raise a matter on the Adjournment? If it is possible, I should like so to do because of the intense dissatisfaction I feel about what the Minister said.

PART III

◦∞◊∞◦

THE FALKLANDS CAMPAIGN:
THE OPERATION

PRESENTED TO PARLIAMENT
BY THE SECRETARY OF STATE
FOR DEFENCE

DECEMBER 1982

On 2 April 1982 in an act of unprovoked aggression against British sovereign territory and British people Argentine forces invaded the Falkland Islands. The next day they invaded South Georgia. These invasions were launched despite urgent calls upon the Argentine Government from the President of the USA, the President of the United Nations (UN) Security Council and the Secretary General of the UN to desist from military action. The invasion was immediately condemned by the UN Security Council in its

Resolution 502. That Resolution went on to call for an immediate withdrawal of the Argentine forces occupying the Falkland Islands, and for a peaceful settlement of the dispute.

The Government made clear from the first its willingness to accept and abide by Resolution 502. We engaged in intense and prolonged diplomatic activity in pursuit of a peaceful solution. But we could not depend upon it. We therefore took military steps intended to put pressure on Argentina to withdraw and to make possible our repossession of the Islands by force if that should ultimately prove necessary. Three days after the invasion, HMS *Hermes* and HMS *Invincible* left the United Kingdom to head what was to become the largest task force in recent history.

While diplomatic efforts continued the net was gradually drawn more tightly around the Argentine garrison on the Falklands. On 12 April we imposed a maritime exclusion zone of 200 miles around the Falklands against Argentine naval ships. On 23 April we warned that any approach by Argentine forces which could amount to a threat to interfere with the mission of British forces in the South Atlantic would be dealt with appropriately. On 25 April the task force repossessed South Georgia. The recapture of South Georgia dealt a psychological blow to the Argentine Government and provided clear evidence of the United Kingdom's resolve and willingness to resort to military action if all other courses were closed. It also gave the task force an anchorage in the South Atlantic. On 29 April we warned that all Argentine vessels shadowing the task force would be liable to attack. Despite this increasing military pressure, however, Argentine showed no signs of yielding on any points which could make negotiations possible.

We took further measures: on 30 April a total exclusion zone was imposed; on 1 May Port Stanley airfield was bombed; and on 7 May we warned that any Argentine warship or military aircraft over 12 miles from the Argentine coast would be treated as hostile. Even at this stage the way was open for the Argentine Government to accept a peaceful withdrawal of their troops. They declined, and it became clear that the Falklands would have to be retaken by force.

The first major landing on the Falkland Islands was made at San Carlos Water on the night of 20/21 May. In the actions which followed there were inevitably setbacks and casualties. Nevertheless, just over three weeks later Major General Moore, the Land Force Commander accepted the surrender of General Menendez and his force at Port Stanley. It was by any standards a brilliant campaign, marked by exceptional logistic planning and improvisation, and carried through with outstanding skill and fortitude.

DEPLOYMENT

To despatch a task force in such a short space of time was a remarkable achievement. It was the result of close co-operation between the Services, the Merchant Navy, the Royal Dockyards and commercial ports, the stores and transport organisations of the Ministry of Defence, and Industry. The task force had to be stocked and provisioned for at least three months at sea. Many of the merchant ships required extensive modification to prepare them for their new rôle. Eventually over 110 ships were deployed. These included 44 warships; 22 from the Royal Fleet Auxiliary (RFA); and 45 merchant ships whose civilian crews were all volunteers.

The Falkland Islands lie 8,000 miles south-west of the United Kingdom and over 3,500 miles from Ascension Island; but only 400 miles from the Argentine mainland. The task force needed to be self-sufficient in food, water, fuel, ammunition and all the other military equipment it might require. Sound transport and logistic arrangements were vitally important. The ships of the RFA and the Merchant Navy and the Royal Air Force's transport aircraft were to be the task force's lifeline. Merchant shipping alone transported 9,000 personnel, 100,000 tons of freight and 95 aircraft to the South Atlantic. The supply chain carried 400,000 tons of fuel. RFA support ships transferred ammunition, dry cargo and fuel on some 1,200 occasions, in addition to more than 300 helicopter transfers. British forces established a joint forward operating base at Ascension Island. The Royal Air Force moved over 5,800 people and 6,600 tons of stores through Ascension Island in more than 600 sorties by Hercules and VC10 aircraft. Hercules aircraft also made some 40 supply drops to the task force, which entailed mid-air refuelling in round-trips lasting, in many cases, over 25 hours. This massive logistic effort enabled the warships and the aircraft of the task force to operate continuously without returning to distant bases for provisions.

In the space of seven weeks a task force of 28,000 men and over 100 ships had been assembled, sailed 8,000 miles, effectively neutralised the Argentine Navy and fought off persistent and courageous attacks from combat aircraft which outnumbered its own by more than six to one. This in itself was no mean feat, but the task force then put ashore 10,000 men on a hostile coast while under threat of heavy air attack; fought several pitched battles against an entrenched and well-supplied enemy who at all times outnumbered our forces; and brought them to surrender within three and a half weeks.

FROM SOUTH GEORGIA TO SAN CARLOS ON THE FALKLANDS

The first action at sea took place off South Georgia when on 25 April the Argentine submarine *Santa Fé* was attacked on the surface some five miles from the main harbour at Grytviken. She was badly damaged and subsequently beached. The same day the island was repossessed by Royal Marines and Special Forces (the Special Air Service (SAS) and the Special Boat Squadron (SBS) of the Royal Marines (RM)). On 1 May a Vulcan followed by Sea Harriers carried out their first attacks on the Falklands, and the first Argentine aircraft were shot down. The carrier group made a major demonstration of force, simulating an amphibious landing off Port Stanley which successfully drew the Argentines and revealed some of their defensive positions.

On 2 May HMS *Conqueror* detected the Argentine cruiser, *General Belgrano*, accompanied by two destroyers, sailing near to the total exclusion zone. Other Argentine ships were also thought to be probing our defences to the north of the zone. The *Belgrano*, and her escorts armed with Exocet missiles, posed a clear threat to the ships of the task force. She was therefore attacked and sunk by torpedoes. Thereafter major Argentine warships remained within 12 miles of the Argentine coast and took no further part in the campaign. Argentine submarines continued to pose a serious threat, but no task force ships were successfully attacked.

The task force suffered its first major loss on 4 May. HMS *Sheffield*, while on forward radar picket duty, was hit

The Falklands Campaign, 1982

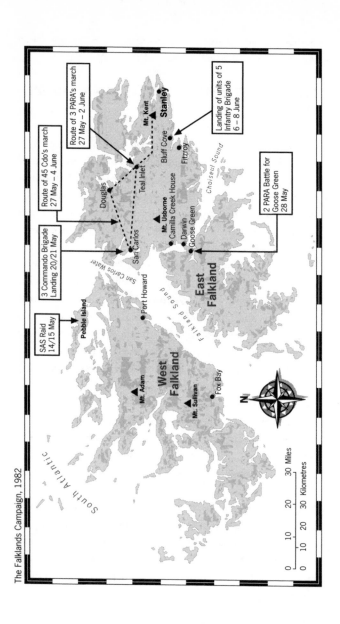

by an Exocet missile launched from an Argentine Super Etendard aircraft. The missile hit fuel tanks amidships and serious fires started, which filled the central section of the ship with acrid smoke. After nearly four hours, with the fires increasing in intensity, the Captain gave orders to abandon ship. Twenty members of her crew died.

By mid-May the task force had accomplished two of its main tasks: the movement of the troops safely to the South Atlantic and the establishment of control of the seas around the Islands. The rôle of the carriers, HMS *Hermes* and HMS *Invincible*, was crucial at this and subsequent stages in providing air defence and the means of attacking enemy ships and ground positions, while their helicopters provided constant anti-submarine protection.

It was now necessary to put land forces ashore in sufficient strength to repossess the Islands. San Carlos was chosen as the site for the amphibious landing because it offered a good anchorage which could be protected against submarine attack and was known to be lightly defended by the enemy and difficult for him to reinforce rapidly. The low hills surrounding the inlet afforded good protection against the risk of Exocet attack. The SAS and the SBS had for some time been reconnoitring East and West Falkland. Taking advantage of the intelligence they had gained, and under cover of a naval bombardment, the SAS carried out a daring night raid on Pebble Island on 15 May. They destroyed 11 Argentine aircraft on the ground.

On 20 May the main amphibious force moved towards San Carlos Water, taking advantage of an overcast sky and poor visibility, and keeping strict radio silence. Meanwhile Special Forces mounted a series of diversionary raids at various points around East Falkland. Under cover of naval gunfire, men of the 3rd Commando Brigade RM (3 Cdo Bde), including the 2nd and 3rd Battalions, the Parachute Regiment (2 PARA and 3 PARA), embarked in their landing craft. The landing was made over four beaches. Helicopters operated continuously, moving stores and helping to establish the beach-head. The operation achieved complete tactical surprise. 5,000 men were safely landed, and what little opposition there was quickly collapsed. British losses in this phase were two helicopters and their crews.

The next morning brought clear skies, but the landing force had won a vital few hours to establish defensive positions and begin to set up their Rapier units. At mid-day the Argentine Air Force began a series of fierce and protracted attacks against the beach-head and the ships supporting it.

The Sea Harriers on combat air patrol provided the outer layer of defence. The second layer was provided by a pair of ships known as the "missile trap", positioned off the northern entrance to Falkland Sound. These were usually a Type 42 destroyer armed with Sea Dart and a Type 22 frigate with Sea Wolf. The next layer of defence, which became known as the "gunline", was a group of three or four ships inside the entrance to the Sound using every gun and missile system they possessed to fight off the incoming Argentine aircraft. Finally within the anchorage itself (nicknamed "bomb alley"), where there were often up to eight troop or stores ships at any one time, the small calibre guns and Seacat missiles from the assault ships, HMS *Intrepid* and HMS *Fearless*, together with Blowpipe missiles, machine guns and notably the Rapier fire units on shore provided the final layer of defence.

The Argentine pilots were courageous and persistent in their attacks and ships of the task force suffered loss and damage during the first few days after the landing. On the "gunline" we lost HMS *Ardent* and HMS *Antelope* on 21 and 23 May; 24 men died. Six other ships were damaged between 21 and 24 May. But the Argentines paid a heavy price. On 21 May British forces shot down some 15 attacking aircraft. When attacks resumed on 23 May, 10 attacking aircraft were destroyed; on 24 May a further 18 were shot down.

On 25 May, Argentina's National Day, the Argentine Air Force made a major effort against the task force. HMS *Coventry* had been in the "missile trap" to the north-west and had successfully controlled Sea Harriers and shot down three aircraft herself. She was attacked at low level by waves of Skyhawk aircraft which overwhelmed her defences. She capsized quickly. Survivors were rescued by HMS *Broadsword* and helicopters; 19 men died. Air attacks on the beach-head now became much less frequent and British forces were safely established ashore. The battle of San Carlos had been won.

Away from the beach-head air attacks continued. On 25 May the merchant ship, *Atlantic Conveyor*, which was carrying much needed supplies, including helicopters, was north-east of the Falklands. Two Exocet missiles, launched from Argentine Super Etendard aircraft, hit the *Atlantic Conveyor*. The ship was set on fire. The fire spread rapidly and the ship was abandoned with the loss of 12 lives. A third attack on the task force by air-launched Exocet on 30 May was successfully countered.

FROM SAN CARLOS TO FITZROY

With the establishment of a firm bridge-head the advance on Port Stanley became the next objective. One threat to the flank of any attack on Port Stanley lay in the significant Argentine garrison and airfield at Darwin and Goose Green. 2 PARA was given the task of removing that danger and seeking an early victory. Overnight on 26/27 May one company of 2 PARA secured Camilla Creek House. After a 12-mile night-approach march the rest of the battalion joined them and lay up for the day. An artillery troop of three 105mm light guns was flown into position to assist in the impending assault which started at 0200 hours on 28 May.

2 PARA began by attacking Darwin, supported by naval gunfire. The settlement was secured by mid-afternoon but the battalion was then faced with an advance on Goose Green, where the enemy were dug into strong defensive positions which had to be approached across the open ground of a narrow isthmus. Harrier aircraft were called in to attack the Argentine positions. The battalion was attacked by Pucara light aircraft from Goose Green, one of which was shot down by a Blowpipe missile. The battalion eventually overcame stiff resistance and pushed the enemy back into the settlement. A timely strike by the Harriers considerably helped the progress of the paratroopers and the next day the Argentine commander surrendered. British dead totalled 17.

Besides securing the flank the battle was significant for two reasons. First it gave us a chance to assess the fighting qualities of the enemy. Second, and more importantly, by their outstanding performance against a numerically superior enemy 2 PARA established a psychological ascendancy over the Argentines which our forces never lost.

In the course of a remarkable march of 50 miles over difficult terrain in inhospitable conditions, 45 Cdo and 3 PARA secured Douglas Settlement and Teal Inlet on 30 May. Meanwhile the SAS had established a patrol base

Advance on Port Stanley, June 1982

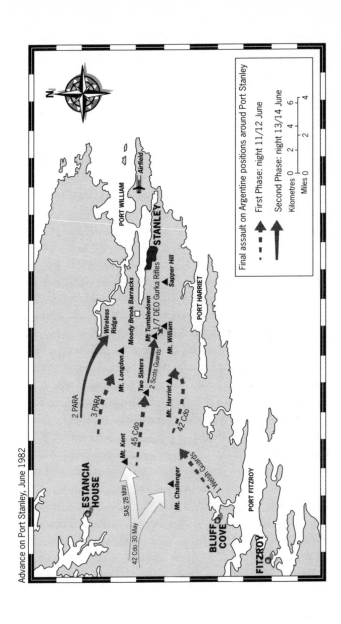

Final assault on Argentine positions around Port Stanley

First Phase: night 11/12 June

Second Phase: night 13/14 June

Kilometres 0 2 4 6

Miles 0 2 4

PORT WILLIAM

Airfield

STANLEY

Wireless Ridge

Moody Brook Barracks

Mt. Longdon

Two Sisters

Mt Tumbledown

1/7 DEO Gurka Rifles

2 Scots Guards

Sapper Hill

Mt. William

PORT HARRIET

Mt. Harriet

2 PARA

3 PARA

Mt. Kent

45 Cdo

42 Cdo

Mt. Challenger

SAS 28 May

42 Cdo 30 May

1 Welsh Guards

ESTANCIA HOUSE

BLUFF COVE

PORT FITZROY

FITZROY

forward on Mount Kent. 42 Cdo, making best use of the helicopter lift available, leap-frogged forward to secure Mount Kent and Mount Challenger, the western approaches to Port Stanley. On the same day Major General Moore assumed command of all land operations. The 5th Infantry Brigade (5 Bde) came ashore on 1 June.

The Land Force Commander decided to press on quickly with the advance on Port Stanley and to commit 5 Bde to the South. When it was discovered that the Argentines had evacuated Fitzroy settlement, 2 PARA moved forward rapidly to secure the area, which was an important point in the advance on Stanley. The 1st Battalion 7th Duke of Edinburgh's Own Gurkha Rifles and the rest of 2 PARA advanced by sea and by air while the 2nd Battalion Scots Guards, the 1st Battalion Welsh Guards and logistic support units were transported to Fitzroy by sea. The loss of Chinook helicopters on the *Atlantic Conveyor* had effectively precluded the option of air-lifting the bulk of 5 Bde. Passage by sea was therefore the only way to move forward quickly, maintaining the impetus of the advance and minimising the risk of Argentine counter-attack. On the nights 5/6 and 6/7 June the Scots Guards and elements of the Welsh Guards were successfully moved by HMS *Intrepid* and HMS *Fearless*.

The deployment of the balance of the Welsh Guards was thwarted by appalling weather. On the night 7/8 June RFA *Sir Galahad* was despatched with support units and the remaining Welsh Guards. On 8 June the cloud lifted and, before the final elements had been disembarked from the landing ships, RFA *Sir Galahad* and RFA *Sir Tristram* were hit by an air strike at Fitzroy. Both ships were abandoned. The *Sir Galahad*, which had a large number of men on board, was burnt out. 50 men lost their lives, of whom 32 were from the 1st Battalion Welsh Guards. The courageous efforts of the helicopter pilots and rescue boat crews, who took their craft again and again into the flames and blinding smoke rising from the stricken vessel, prevented greater loss of life. But for the bravery of the seamen and the dedication of all those who assisted ashore the loss of life would have been much greater. Later that day a pair of patrolling Sea Harriers destroyed four Mirages over Choiseul Sound.

ADVANCE ON PORT STANLEY

Despite previous set-backs through loss of men and equipment, particularly helicopters, the first phase of the main battle for Port Stanley began on 11/12 June when 3 Cdo Bde mounted a three battalion night attack. Simultaneously targets further to the east were bombarded by naval vessels. As a result of vigorous and aggressive patrolling the troops were able to achieve initial surprise, and after a night of stiff fighting 3 PARA took Mount Longdon, 45 Cdo captured Two Sisters, and 42 Cdo captured Mount Harriet. British casualties were 22 killed and 44 wounded. Throughout the following day, all these positions came under considerable enemy artillery fire, causing more casualties. The shelling was not, however, all one way: the Argentine defences were heavily bombarded by our own artillery and at night by naval guns.

During the night of 11/12 June HMS *Glamorgan* was withdrawing from a bombardment of shore positions near Port Stanley when she was hit by a shore-launched Exocet missile. Her company extinguished severe fires and the ship continued to be available for action. 13 men died. It was the last direct attack on a British ship in the campaign.

The second phase took place on the night of 13/14 June. In the north, in another superbly executed night attack, 2 PARA captured Wireless Ridge. Further south the Scots Guards had a hard fight to capture Tumbledown Mountain from a regular Argentine Marine battalion whose heavily defended machine gun emplacements put up fierce resistance for a number of hours. The Scots Guards secured their objectives and the Gurkhas moved through to take Mount William to the south-east. In this final phase we lost 20 men.

Large numbers of the enemy abandoned their positions, discarded their weapons and stood around disconsolately. British troops followed up to the edge of Port Stanley where they were ordered to halt and fire only in self-defence, to avoid fighting in the town and among the civilian population. Soon afterwards white flags were reported over Stanley and General Moore accepted the Argentine surrender.

Chronology

2 April	Argentina invades the Falkland Islands.
3 April	Argentina invades South Georgia; UN passes Security Council Resolution 502; first RAF transport aircraft deploy to Ascension Island.
5 April	First task force ships sail from the United Kingdom.
12 April	200-mile maritime exclusion zone comes into effect.

23 April	The Government warns Argentina that any approach by Argentine warships or military aircraft which could amount to a threat to the task force would be dealt with appropriately.
25 April	British forces recapture South Georgia; submarine *Santa Fé* attacked and disabled.
30 April	Total exclusion zone comes into effect.
1 May	First attack on Falklands by Vulcan, Sea Harriers and warships; first Argentine aircraft shot down.
2 May	*General Belgrano* sunk by HMS *Conqueror*.
4 May	HMS *Sheffield* hit by Exocet missile; later sinks.
7 May	The Government warns Argentina that any Argentine warships and military aircraft over 12 miles from the Argentine coast would be regarded as hostile and liable to be dealt with accordingly.
9 May	Two Sea Harriers sink trawler, *Narwal*, which had been shadowing task force.
11 May	HMS *Alacrity* sinks store ship *Cabo de los Estados* in Falkland Sound.
14/15 May	Special Forces night raid on Pebble Island; 11 Argentine aircraft destroyed on the ground.

21 May	3 Cdo Bde establish beach-head at San Carlos; HMS *Ardent* lost; some 15 Argentine aircraft destroyed.
23 May	HMS *Antelope* crippled (sinks on 24 May); 10 Argentine aircraft destroyed.
24 May	18 Argentine aircraft destroyed; some damage to ships.
25 May	HMS *Coventry* lost and *Atlantic Conveyor* hit by Exocet (sinks 28 May); 8 Argentine aircraft destroyed.
28 May	2 PARA recapture Darwin and Goose Green.
30 May	45 Cdo secure Douglas settlement; 3 PARA recapture Teal Inlet; 42 Cdo advance on Mount Kent and Mount Challenger.
1 June	5 Bde land at San Carlos.
8 June	RFAs *Sir Galahad* and *Sir Tristram* hit at Fitzroy; 10 Argentine aircraft destroyed.
11/12 June	Mount Harriet, Two Sisters and Mount Longdon secured; HMS *Glamorgan* hit by shore-based Exocet—damaged but seaworthy.
13/14 June	Tumbledown Mountain, Wireless Ridge and Mount William secured; General Menendez surrenders.
20 June	Southern Thule secured.
25 June	Mr Hunt, Civil Commissioner, returns to Port Stanley.

PART IV

∞∞❈∞∞

THE FALKLANDS CAMPAIGN:
A DIGEST OF DEBATES IN THE
HOUSE OF COMMONS

APRIL TO JUNE 1982

The extracts which follow have been taken from Kenneth Morgan's book The Falklands Campaign *(HMSO, 1982), which presented a digest of the six debates and numerous questions and answers that occupied the attention of the House of Commons from 2 April to 15 June 1982. The extracts chosen are from the discussions which took place on 3 April, 4 May and 15 June 1982. The editing of these debates was expertly carried out by Mr Morgan, who has made linking additions and in some cases judicious omissions from the original debate. For a fuller report the reader should refer to Mr Morgan's original text and, if necessary, the Official Hansard Report for a verbatim record.*

SATURDAY 3 APRIL 1982

Parliament was recalled on a Saturday for the first time in more than 20 years on 3 April for an emergency debate.

The Prime Minister (Mrs Margaret Thatcher): The House meets this Saturday to respond to a situation of great gravity. We are here because, for the first time for many years, British sovereign territory has been invaded by a foreign power. After several days of rising tension in our relations with Argentina, that country's armed forces attacked the Falkland

Islands yesterday and established military control of the islands.

Yesterday was a day of rumour and counter-rumour. Throughout the day we had no communication from the Government of the Falklands. Indeed, the last message that we received was at 21.55 hours on Thursday night, 1 April. Yesterday morning at 8.33 we sent a telegram which was acknowledged. At 8.45 a.m. all communications ceased. I shall refer to that again in a moment. By late afternoon yesterday it became clear that an Argentine invasion had taken place and that the lawful British Government of the islands had been usurped.

I am sure that the whole House will join me in condemning totally this unprovoked aggression by the Government of Argentina against British territory. [HON. MEMBERS: "Hear, hear."] It has not a shred of justification and not a scrap of legality.

It was not until 8.30 this morning, our time, when I was able to speak to the governor, who had arrived in Uruguay, that I learnt precisely what had happened. He told me that the Argentines had landed at approximately 6 a.m. Falkland's time, 10 a.m. our time. One party attacked the capital from the landward side and another from the seaward side. The governor then sent a signal to us which we did not receive.

Communications had ceased at 8.45 a.m. our time. It is common for atmospheric conditions to make communications with Port Stanley difficult. Indeed, we had been out of contact for a period the previous night.

The governor reported that the marines, in the defence of Government House, were superb. He said that they acted in the best traditions of the Royal Marines. They inflicted casualties, but those defending Government House suffered none. He had kept the local people informed of what was happening through a small local transmitter which he had in Government House. He is relieved that the islanders heeded his advice to stay indoors. Fortunately, as far as he is aware, there were no civilian casualties. When he left the Falklands, he said that the people were in tears. They do not want to be Argentine. He said that the islanders are still tremendously loyal. I must say that I have every confidence in the governor and the action that he took.

I must tell the House that the Falkland Islands and their dependencies remain British territory. No aggression and no invasion can alter that simple fact. It is the Government's objective to see that the islands are freed from occupation and are returned to British administration at the earliest possible moment.

Argentina has, of course, long disputed British sovereignty over the islands. We have absolutely no doubt about our sovereignty, which has been continuous since 1833. Nor have we any doubt about the unequivocal wishes of the Falkland Islanders, who are British in stock and tradition, and they wish to remain British in allegiance. We cannot allow the democratic rights of the islanders to be denied by the territorial ambitions of Argentina ...

There had, of course, been previous incidents affecting sovereignty before the one in South Georgia, to which I shall refer in a moment. In December 1976 the Argentines illegally set up a scientific station on one of the dependencies within the Falklands group—Southern Thule. The Labour Government attempted to solve the matter through diplomatic exchanges, but without success. The Argentines remained there and are still there ...

In the meantime, we had been in touch with the Argentine Government about the [South Georgia] incident. They claimed to have had no prior knowledge of the landing and assured us that there were no Argentine military personnel in the party. For our part we made it clear that, while we had no wish to interfere in the operation of a normal commercial contract, we could not accept the illegal presence of these people on British territory.

We asked the Argentine Government either to arrange for the departure of the remaining men or to ensure that they obtained the necessary permission to be there. Because we recognised the potentially serious nature of the situation, HMS *Endurance* was ordered to the area. We told the Argentine Government that, if they failed to regularise the position of the party on South Georgia or to arrange for their departure, HMS *Endurance* would take them off, without using force, and return them to Argentina.

This was, however, to be the last resort. We were determined that this apparently minor problem of 10 people on South Georgia in pursuit of a commercial contract should not be allowed to escalate and we made it plain to the Argentine Government that we wanted to achieve a peaceful resolution of the problem by diplomatic means. To help in this, HMS *Endurance* was ordered not to approach the Argentine party at Leith but to go to Grytviken.

But it soon became clear that the Argentine Government had little interest in trying to solve the problem. On 25 March another Argentine Navy ship arrived at Leith to deliver supplies to the 10 men ashore. Our ambassador in Buenos Aires sought an early response from the Argentine Government to our previous requests that they should arrange for the men's departure. This request was refused. Last Sunday, 28 March, the Argentine Foreign Minister sent a message to my right hon. and noble Friend the Foreign Secretary refusing outright to regularise the men's position. Instead it restated Argentina's claim to sovereignty over the Falkland Islands and their dependencies.

My right hon. and noble Friend the Foreign and Commonwealth Secretary then sent a message to the United States Secretary of State asking him to intervene and to urge restraint.

By the beginning of this week it was clear that our efforts to solve the South Georgia dispute through the usual diplomatic channels were getting nowhere. Therefore, on Wednesday 31 March my right hon. and noble Friend the Foreign Secretary proposed to the Argentine Foreign Minister that we should dispatch a special emissary to Buenos Aires.

Later that day we received information which led us to believe that a large number of Argentine ships, including an aircraft carrier, destroyers, landing craft, troop carriers and submarines, were heading for Port Stanley. I contacted President Reagan that evening and asked him to intervene with the Argentine President directly. We promised, in the meantime, to take no action to escalate the dispute for fear of precipitating—*[Interruption]*—the very event that our efforts were directed to avoid. May I remind Opposition Members—*[Interruption]*—what happened when, during the lifetime of their Government ... Southern Thule was occupied. It was occupied in 1976. The House was not even informed by the then Government until 1978 ...

Mr Edward Rowlands (Merthyr Tydfil): The right hon. Lady is talking about a piece of rock in the most southerly part of the dependencies, which is totally uninhabited and which smells of large accumulations of penguin and other bird droppings. There is a vast difference—a whole world of difference—between the 1,800 people now imprisoned by Argentine invaders and that argument. The right hon. Lady should have the grace to accept that.

The Prime Minister: We are talking about the sovereignty of British territory—*[Interruption]*—which was infringed in 1976. The House was not even informed of it until 1978. We are talking about a further incident in South Georgia which—as I have indicated—seemed to be a minor incident at the time. There is only a British Antarctic scientific survey there and there was a commercial contract to remove a whaling station. I suggest to the hon. Gentleman that had I come to the House at that time and said that we had a problem on South Georgia with 10 people who had landed with a contract to remove a whaling station, and had I gone on to say that we should send HMS *Invincible*, I should have been accused of warmongering and sabre-rattling.

Information about the Argentine fleet did not arrive until Wednesday. Argentina is, of course, very close to the Falklands—a point that the hon. Member for Merthyr Tydfil cannot and must not ignore—and its Navy can sail there very quickly. On Thursday, the Argentine Foreign Minister rejected the idea of an emissary and told our ambassador that the diplomatic channel, as a means of solving this dispute, was closed. President Reagan had a very long telephone conversation, of some 50 minutes, with the Argentine President, but his strong representations fell on deaf ears. I am grateful to him and to Secretary Haig for their strenuous and persistent efforts on our behalf.

On Thursday, the United Nations Secretary-General, Mr Perez de Cuellar, summoned both British and Argentine permanent representatives to urge both countries to refrain from the use or threat of force in the South Atlantic. Later that evening we sought an emergency meeting of the Security Council. We accepted the appeal of its President for restraint. The Argentines said nothing. On Friday, as the House knows, the Argentines invaded the Falklands and I have given a precise account of everything we knew, or did not know, about that situation. There were also reports that yesterday the Argentines also attacked South Georgia, where HMS *Endurance* had left a detachment of 22 Royal Marines. Our information is that on 2 April an Argentine naval transport vessel informed the base commander at Grytviken that an important message would be passed to him after 11 o'clock today our time. It is assumed that this message will ask the base commander to surrender.

Before indicating some of the measures that the Government have taken in response to the Argentinian invasion, I should like to make three points. First, even if ships had been instructed to sail the day that the Argentines landed on South Georgia to clear the whaling station, the ships could not possibly have got to Port Stanley before the invasion. *[Interruption]* Opposition Members may not like it, but that is a fact.

Secondly, there have been several occasions in the past when an invasion has been threatened. The only way of being certain to prevent an invasion would have been to keep a very large fleet close to the Falklands, when we are some 8,000 miles away from base. No Government have ever been able to do that, and the cost would be enormous.

Mr Eric Ogden (Liverpool, West Derby): Will the right hon. Lady say what has happened to HMS *Endurance*?

The Prime Minister: HMS *Endurance* is in the area. It is not for me to say precisely where, and the hon. Gentleman would not wish me to do so.

Thirdly, aircraft unable to land on the Falklands, because of the frequently changing weather, would have had little fuel left and, ironically, their only hope of landing safely would have been to divert to Argentina. Indeed, all of the air and most sea supplies for the Falklands come from Argentina, which is but 400 miles away compared with our 8,000 miles.

That is the background against which we have to make decisions and to consider what action we can best take. I cannot tell the House precisely what dispositions have been made—some ships are already at sea, others were put on immediate alert on Thursday evening.

The Government have now decided that a large task force will sail as soon as all preparations are complete. HMS *Invincible* will be in the lead and will leave port on Monday ...

We are now reviewing all aspects of the relationship between Argentina and the United Kingdom. The Argentine *Chargé d'Affaires* and his staff were yesterday instructed to leave within four days.

As an appropriate precautionary and, I hope, temporary measure, the Government have taken action to freeze Argentine financial assets held in this country ...

Mr Michael Foot (Ebbw Vale): ... I first wish to set on record as clearly as I possibly can what we believe to be the international rights and wrongs of this matter, because I believe that one of the purposes of the House being assembled on this occasion is to make that clear not only to the people in our country but to people throughout the world.

The rights and the circumstances of the people in the Falkland Islands must be uppermost in our minds. There is no question in the Falkland Islands of any colonial dependence or anything of the sort. It is a question of people who wish to be associated with this country and who have built their whole lives on the basis of association with this country. We have a moral duty, a political duty and every other kind of duty to ensure that that is sustained.

The people of the Falkland Islands have the absolute right to look to us at this moment of their desperate plight, just as they have looked to us over the past 150 years. They are faced with an act of naked, unqualified aggression, carried out in the most shameful and disreputable circumstances. Any guarantee from this invading force is utterly worthless— as worthless as any of the guarantees that are given by this same Argentine junta to its own people.

We can hardly forget that thousands of innocent people fighting for their political rights in Argentine are in prison and have been tortured and debased. We cannot forget that fact when our friends and fellow citizens in the Falkland Islands are suffering as they are at this moment.

On the merits of the matter, we hope that the question is understood throughout the world. In that respect I believe that the Government were right to take the matter to the United Nations. It would have been delinquency if they had not, because that is the forum in which we have agreed that such matters of international right and international claim should be stated.

Whatever else the Government have done—I shall come to that in a moment—or not done, I believe that it was essential for them to take our case to the United Nations and to present it with all the force and power of advocacy at the command of this country. The decision and the vote in the United Nations will take place in an hour or two's time. I must say to people there that we in this country, as a whole, irrespective of our party affiliations, will examine the votes most carefully.

I was interested to hear how strongly the President of France spoke out earlier this morning. I hope that every other country in the world will speak in a similar way.

If, at the United Nations this afternoon, no such declaration were made—I know that it would be only a declaration at first, but there might be the possibility of action there later—not merely would it be a gross injury to the rights of the people of the Falkland Islands, not merely would it be an injury to the people of this country, who have a right to have their claims upheld in the United Nations, but it would be a serious injury to the United Nations itself. It would enhance the dangers that similar, unprovoked aggressions could occur in other parts of the world.

That is one of the reasons why we are determined to ensure that we examine this matter in full and uphold the rights of our country throughout the world, and the claim of our country to be a defender of people's freedom throughout the world, particularly those who look to us for special protection, as do the people in the Falkland Islands . . .

What has happened to British diplomacy? The explanations given by the right hon. Lady, when she managed to rise above some of her own party arguments—they were not quite the exclusive part of her speech—were not very full and not very clear. They will need to be made a good deal more ample in the days to come ...

The right hon. Lady, the Secretary of State for Defence and the whole Government will have to give a very full account of what happened, how their diplomacy was conducted and why we did not have the information to which we are entitled when expenditure takes place on such a scale. Above all, more important than the question of what happened to British diplomacy or to British intelligence is what happened to our power to act. The right hon. Lady seemed to dismiss that question. It cannot be dismissed. Of course this country has the power to act—short, often, of taking military measures. Indeed, we have always been told, as I understand it, that the purpose of having some military power is to deter. The right to deter and the capacity to deter were both required in this situation.

The previous Government had to deal with the same kind of dictatorial regime in the Argentine, the same kind of threat to the people of the Falkland Islands, and the same kinds of problems as those with which the Government have had to wrestle over the past weeks and months ...

No one can say for certain that the pacific and honourable solution of this problem that was reached in 1977 was due to the combination of diplomatic and military activity. These things cannot be proved. There is, however, every likelihood that that was the case. In any event, the fact that it worked on the previous occasion was surely all the more reason for the Government's seeking to make it work on this occasion, especially when, according to the Secretary of State for Foreign and Commonwealth Affairs—I refer again to the diplomatic exchanges—it had been going on for some time. According to the diplomatic exchanges, the Argentine Government were still awaiting an answer from the Secretary of State on some of the matters involved ...

I have not the slightest doubt that, at some stage, an inquiry ... without any inhibitions and restraints, that can probe the matter fully will have to be undertaken ...

We are paramountly concerned ... about what we can do to protect those who rightly and naturally look to us for protection. So far, they have been betrayed. The responsibility for the betrayal rests with the Government. The Government must now prove by deeds—they will never be able to do it by words—that they are not responsible for the betrayal and cannot be faced with that charge. That is the charge, I believe, that lies against them. Even though the position and the circumstances of the people who live in the Falkland Islands are uppermost in our minds—it would be outrageous if that were not the case—there is the longer-term interest to ensure that foul and brutal aggression does not succeed in our world. If it does, there will be a danger not merely to the Falkland Islands, but to people all over this dangerous planet.

Mr Edward du Cann (Taunton): There are times, Mr Speaker, in the affairs of our nation when the House should speak with a single, united voice. This is just such a time. The Leader of the Opposition spoke for us all. He did this nation a service when, in clear and unmistakable terms, he condemned what he called this brutal aggression and when he affirmed the rights of the Falkland Islanders to decide their own destiny. I warmly applaud that part of his speech. I resent and reject his charge of betrayal.

I have a single simple point to make and I can make it shortly. It is right that the House should also, at this moment of crisis for our nation and for the Government, pledge full support to my right hon. Friend the Prime Minister and her colleagues in their heavy and awesome responsibility. As the Leader of the Opposition said, we must do what is necessary and what is right. However, let us see that what we do is well done.

Undoubtedly, there will be questions to be asked. There will also be questions to be answered. I agree with the Leader of the Opposition that there will be a need for a full account of this affair ...

It is astounding that, for all our defence expenditure, which in absolute and proportional terms is huge, and for all our capacity for diplomatic activity and intelligence, we appear to have been so woefully ill prepared. It is extraordinary that conventional forces were not deployed on standby against an occupation ...

Let us declare and resolve that our duty now is to repossess our possessions and to rescue our own people. Our right to the Falkland Islands is undoubted. Our sovereignty is unimpeachable. British interest in that part of the world ... is substantial ...

If one tolerates a single act of aggression, one connives at them all. In the United Kingdom we must accept reality. For all our alliances and for all the social politenesses which the diplomats so often mistake for trust, in the end in life it is self-reliance and only self-reliance that counts. Suez, when I first came into the House 25 and more years ago, surely taught us that not every ally is staunch when the call comes. We have one duty only, which we owe to ourselves—the duty to rescue our people and to uphold our rights. Let that be the unanimous and clear resolve of the House this day.

Let us hear no more about logistics—how difficult it is to travel long distances. I do not remember the Duke of Wellington whining about Torres Vedras. [HON. MEMBERS: "Hear, hear."] We have nothing to lose now except our honour. I am clear that that is safe in the hands of my right hon. Friend.

Mr J. Enoch Powell (Down, South): ... I agree with the right hon. Member for Taunton (Mr du Cann) that the House today is not primarily concerned with inquests—there will be a time for inquests and more abundant material for them—but with what is now to be done. Those who take part in this debate ought to declare clearly what they believe ought now to be done ...

When the sovereign territory of a country is invaded without warning, without provocation and without excuse, there is nothing which requires us to wait upon the decisions or upon the condition or upon the deliberations or upon the resolutions of the United Nations before we take the appropriate steps which ought to follow ...

There is only one reaction which is fit to meet unprovoked aggression upon one's own sovereign territory; that is direct and unqualified and immediate willingness—not merely willingness, but willingness expressed by action—to use force. The Government have set in train measures which will enable them to do that; but there must be nothing which casts doubt upon their will and their intention to do it.

The Prime Minister, shortly after she came into office, received a soubriquet as the "Iron Lady". It arose in the context of remarks which she made about defence against the Soviet Union and its allies; but there was no reason to suppose that the right hon. Lady did not welcome and, indeed, take pride in that description. In the next week or two this House, the nation and the right hon. Lady herself will learn of what metal she is made.

Dr David Owen (Plymouth, Devonport): The Government have the right to ask both sides of the House for the fullest support in their resolve to return the Falkland Islands and the freedom of the islanders to British sovereignty. They will get that support and they deserve it in every action that they take in the Security Council and elsewhere. However, the Government must restore the confidence of the country and the House in their ability to carry out that mission.

I agree with the Leader of the Opposition that this is not the time to have an examination. There will come a time when an inquiry will be necessary and we must examine in great detail all that has happened or not happened during the past six weeks. However, it is necessary to examine a central question: why was no preparatory action taken a month ago? ...

There was ample warning that the position was deteriorating. We knew of the horror of the military junta in the Argentine and we knew of its actions. Only a few days ago, 3,000 political prisoners were taken, only to be released amid the euphoria of the invasion of the Falkland Islands. We knew that the military were jockeying for position in the Navy, the Army and the Air Force. We have known that for many years. It was for that reason four years ago, when a similar position developed, that naval forces were sent ...

We all know that there will be great difficulties in a resisted offensive against the Falkland Islands. There are massive forces on the islands, but nothing said in the House should exclude any possibility of repossessing them. I believe that they will be repossessed by a combination of firm diplomacy backed by the use of the Navy ...

The Prime Minister misjudged the atmosphere of the House most seriously. It is now necessary for the message to come from the House that we are grossly dissatisfied with the conduct of the Government during the past month. We shall sustain them despite that, because we recognise that our Service men's lives might be put at risk ...

[The absence of a decision to send forces a month ago has meant humiliation.] The House must now resolve to sustain the Government in restoring the position.

The Secretary of State for Defence (Mr John Nott): ... Two main criticisms of the Government have emerged in the debate, certainly in my area of responsibility ...

The first main criticism is that in some way the changes that we have made to our naval programme and our other defence arrangements have diminished our capability to respond to such a crisis. The second criticism is that the specific events that developed 14 days ago in South Georgia have caught us unprepared militarily.

The pledge of the right hon. Member for Deptford (Mr Silkin) yesterday that we could count on the support of the official Opposition was welcome. Of course, there is much criticism of the Government on both sides of the House, but I hope that we can unite behind our Armed Forces and that they will have the full backing of the House in the difficult circumstances that we face. It is clear that the whole House accepts that the guarantee of political integrity granted to the Falkland Islands by successive Governments has been breached by an act of flagrant territorial aggression in the face of a determined diplomatic effort to solve the problem peacefully—without any sabre-rattling by the British Government. Our attempt to achieve a peaceful resolution of a long-standing dispute stretching back for many years under Governments of both parties might have been expected to appeal to the Leader of the Opposition. He welcomed our peaceful attempts to resolve the dispute. We shall all remember that, speaking for the whole House, he said that we would not wish to see foul, brutal aggression succeed anywhere in the world. My right hon. Friend the Member for Taunton (Mr du Cann) and the whole House applauded him for that remark, which we shall remember ...

The other major criticism that has been echoed on both sides of the House is that we should have reacted earlier with the despatch, either covertly or overtly, of some surface ships. There are two questions on that issue. First, should we have despatched earlier than we did a naval task force? [HON. MEMBERS: "Yes."] Secondly, should we have deployed covertly some frigates, as the right hon. Member for Cardiff, South-East (Mr Callaghan) did in 1977? With the wisdom of hindsight, the despatch of a large surface task force sufficient to deter or destroy the Argentine Navy might have given pause to the Argentines. *[Interruption]* Perhaps the House will allow me to argue the point through. As the incident at South Georgia began just 14 days ago, such a task force would not have reached the Falkland Islands in order to perform its task. It is impossible, as the right hon. Gentleman said, to know what psychological impact such a force might have had on Argentine intentions, but certainly in deterrence terms, had it been successful, that large task force would have had to remain perhaps indefinitely in Falkland waters, in detriment to its other tasks. But, as my right hon. Friend the Prime Minister said in opening this debate, we were throughout seeking a peaceful solution through the United Nations and by other means ... Such an act, at a moment when we might have been going to the United Nations, would have seemed highly provocative ...

The other option would have been the deployment of a small force insufficient to resist the Argentine Navy, as was done in 1977 ...

Presumably to deter, the presence of the force must have been known. If so, to have sent it, then it would have had precisely the same objections to a peaceful solution. *[Interruption]* If this were a covert deployment, which I believe that it was, it could not have deterred if its presence was not known; and even if the size of the force had been revealed, it could have provided nothing more than a trip-wire of exactly the same kind provided by HMS *Endurance* and provided by the Royal Marine garrison on Port Stanley.

Mr Foot: The right hon. Gentleman is trying to say that there was some difference of opinion, but it was clearly stated by my right hon. Friend when the fact became known without fuss and publicity, and it had a success. That is the difference. What happened in 1977 was a success. This is a terrible failure.

Mr Nott: I do not think that one is able to draw that conclusion.

Dr Owen: If the right hon. Gentleman as Secretary of State for Defence has not understood the value to a Foreign

Secretary of being able to negotiate in a position of some military influence and strength, he should not be Secretary of State for Defence.

Mr Nott: Of course I understand that. However ... there can be no evidence that the position of the frigates in the South Atlantic at that time brought about the settlement of that dispute.

Several hon. Members have spoken of the problems that we now face. I do not seek to hide from Parliament the formidable difficulties with a crisis 8,000 miles away. However, the United Kingdom has the ability to mount a major naval task force and to sustain it for a period at that distance. The charge that the Royal Navy cannot do this is flagrantly and patently untrue. We have that capability, as will certainly be evident, and it amounts to a formidable force which no other nation in the world possesses with the exception of the Soviet Union and the United States ... The Government do not pretend that the situation is anything but extremely grave. The resolution of this problem will undoubtedly be all the more difficult since the occupation. We intend to solve the problem and we shall try to solve it continuingly by diplomatic means, but if that fails, and it will probably do so, we shall have no choice but to press forward with our plans, retaining secrecy where necessary and flexibility to act as circumstances demand.

The military problems are formidable, but they are certainly not insoluble because of the professionalism, the preparedness and the quality of our defences, which for our nation's size are unique in the free world ...

4 MAY 1982

Following week-end reports of naval and air encounters, on Tuesday 4 May the Prime Minister answered questions about the sinking of an Argentine cruiser, General Belgrano, and Mr Pym and Mr Nott made further statements. Later that night Mr Nott returned to the House with a statement on the loss of HMS Sheffield.

Mr Roberts: In view of the terrible loss of life in the South Atlantic, and the rapidly escalating military confrontation, will the Prime Minister make a further effort today to reach a peaceful solution to the situation, involving probably the United Nations?

The Prime Minister: We all regret the loss of human life in the South Atlantic, but our first duty is to protect, and to minimise the danger to, our own forces in the South Atlantic, who are there because we all agreed that we should send a task force ... because we all agreed that we must stop the invader, and because the vast majority of people in this House recognise that the best way to stop the trouble is to withdraw the forces from the Falkland Islands ...

Sir Peter Emery: Will my right hon. Friend say over and over again that until the Argentine Government withdraw their troops from the Falkland Islands, every injury and fatality in the Southern Atlantic is absolutely due to the action of the Argentine junta?

The Prime Minister: Yes, it was the Argentines who broke the peace with unprovoked aggression. They are on British sovereign territory and there are British people under the heel of the junta. We sent the task force to rectify that situation. We hope to do so by all peaceful means and shall continue to try to do so. In the meantime, our first duty must be to protect our boys.

Mr Foot: May I press the right hon. Lady on the question of the sinking of the cruiser and the tragic loss of life involved. We are all deeply concerned about it, just as we all are deeply aware that the origin of the crisis was the aggression by the Argentine. None the less, the Government have direct responsibilities in this matter, and the right hon. Lady especially so. Can she tell us what political control there was over this development, which was a major development? Can she say what calculations about the minimum use of force entered into those considerations? ... What are the next steps that will be taken by the Government to try to deal with the situation? ...

The Prime Minister: ... I want to make it perfectly clear that after the announcement of the maritime exclusion zone— I referred to the matter in the House last week—there was another announcement on 23 April, which was communicated to the Argentine Government and also to the United Nations. It may help if I read it in full:

> In announcing the establishment of a maritime exclusion zone around the Falkland Islands, Her Majesty's Government made it clear that this measure was without prejudice to the right of the United Kingdom to take whatever additional measures may be needed in the exercise of its right of self-defence under Article 51 of the United Nations Charter. In this connection, Her Majesty's Government now wishes to make clear that any approach on the part of Argentine warships, including submarines, naval auxiliaries, or military aircraft, which could amount to a threat to interfere with the mission of the British forces in the South Atlantic will encounter the appropriate response.

The warning was given to the Argentine Government, I repeat, on 23 April. It was reported to the United Nations on 24 April.

Mr Foot: . . .The right hon. Lady has not fully explained why such a development as this occurred in the circumstances in which it did occur; nor has she explained why the maximum amount—or, at any rate, a considerable amount—of force was used to carry it out. None of these things has been explained. They will need to be explained much more fully to the country and to others. Does the right hon. Lady appreciate that these are important matters for our own Service men, whom we wish to protect as much as anyone? They are also important for the support that this Government may command throughout the world in these matters. If the right hon. Lady and the Government do not appreciate that the sinking of the cruiser raises great questions of this kind, she does not understand the situation.

The Prime Minister: May I make it perfectly clear that the worry that I live with hourly is that attacking Argentine forces, either naval or air, may get through to ours and sink some of our ships. I am sure that that will also be in the right hon. Gentleman's mind. There was clear aggressive intent on the part of the Argentine fleet and Government. It could be seen first in their claims. They previously claimed that they had sunk HMS *Exeter,* that they had damaged HMS *Hermes,* leaving it inoperative and badly damaged, and that they had brought down 11 Harriers. That was clear evidence of Argentine aggressive intent. The right hon. Gentleman may also remember the persistent attacks throughout the whole of Saturday on our task force, which were repelled only by the supreme skill and courage of our people. He may also know, or will hear from my right hon. Friend, of the very heavy armaments that the cruiser carried, and, of course, the cruiser was accompanied by two destroyers, which were not attacked in any way.

Mr Mates: Does my right hon. Friend agree that of all the uses to which the word has been put in the last weeks the word "paramount" applies most of all now to the safety and lives of our Service men in the South Atlantic? ...

The Prime Minister: I wholly agree with my hon. Friend. Our first duty is to our own forces, who are there on our orders and with our support. We must look after their safety. Our second duty is to see that we try to use minimum force. However, that cruiser and the associated destroyers—and, of course, there are other task forces of the Argentine Navy also at large in the South Atlantic, not far from the exclusion zone—posed a very obvious threat to the men in our task force. Had we left it any later, it would have been too late, and I might have had to come to the House with the news that some of our ships had been sunk ...

Mr Dalyell: When the Prime Minister referred to political control, did she herself, personally and explicitly, authorise the firing of the torpedoes on the *General Belgrano*?

The Prime Minister: I assure the hon. Gentleman that the task force is and was under full political control.

Sir John Biggs-Davison: Would not some of the ignorant and irresponsible questions coming from the Opposition have been avoided if the Leader of the Opposition had done his duty to his party, to the country, and as a Privy

Counsellor, by availing himself of the invitation from my right hon. Friend the Prime Minister to acquaint him with matters to which we, who are not sworn of the Privy Council, do not wish to have access because we have confidence in her handling of this affair and in Her Majesty's Forces?

The Prime Minister: It is for the right hon. Gentleman to say whether he will avail himself of any offer to talk on Privy Counsellor terms ...

Mr Foot: Would the right hon. Lady care to read to the House what she said about the matter of consultations on *Panorama* a few days ago? Will she also repeat to the House what I think she understood well before, the attitude that has been taken by many Opposition leaders in previous times, who thought that they would be failing in their duty to the House of Commons to gag themselves? ...

The Prime Minister: I do not quarrel with the right hon. Gentleman's decision in any way. I made an offer available to him on the same basis as I did to the right hon. Gentleman the leader of the Liberal Party and to the leader of the SDP in this House. Whether or not he takes it up is a matter for him. I have been in a similar position. There have been times when I have taken the offer up and times when I have not.

Sir Anthony Kershaw: On the subject of the cruiser, how can anyone maintain that such a ship, armed in that way, and accompanied by those destroyers, was not a threat to our forces? ...

The Prime Minister: ...The cruiser posed a real threat to our forces then, and would have continued to do so in the coming days ...

Mr Grimond: ...Has not the time now come for a fresh, direct approach by Her Majesty's Government to the junta proposing that the Argentines evacuate the Falkland Islands, so that negotiations can then be entered into directly between us? After all, we are still not at war with the Argentine.

The Prime Minister: At the moment we prefer to make our approaches through a third party. Mr Haig did valiant work, and it is clear that he is still interested in trying to bring about a solution, both through his own efforts and, as the right hon. Gentleman may have read, through certain initiatives that are being undertaken by Mr Haig through the Peruvian Government, and which we are pursuing vigorously ...

Mr Brinton: ...Is my right hon. Friend also aware that there are two former colonies in the world today with populations of fewer than 8,000 and about 20 countries which have less land area than the Falkland Islands? Will she ensure that Britain does not deviate from its determination to demonstrate that armed, unprovoked aggression must never pay?

The Prime Minister: I believe that what my hon. Friend says about there being small countries in the Commonwealth and countries with smaller areas than the Falkland Islands is correct. I entirely agree that unless Britain manages to stop and undo the Argentine aggression, many other small countries and territories will go in fear that they may suffer the same fate ...

*The Secretary of State for Foreign and Commonwealth Affairs
(Mr Francis Pym):* Since we debated the Falklands crisis last
Thursday, there have been some important military developments. My right hon. Friend the Secretary of State for
Defence will report on those in a few minutes. Meanwhile,
I wish to pay tribute to the efficiency and courage of our
forces. Our relief that British lives have not been lost is
inevitably tempered by our deep regret at Argentine casualties. I know that the whole House would wish to be
associated with these sentiments.

These military achievements have been in support of
our overall strategy; they have not been and will not
become a substitute for it. As the House knows, we are
maintaining the maximum pressure on Argentina in the
diplomatic, economic and military fields with the objective
of securing Argentine withdrawal at the earliest possible
moment and in compliance with the mandatory resolution
of the United Nations Security Council.

The military pressure that we have exercised has been
challenged despite our clear warnings and our desire to use
the minimum force. Our response in the circumstances was
as inevitable as it was right. However, I can assure the House
that what we are seeking is not the military humiliation of
Argentina but a victory for the rule of law in international
affairs.

Since the House last met, I have visited Washington
and New York to reinforce our diplomatic efforts to
achieve a negotiated settlement as soon as possible. I had
extensive talks with Secretary Haig. These covered the
diplomatic, economic and military dimensions of the crisis.

On the diplomatic side, Mr Haig made it clear that,
just as we have not abandoned our diplomatic endeavours

following Argentina's rejection of the earlier American proposals, nor has he. We discussed a range of ideas for a settlement. We are continuing our work with all urgency. As the House will be aware, other Governments have also been active in promoting a settlement. We welcome this and are in close touch with them. Therefore, we are working actively on various ideas, including those put forward by the President of Peru. I can assure the House that we are losing no time in developing our thoughts about them and communicating our constructive views to those concerned. The framework for a settlement remains as I have outlined it to the House.

Proposals are needed which cover the essential elements of resolution 502—withdrawal, and negotiations on the future, unprejudiced in any way. They must also address the interim arrangements and guarantees required.

On the economic front, Mr Haig described the measures which the United States has recently announced. They are a tangible sign of American support for our cause. I know that the Americans have not closed their mind to additional steps.

On the military front, Mr Haig and Mr Weinberger confirmed that they are ready to provide material support for our forces and I welcomed this. We are following it up in detail and urgently.

In New York I discussed diplomatic possibilities with the Secretary-General of the United Nations and with the President of the Security Council. I made it clear to them that our immediate concern is the implementation of resolution 502, and that we are open to any ideas which would achieve this on a satisfactory basis, namely, an Argentine withdrawal followed by negotiations on the long-term solution without prejudice to basic principles.

We were able to consider together the various possible ways of involving the United Nations. We recognised that a solution will require not only the right ideas but the right timing and the right sequence of events. I know that the Secretary-General is in touch with the Argentine Government. The burden of compliance with what has already been decided, of course, rests squarely with them.

It must not be forgotten that we remain the victims of a totally unprovoked act of aggression in defiance of the United Nations Charter. We are seeking to ensure that Argentina does not profit from aggression and to uphold the rule of law in international affairs. That is an interest which all members of the United Nations must share.

Our resolve should not be doubted; nor should our readiness to talk and our will for peace.

Mr Denis Healey (Leeds, East): I shall not be drawn into discussing now the military operations of the weekend as the Secretary of State for Defence is about to make a statement on them, except to join the Foreign Secretary in paying tribute to the courage and efficiency shown by our forces.

I remind the right hon. Gentleman that Mr Haig, in announcing the shift in American policy on Friday, said that

> a purely military outcome cannot endure over time. There will have to be a negotiated solution. Otherwise we will all face unending hostility and insecurity in the South Atlantic.

I hope that Her Majesty's Government share those views, because they are shared unanimously by Labour Members.

There is deep concern among Labour Members and many of our allies in case certain types of military action—

the attack on the cruiser *General Belgrano* may be such an instance—intended, as the Foreign Secretary said, to back up negotiations, may weaken or even destroy the possibility of negotiations for a long-term solution. He must be aware from telegrams that have been received in the Foreign Office this morning that the operations of the last few days have already cost us a great deal of support among our European allies.

On Friday Mr Haig said that he had reason to hope that the United Kingdom would consider a settlement along the lines of his proposals. We understand from newspaper reports that Mr Haig's proposals were put again, although perhaps in a modified form, by the Peruvian Government in the past two days.

Has not the time now come when the Foreign Secretary should tell us a little bit about those proposals as it is the Argentine failure to accept them which has led to the military action over the past few days and the shift in American policy? The House has the right to that information at this time because it is now being made available to Governments in many other parts of the world.

Finally, may I ask the Foreign Secretary about his visit to the United Nations? I understand from newspaper reports that the Common Market Commission will put to the Council of Ministers this week the proposal that the continuing support of the Common Market for the British position over the Falkland Islands should depend on our asking the Secretary-General of the United Nations to provide his good offices. The Foreign Secretary will be aware that the Argentine Foreign Minister, at a meeting last Friday, invited the Secretary-General to give his good offices. He will know that the Secretary-General is able to do so if we, as the other party to the dispute, ask him to do so ... Has the right hon. Gentleman asked the United Nations Secretary-General to take over the role of intermediary at this time? If he has not, why not?

Over the weekend the Foreign Secretary said that it was Her Majesty's Government's intention to secure the withdrawal of Argentine forces by negotiation. The Government refuse to negotiate directly with the Argentine Government so long as Argentine troops are still on the Falkland Islands. If they are not prepared to negotiate directly, will they ask the United Nations to take over the role of intermediary?

I hope that there is no truth in the newspaper reports of the past two days that the only reason why the right hon. Gentleman visited the United Nations this weekend was to appease opinion in the United Kingdom and elsewhere. We believe that the time has come when the United Nations must play the central role in securing the withdrawal of Argentine troops from the Falkland Islands and that it will have a very important role in implementing the ultimate settlement.

Mr Pym: The right hon. Gentleman is less than fair when he suggests that what I have done during this weekend and in previous weeks is anything other than to do everything that I conceivably can to bring about "a negotiated settlement as soon as possible", the words that I used in my statement. We do not yet know whether that can be achieved, but I agree with the right hon. Gentleman that in the end, whenever that is, there must be a negotiated settlement. The sooner that it comes, the better it will be. That is what my expedition was intended to try to further.

I assure the right hon. Gentleman that the Secretary-General is in touch with the Argentine Government and is talking with them in the same way as he is talking with me. He did not describe himself as an intermediary, but, as he is in touch with both Governments, I suppose that one could describe that as his position. I have had many talks with him about the various possibilities, but the essential point remains that the Argentines are already under a mandatory obligation to withdraw. One problem that the United Nations faces is how to ensure that that withdrawal is carried out. That must be a precondition for taking matters further. The other essential condition is that the Argentines must come off their hook of saying that the outcome of the negotiations should be predetermined in favour of Argentina. That clearly cannot be acceptable. It may be that the Argentines will move from both those positions, in which case we may make a real advance.

I visited not only the United Nations but Mr Haig to explore all those matters. Although the United Nations is a possible forum and can help in many ways, there are other possibilities, and I referred in my statement to the work that is going on, based on ideas that originated with Peru. The original American proposals were rejected last week by the Argentines. We are now working on a new series of proposals. I shall make a constructive input to those proposals and I am already doing so. They are different in character, but they cover the same area that I mentioned in last week's debate—withdrawal, what happens in the interim, and the final negotiations. Whatever detail is discussed, it must cover those areas. That is what we are pursuing actively, constructively and positively, as I am sure the House wishes.

That is the present position. It is difficult in the United Nations at the moment for the simple reason that the mandatory resolution has not been fulfilled by the Argentines. The right hon. Gentleman is right in intimating that one member of the European Community raised a matter with the President of the Security Council today. There may be a meeting, but I do not yet know what specific proposal will be put to the Security Council. That is perhaps not as important as the search for the means by which we can achieve a negotiated settlement ...

Mr Healey: The Foreign Secretary has made two important statements. First, he said that he believed that the word "intermediary" might be appropriate to describe the function that is now being carried out by the United Nations Secretary-General. Secondly—I am surprised that he did not tell the House this in his original statement—he said that a member of the European Community was already in touch with the United Nations Secretary-General with a view to calling a meeting of the Security Council ...

In the light of the information that the Foreign Secretary gave us about another possible meeting of the Security Council, it is now very urgent, in the interests of the United Kingdom, that, the Argentine Foreign Minister having already asked the Secretary-General to assume that role, we should do the same now so that no time is lost and the future is not prejudiced, as I warned the right hon. Gentleman in our debate last week it might be, by a decision of the Security Council which might be much more hostile to our interests than the present one.

Mr Pym: The Security Council has already passed resolution 502, which requires the Argentines to withdraw. That is the basic position. British sovereign territory has been invaded and during the past three weeks the Argentine forces have been heavily reinforced. Clearly, the first move must be an Argentine withdrawal from that territory. The Secretary-General is in touch with the Argentine Government, as I made clear in my statement, and one of his objectives is to ensure that resolution 502 is implemented ...

I have had no direct communication from any member of the European Community. However, it is on the tapes and it has been made public knowledge that one member has taken certain action. I shall comment upon that and react to it when I hear from the member State what it intends. However, not only the Secretary-General but the President of the Security Council had consultations throughout yesterday—no doubt they continued today—with all the members of the Security Council. Therefore, the United Nations' work on this important crisis is very active ...

Dr David Owen (Plymouth, Devonport): May I associate the SDP with the expressions of regret at the loss of life of the Argentine Service men and also pay tribute to the courage and skill of the British Service men who have been operating in very difficult circumstances? ... *[Is]* not Peru uniquely well placed to act in that way, as a friend of the Argentine and with close relations with the United States and friendly relations with Britain—quite apart from its association with the Secretary-General of the United Nations? What does the right hon. Gentleman intend to do about taking up that initiative? Is he ready to negotiate without precondition, and would such negotiations include the acceptance of a readiness to talk about the trusteeship council provision?

Mr Pym: ... The President of Peru formulated a series of proposals which he communicated to the United States and directly to the Argentines, who turned them down. With Mr Haig, I am responding positively to the ideas contained in the proposal and I will communicate some ideas of my own which may lead to a possible basis. I should not like to raise undue hopes, but I will do everything that I can.

The right hon. Gentleman spoke of negotiations without preconditions, but there must be the precondition of the withdrawal of Argentine forces, who have no right to be in the Falkland Islands, and no prejudice to the ultimate negotiations. Then we could start talking ...

Mr Tony Benn (Bristol, South-East): Has the Foreign Secretary's attention been drawn to the fact that in *The Sunday Times* a public opinion poll showed that six out of 10 people in Britain were not prepared to see one Service man's life or a Falkland Islander's life put at risk and that such a majority in Britain will not be rejoicing with the Prime Minister at the loss of life when the ship—[HON. MEMBERS: "Withdraw."]—was torpedoed without a declaration of war well outside the exclusion zone? Will the Foreign Secretary take account of the desire for peace in Britain by agreeing to a ceasefire and to the transfer at once to the United Nations of sovereignty of the Falkland Islands and its administration pending a settlement under United Nations auspices?

Mr Pym: In making those points and others that he makes from time to time, which may be controversial and with which many people disagree, it is disgraceful for the right hon. Gentleman to attribute to my right hon. Friend the Prime Minister the reaction that he has alleged. I believe that it is utterly wrong to impute such motives or thoughts when they are untrue. That spoils the validity of everything else that the right hon. Gentleman says.

The Secretary of State for Defence (Mr John Nott): ... In the House on 7 April I announced that our first naval action would be to deny the Argentine forces on the Falklands the means of sea reinforcement and resupply from the mainland. British submarines have achieved that objective. With the arrival of our task force on 30 April our next move was to stop reinforcement and resupply from the air, as well as by sea. Since the passing of resolution 502 the Argentines, instead of withdrawing, had continuously reinforced the islands. We gave two days' prior warning to the Argentine Government of the imposition of this total exclusion zone, and our task force is now enforcing it.

The task force was dispatched to the South Atlantic with the support of the House and, I believe, of the country. Since its arrival in these waters our overriding duty has been to protect our task force against attack by Argentine forces ...

I shall now describe the military sequence of events. Air attacks by Vulcan and Sea Harrier aircraft against Port Stanley airfield were launched early on 1 May. The runway was cratered and rendered unusable by transport aircraft from the Argentine mainland. A further sortie was made today to render the airstrip unusable for light supply, communications and ground attack aircraft operating within the Falkland Islands themselves. The other main airfield on East Falkland at Goose Green has also effectively been put out of action.

On 1 May the Argentines launched attacks on our ships during most of the daylight hours. The attacks by Argentine Mirage and Canberra aircraft operating from the mainland were repulsed by British Sea Harriers. Had our Sea Harriers failed to repulse the attacks on the task force, our ships could have been severely damaged or sunk. In fact, one Argentine Canberra and one Mirage were shot down and others were damaged. We believe that another Mirage was brought down by Argentine anti-aircraft fire. One of our frigates suffered splinter damage as a result of the air attacks and there was one British casualty, whose condition is now satisfactory. All our aircraft returned safely. On the same day our forces located and attacked what was believed to be an Argentine submarine which was clearly in a position to torpedo our ships. It is not known whether the submarine was hit.

The prolonged air attack on our ships, the presence of an Argentine submarine close by, and all other information available to us, left us in no doubt of the dangers to our task force from hostile action.

The next day, 2 May, at 8 p. m. London time, one of our submarines detected the Argentine cruiser, *General Belgrano* escorted by two destroyers. This heavily armed surface attack group was close to the total exclusion zone and was closing on elements of our task force, which was only hours away. We knew that the cruiser itself has substantial fire power, provided by 15 6in guns, with a range of 13 miles, and Seacat anti-aircraft missiles. Together with its escorting destroyers, which we believe were equipped with Exocet anti-ship missiles with a range of more than 20 miles, the threat to the task force was such that the task force commander could ignore it only at his peril.

The House will know that the attack by our submarine involved the capital ship only and not its escorting destroyers, so that they should have been able to go to the assistance of the damaged cruiser. We do not know whether they did so, but, in so doing, they would not have been engaged.

On 3 May, at about 4 a.m. London time, a Sea King helicopter keeping watch against submarine attack around the task force was fired on by an Argentine ocean-going patrol craft. This vessel was then attacked and sunk by a Lynx helicopter. A second Lynx then came under attack from another Argentine vessel, which was itself attacked and damaged.

It must be a matter of deep concern to the House that there has been loss of life from these engagements including the sinking of the *General Belgrano*, but our first duty must be the protection of our own ships and men. There may be further attacks on our forces and they must be allowed to act in self-defence. We cannot deny them that right. Nor must we forget that military action began by an attack on British marines and the forcible seizure of British territory. The way of stopping the fighting forthwith is for the Argentines to withdraw their garrison from the Falkland Islands in compliance with the United Nations resolution 502.

Mr Denis Healey (Leeds, East): The right hon. Gentleman rightly said ... that his policy was and would always be to use minimum force under strict political control to achieve a diplomatic solution. I confess that it is not always easy to achieve that in the stress of battle. Nevertheless, on the evidence that he has just given, it seems that he has successfully achieved that objective, first, in the reoccupation of South Georgia; secondly, in the attacks on the airfields and military facilities on the Falkland Islands; and, thirdly, in the actions that he has just described within the total exclusion zone.

I shall address my questions entirely to the action against the Argentine cruiser *General Belgrano*. The right hon. Gentleman said that the Government were concerned about the loss of life that had occurred. I understand that the action took place 36 miles outside the total exclusion zone. Although it appears now that there have not been 1,000 lives lost, as we feared earlier, the number must run into many hundreds ...

Almost two days after the event it should be possible for the Secretary of State to give the House more details than were in his statement ...

First, will the right hon. Gentleman say how far the Argentine ships were from the task force? ... It makes a big difference whether they were 50, 100 or 300 miles away. Any of those distances could be described as "hours away".

Secondly, what were the two escorting destroyers? Were they by any chance the type 42 frigate that Britain sold to the Argentine?

Thirdly, if the attack was necessary to protect our forces, could not action have been taken to cripple rather than to sink the cruiser? ... I accept that it is not easy for submarines that were designed for global war against a great power to exercise the use of minimum force in a police action against a minor power. There remains the question whether it was possible to cripple the cruiser rather than to sink it, as was done to the submarine off South Georgia. That question deserves to be answered . . .

I ask these questions in no carping spirit. If it is indeed the Government's intention at all times to use minimum force to achieve a political solution, they must avoid risking the lives of half of the population of the Falkland Islands in a single engagement.

Mr Nott: . . . I said at a press conference yesterday that it was our policy to use minimum force. The task force remains under the political control of the Government. It operates within a political framework. Nevertheless, in exercising minimum force it must bear in mind the overriding need not to endanger itself—our own men and our own ships.

We believe that the action took place just outside—about 35 miles—the total exclusion zone. However, as I said in my statement, the cruiser and the escorting destroyers were only hours' steaming time away. [HON. MEMBERS: "How many hours?"] The right hon. Gentleman asked for the precise distance. I cannot give it, as I am not prepared to reveal the position of our task force. Nor can I give full details of the exact composition of the Argentine forces operating against us. The right hon. Gentleman will know, because he, too, has been Secretary of State for Defence, that communications are not necessarily received instantly by a submarine. It sometimes takes time for communications to be made, for reasons that have to do with the natural concealment of the submarine, but the group was hours away from our task force.

Only two torpedoes were fired at the cruiser. It is impossible to say whether that would have crippled the cruiser—that could not be predicted—but, having fired its torpedoes, the submarine clearly could not remain in the area without endangering itself. Therefore, in accordance with normal procedures, it fired the two torpedoes and then left the area ... I can tell the House that in this case, due to the serious threat that the group of Argentine naval vessels posed to our task force, our submarine was ordered to fire some torpedoes at the cruiser.

Mr Healey: With great respect, the right hon. Gentleman's answer about the distance between the task force and the Argentine forces is inadequate. First, the action took place nearly two days ago. No one could assume that our task force would still be in the position in which, according to the right hon. Gentleman, it was identified by the Argentine destroyers at that time ...

I did not ask where the submarine was. I asked where the task force was. The task force is a surface force in continuous communication with the Ministry of Defence in London, as we know from the hourly press reports from correspondents aboard some of the ships.

Mr Nott: I realise that the right hon. Gentleman asked where our task force was, but that is not information that I think it would be prudent to give to the House. As he will know, the task force is within the region of the Falkland Islands, around the area of the total exclusion zone, but I cannot be asked to give precise nautical miles in a case of this kind ...

Mr David Steel (Roxburgh, Selkirk and Peebles): I join in the congratulations extended to our forces on the success of the operation so far.

Will the Secretary of State confirm that the military policy remains as described by the Prime Minister in the debate last Thursday as being measured and controlled? The right hon. Gentleman presumably accepts that if the scale of loss of life already suffered by the Argentines were repeated against us in retaliation it would quickly equal the total population of the Falkland Islands. Will he therefore tell us whether there is a general directive to the Fleet Commander that all action must be taken only if it is totally unavoidable?

Mr Nott: I am grateful to the right hon. Gentleman for his remarks about the skill of our men with the task force.

The right hon. Gentleman is quite right. The action of our Fleet in the South Atlantic must at all times be measured and controlled ...

I am sure that he will accept from me, however, that in the conditions in which our forces find themselves— repeated air attacks had been launched on them the previous day; we have reason to believe that there is a submarine or perhaps two operating in the area; and the Argentines themselves announced that they had sunk HMS *Exeter*, brought down 11 of our aircraft and severely damaged HMS *Hermes*, all of which is clear evidence that the orders of the Argentine fleet are to sink our ships—we must do nothing that endangers our task force, which went there and is there with, I believe, the consent of the majority of Members of the House.

Mr Robert Atkins (Preston, North): Does my right hon. Friend begin to agree with the remarks attributed to Air Chief Marshal "Bomber" Harris ... when he suggested that too much publicity was given to the nitty-gritty of strategic and tactical decisions taken by the people on the high seas facing difficulties in protecting our interests and our troops? If he does agree, what steps does he think can be taken to rebut some of the nonsensical remarks by right hon. and hon. Gentlemen opposite?

Mr Nott: It would be of assistance to us if retired Service officers and others would not speculate so widely on all the military options that are open to us. It would also, naturally, be of help to us if the BBC and other media could have rather fewer programmes of this kind, because we are talking about lives, and the lives of our own Service men, and at the moment some of these programmes go rather too far.

Mr William Hamilton (Fife, Central): Will the Minister confirm what the Prime Minister said earlier this afternoon, namely, that the decision to launch the torpedoes was a political decision—in other words, it was made by either the Prime Minister or the right hon. Gentleman, or both of them together? Or was it made by the admiral on the spot? It is extremely important that the country should know who is making decisions to kill in the South Atlantic.

Mr Nott: Throughout this affair we have kept close control of the rules of engagement that go to the task force, and that must be obvious. The overall political control remains with the Government, and my right hon. Friend the Prime Minister was, of course, confirming that. That must be the case. We did not fire the first shot, and the day before the *General Belgrano* was sunk there was launched upon our ships a substantial and dangerous air attack. It was only because of the superior skill and the better aircraft that we have available that our ships were not sunk the day before. I hope that the country understands that very clearly. We cannot allow Argentine naval or air assets to be left free to attack and sink our ships.

Mr Healey: May I ask the right hon. Gentleman once more if he can give us more details about the distance between the opposing forces, because this is critical in establishing the necessity to attack the cruiser in self-defence? The right hon. Gentleman told the House a moment ago that the Argentine ships were closing on elements of our task force, so presumably they knew where it was, and, since two of them survived, presumably the Argentine Government knows. The Soviet Government certainly knows, because it has three spy satellites over the area. Will the right hon. Gentleman tell us where the task force was 40 hours ago?

Mr Nott: I have noted that the right hon. Gentleman thinks that the Soviets know where our task force is. I rather doubt that that is the case. The *General Belgrano* was sunk about 30 miles south of the exclusion zone. I repeat that I cannot tell the right hon. Gentleman where our task force was then or where it is now. With respect to the right hon. Gentleman's natural wish to know how close the forces were, given the delay in communications that can arise between London and a submarine, the fact that I have told him and the House that this group was only hours of steaming time away surely gives him sufficient information to appreciate that these ships were a threat to our Fleet.

Later—

Mr Dennis Skinner (Bolsover): On a point of order, Mr Deputy Speaker. About an hour ago it was mentioned on television that one of the British ships, HMS *Sheffield*, had been destroyed in the South Atlantic. Has the Prime Minister indicated whether she intends coming to the House tonight to explain precisely what happened?

Mr Deputy Speaker (Mr Bernard Weatherill): As soon as there is any such information, it will be given to the House.

Mr Leo Abse (Pontypool): Further to that point of order, Mr Deputy Speaker. While it may be that such information will be given in due course, the alarm, concern and distress that exist as a consequence of the massive folly that is occurring demand that there should be an immediate statement in the House. Surely it is necessary that the Prime Minister should come to the House and tell us precisely what has occurred, so that the House can give a firm indication of the need for a cessation of hostilities on the initiative of this Government and the need for far more urgent attempts to negotiate ...

Mr Frank Allaun (Salford, East): Further to that point of order, Mr Deputy Speaker ...

I put it to you that the sinking of HMS *Sheffield* is so serious, is such a dramatic and tragic event, that hon. Members on both sides of the House really want to hear a statement from the Ministry ...

Mr David Winnick (Walsall, North): Further to that point of order, Mr Deputy Speaker ...

We require the Leader of the House to tell us as quickly as possible when the Defence Minister is going to be at the Despatch Box, and we certainly expect a statement tonight ...

Mr John Stokes (Halesowen and Stourbridge): On a point of order, Mr Deputy Speaker. I think that it would be a great mistake if the House were to panic. This great and ancient nation has been through many wars and struggles and it does not need a debate and a statement every five minutes because a ship has been sunk ...

The Lord President of the Council and Leader of the House of Commons (Mr John Biffen): The loss of HMS *Sheffield* and recent events reported from the Falklands very properly excite the deep concern of the House. Throughout the whole of the Falklands episode the Government have sought to keep the House informed in as comprehensive a fashion as possible for the convenience of the House. The situation concerning the loss of the *Sheffield* is still not totally clarified, but, as my right hon. Friend the Secretary of State for Defence has said that he wishes to make a statement first thing after Questions tomorrow, I am certain that he will then be in a position—

Mr Winnick: We must have it now.

Mr Biffen: —to give the House the most up-to-date information that is available, which is consistent with the tradition of informing the House as well as having regard to sheer practicalities.

Mr George Foulkes (South Ayrshire): Further to that point of order, Mr Deputy Speaker. The House will not adjourn in the near future ...

Mr Abse: ... What possible condition exists to justify the right hon. Gentleman's statement that tomorrow is the day to make a statement and not tonight when we are all assembled and when the nation expects a statement from a Minister, so that we all know who is responsible, what is to occur and what fresh initiative will take place before further lives are lost? ...

Sir John Eden (Bournemouth, West): ... May I respectfully appeal to hon. Members on the Opposition Benches for a moment of calm? Is it not absolutely clear that in a military engagement it is inescapable that there will be casualties on both sides?

Mr Biffen: I very much wish to assist the House in making progress this evening in the way in which it feels most congenial and orderly. I appreciate that in all parts of the House there is deep concern over the recent news. There is great anxiety that the matter should be fully ventilated in the Chamber. Some feel that it must happen this evening. I believe that the majority feel that the most appropriate occasion would be for my right hon. Friend the Secretary of State for Defence to make a comprehensive statement tomorrow afternoon with all the available information that he will then have. I believe that that would be a gesture consistent with the traditions of the House and with the nature of the situation ...

If it will help, I shall convey to my right hon. Friend the Secretary of State for Defence the opinions expressed and the hope that he might be able to come to the House for what I am sure will be understood to be a brief holding statement ...

Mr John Nott: On a point of order, Mr Deputy Speaker, I should like to make a statement.

Mr Deputy Speaker: Order. Has the Secretary of State the leave of the House to make a statement?

Hon. Members: Aye.

Mr Nott: In my statement earlier today, I said that we must expect further Argentine attacks on our forces. I deeply regret now to have to inform the House of such attacks.

In the course of its duties within the total exclusion zone around the Falkland Islands, HMS *Sheffield*, a type 42 destroyer, was attacked and hit late this afternoon by an Argentine missile. The ship caught fire, which spread out of control. The order was then given to abandon ship. There were accompanying vessels in the immediate area which picked up those who had abandoned ship. Nearly all the ship's company and the captain are accounted for. However, I regret to say that initial indications are that 12 men are missing and there are likely to be other casualties.

Communications with the operational area are difficult at present and this information must be treated as provisional until further reports are received. Next of kin will, of course, be informed first as soon as full details are received.

Further air operations were also conducted over the Falkland Islands today. In the course of Sea Harrier attacks, one of our aircraft was shot down. The pilot has been killed. His name will be announced after we have confirmation that his next of kin have been informed. All the other Sea Harriers returned safely. The task force is continuing with its operations as planned.

Mr Michael Foot (Ebbw Vale): May I first thank the Leader of the House for having responded to many of the requests from hon. Members that a statement should be made? May I also thank the Secretary of State for Defence for coming to the House to make the statement? As I am sure we all agree, it contains grave and tragic news. All of us deeply deplore the fact that the right hon. Gentleman should have had to come to the House to make it.

When I first heard the news, I thought that it was right that the House should wait for a while because the next of kin had not yet been informed. That is absolutely necessary as the next stage.

For the House to make the right judgment about this matter, it is better that we should have a statement tomorrow. We can consider that, what the Government may say and what we may say. I do not seek in any sense, in this moment of what could be a tragedy for some of our people, to make any political comments, but I hope that tomorrow the Government will be prepared to make a statement on the whole matter ...

There are implications that arise and reflect on some of the things that have been said in the debates over the past few days and to which some of us referred in the debate last Thursday. But I suggest that the best course for the House is that the Secretary of State or perhaps the Prime Minister should come to the House tomorrow and make a further statement in the full light of all these matters ...

Mr Nott: ... It is of course grave and tragic news; I entirely agree with him. I am sure that the Government will wish to make a statement tomorrow.

Mr Ian Mikardo (Bethnal Green and Bow): In the midst of the grief which we all share and which has been expressed from both sides of the House, can the right hon. Gentleman tell us whether the Prime Minister is still inviting us all to rejoice, rejoice?

Mr Nott: I shall not comment on that matter, but I am afraid that I must make one correction to the remarks I made earlier. I said in making my statement that initial indications were that 12 men were missing. I regret to say that the latest news, which I have just had, is rather worse. It is that the number of deaths may be as high as 30. But we really do not have sufficient information at this stage to give firm news to the House, and that is why I think it is better to wait until tomorrow ...

Mr John Stokes: Is my right hon. Friend aware that the eyes of the nation are upon this House tonight? As someone who has been here for only 12 years but who spent six years fighting in the war, I found tonight some signs of panic on both sides of the House. May I assure my right hon. Friend that those signs are only temporary and I am sure that tomorrow the House will be resolved that we should carry through what the Government are determined to do.

Mr Nott: I have noted my right hon. Friend's remarks. I would not wish to comment on them tonight ...

15 JUNE 1982

On Tuesday 15 June the Prime Minister answered her questions and then made a statement formally announcing the surrender of all Argentine forces on the Falkland Islands.

Mr Kenneth Carlisle: In the light of the most welcome news from the Falklands, does my right hon. Friend agree that we should praise and give thanks for the skill, courage and sacrifice of the members of the task force who succeeded so brilliantly in an exercise that was fraught with hazard? Does she agree that it is a fine moment for our country? Does she further agree that it demonstrates that wherever British power can reach, nobody should embark upon aggression?

The Prime Minister: I thank my hon. Friend for his comments. I entirely agree with him. We cannot say enough about how wonderful our Armed Forces and Merchant Marine have been. We salute them all. I hope, as my hon. Friend said, that we have once again restored Britain's dominance and have let every nation know that British sovereign territory will be well and truly defended and that we shall never again be the victim of aggression.

Mr Grimond: Does the welcome ceasefire apply only to hostilities in the Falkland Islands or to all hostilities with Argentina?

The Prime Minister: I shall have something to say about that in my statement. We are endeavouring to achieve a complete ceasefire with Argentina ...

Mr Moate: Does my right hon. Friend agree that the liberation of the Falkland Islands has shown that, although we must be grateful for international support and co-operation, which is always essential, this nation must always retain the freedom, resources and resolve to act independently in defence of the principles for which we stand?

The Prime Minister: I entirely agree. We must have the capacity to act independently. I agree with my hon. Friend that we need both the power to act and the will to see it through.

Mr Foot: We shall have the opportunity to put further questions to the right hon. Lady about the Falkland Islands when she makes a fresh statement on the subject in a few minutes' time. Will she tell us now about the engagement for which I believe she is leaving tonight or tomorrow—the United Nations' special session on disarmament in New York? Does she agree that events both in the South Atlantic and in the Middle East make all the more necessary the effort to ensure that that disarmament conference is successful? Will she use all the strength of the British Government to try to get serious measures passed? Does she agree that the recent war, and particularly the use of certain weapons by the Argentines, make all the more necessary a concerted effort at the United Nations to stop the obscenity of traffic in arms, as a result of which some of our Service men were killed by weapons that we had sold to the Argentines?

The Prime Minister: I am not certain whether I shall be going to New York tomorrow, or possibly later, if it can be arranged. The disarmament conference is in no way a negotiating forum. Negotiations must be carried on elsewhere. I entirely agree that we should like to have security with a lower level of arms, but that lower level must be capable of being verified. The whole world is learning the lesson that unilateral disarmament leads to weakness and liability to attack by the strong, as it always has. Unilateral disarmament of all kinds leads to weakness and liability to be attacked on the part of the nation that undertakes it. Therefore, we need a proper balance of arms, which is what we are trying to obtain.

Mr Kilfedder: As the victory in the South Atlantic was made possible by the supreme sacrifice made by our courageous

Service men and merchant seamen, will the Prime Minister as quickly as possible promote a memorial to those gallant men who epitomise all that is best in our nation?

The Prime Minister: Of course we shall consider that. I think that what they have achieved is their own best memorial. Indeed, none could better it ...

Mr George Gardiner: In the light of today's marvellous news, will my right hon. Friend study the precedent set by Prime Minister and Monarch in May 1940 and consider the designation of a Sunday very soon as a national day of prayer and thanksgiving for our success in freeing the Falkland Islands? ...

The Prime Minister: Of course we shall consider that, but I believe that throughout our land this day and the coming Sunday everywhere there will be thanksgiving.

Mr Campbell-Savours: Will the right hon. Lady give an absolute assurance that neither she nor No. 10 will in any way obstruct the promised inquiry into the events leading up to the invasion of the Falkland Islands and that the determination of the truth will be paramount so that the British people may learn what actually happened as against what the House was told happened?

The Prime Minister: Yes, Sir. I shall shortly be writing to the Leader of the Opposition about the proposed form of the inquiry. I am certain that it needs to go back far further than the events leading up to the conflict.

Mr Faulds: ...As British military abilities have once again rescued British politicians from their failures, will the right hon .... Lady contemplate today whether this is the right time to offer the Argentines a reasonable involvement in the future of the Falkland Islands to prevent a continuing war on our naval and supply communications for the Falkland Islands?

The Prime Minister: No, Sir ...

Later—

The Prime Minister: With permission, Mr Speaker, I should like to make a statement on the Falkland Islands.

Early this morning in Port Stanley, 74 days after the Falkland Islands were invaded, General Moore accepted from General Menendez the surrender of all the Argentine forces in East and West Falkland together with their arms and equipment. In a message to the Commander-in-Chief Fleet, General Moore reported:

> The Falkland Islands are once more under the Government desired by their inhabitants. God Save the Queen.

General Menendez has surrendered some 11,000 men in Port Stanley and some 2,000 in West Falkland. In addition, we had already captured and were holding elsewhere on the islands 1,800 prisoners, making in all some 15,000 prisoners of war now in our hands.

The advance of our forces in the last few days is the culmination of a determined military effort to compel the Argentine Government to withdraw their forces from the Falkland Islands.

On the night of Friday 11 June, men of 42 and 45 Commandos and the 3rd Battalion the Parachute

Regiment, supported by elements of the Royal Artillery and Royal Engineers, mounted an attack on Argentine positions on Mount Harriet, Two Sisters and Mount Longdon. They secured all their objectives, and during the next day consolidated their positions in the face of continuing resistance.

I regret to inform the House that five Royal Marines, 18 Paratroopers and two Royal Engineers lost their lives in those engagements. Their families are being informed. Seventy-two Marines and Paratroopers were wounded. We have no details of Argentine casualties. Hundreds of prisoners and large quantities of equipment were taken in these operations. The land operations were supported by Harrier attacks and naval gunfire from ships of the task force, which made a major contribution to the success of our troops. In the course of the bombardment, however, HMS *Glamorgan* was hit by enemy fire. We now know that 13 of the crew died in this attack or are missing.

Throughout Sunday 13 June, the 3rd Commando Brigade maintained pressure on the enemy from its newly secured forward positions. Meanwhile, men of the 5th Infantry Brigade undertook reconnaissance missions in preparation for the next phase of the operations. HMS *Hermes* flew her one-thousandth Sea Harrier mission since leaving the United Kingdom.

The Argentines mounted two air raids that day. The first was turned back by Harriers of the task force before it could reach the Falklands. In the second raid A4 aircraft made an unsuccessful bombing run and one Mirage aircraft was shot down.

During the night of Sunday 13 June the second phase of the operations commenced. The 2nd Battalion the

Parachute Regiment secured Wireless Ridge and the 2nd Battalion the Scots Guards took Tumbledown Mountain by first light on Monday 14 June. The 1st/7th Gurkhas advanced on Mount William, and the Welsh Guards on Sapper Hill. At 2 p. m. London time large numbers of Argentine troops were reported to be retreating from Mount William, Sapper Hill and Moody Brook in the direction of Port Stanley.

British forces pressed forward to the outskirts of Port Stanley. Large numbers of Argentines threw down their weapons and surrendered.

At 4 o'clock the Argentine garrison indicated its willingness to talk. Orders were given to our forces to fire only in self-defence. Shortly before 5 o'clock a white flag appeared over Port Stanley.

Initial contact was made with the enemy by radio. By midnight General Moore and General Menendez were talking. The surrender of all the Argentine forces of East and West Falkland was agreed at 1 a.m. today London time. Some of our forces are proceeding to West Falkland to organise the surrender of the Argentine forces there.

We are now tackling urgently the immense practical problems of dealing with the Argentine prisoners on the islands. The weather conditions are severe, permanent accommodation is very limited, and much of the temporary accommodation which we had hoped to use was lost when the *Atlantic Conveyor* was sunk on 25 May. We have already repatriated to Argentina almost 1,400 prisoners, and the further 15,000 now in our custody are substantially more than we had expected. With the help of the International Red Cross, we are taking urgent steps to safeguard these prisoners and hope to evacuate them as soon as possible from the islands, in accordance with our responsibilities under the Geneva Convention. This is a formidable task.

We have today sent to the Argentine Government, through the Swiss Government, a message seeking confirmation that Argentina, like Britain, considers all hostilities between us in the South Atlantic—and not only on the islands themselves—to be at an end. It is important that this should be established with clarity and without delay.

We must now bring life in the islands back to normal as quickly as possible, despite the difficult conditions and the onset of the Antarctic winter. Mines must be removed; the water supply in Stanley is not working and there will be other urgent tasks of repair and reconstruction.

Mr Rex Hunt and members of the Islands Council at present in this country will return as soon as possible. Mr Hunt will concentrate on civilian matters. General Moore will be responsible for military matters. They will in effect act as civil and military commissioners and will, of course, work in the closest co-operation.

After all that has been suffered it is too early to look much beyond the beginning of the return to normal life. In due course the islanders will be able to consider and express their views about the future. When the time is right we can discuss with them ways of giving their elected representatives an expanded role in the government of the islands ...

We shall uphold our commitment to the security of the islands. If necessary, we shall do this alone. But I do not exclude the possibility of associating other countries with their security. Our purpose is that the Falkland Islands should never again be a victim of unprovoked aggression.

Recognising the need for economic development, I have asked Lord Shackleton to update his 1976 report on the economic potential of the islands. He has agreed to do this as a matter of urgency. I am most grateful to him.

The House will join me, Mr Speaker, in expressing our deep sense of loss over those who have died, and our sorrow for their families. The final details will not become clear for a few days yet, but we know that some 250 British Service men and civilians have been killed. They died that others may live in freedom and justice.

The battle of the Falklands was a remarkable military operation, boldly planned, bravely executed, and brilliantly accomplished. We owe an enormous debt to the British forces and to the Merchant Marine. We honour them all. They have been supported by a people united in defence of our way of life and of our sovereign territory.

Mr Foot: The Opposition at once wish to join in the thanks and congratulations that the right hon. Lady has given to the Service men and their commanders on the way in which they have discharged their duties throughout these dangerous weeks. We wish that to be emphasised at the outset.

The relief that the House felt and expressed last night when it first heard the news derived partly from the belief that we had been able to avoid not merely the hideousness of a bloody battle at Port Stanley but also the consequences of such a battle. That sense of relief was rightly expressed, and we wish to express it once again.

Even so, as the right hon. Lady emphasised in her final remarks, there have been severe casualties for this country that affect some of our great naval ports such as Plymouth and Portsmouth. There have been severe casualties affecting other places as well. In addition, there have been severe casualties among the Argentine forces. I am sure that we are all concerned about them, too. However, the sense of relief is very great, and we are all grateful for the fact that the bloodshed is now coming to an end.

I hope that we shall have a further statement soon on the casualties when the right hon. Lady has received the further details to which she referred. In the meantime, we extend our deep sympathy to all the families who have suffered the consequences of the casualties and express our determination—I hope the determination of the House of Commons—that proper ways should be found to assist those families and those who have been afflicted by what has happened.

I do not expect the right hon. Lady to deal now with questions about the future, nor do I think that this is the best time to do so. There is bound to be an interval during which we shall deal with the immediate position on the islands, and that interval is bound to mean that normal operations cannot be envisaged. However, it would be right for the right hon. Lady at an early date to express a view about the future. I do not say that she should describe the whole future, but she should give some commitments about it. In our view, it is not possible for the British Government to contemplate that over the years ahead they alone can deal with these matters.

The right hon. Lady said in her statement "I do not exclude the possibility of associating other countries with their security". That is a modest statement of the requirement. I believe that she will have to go considerably further than that, in the interests of the islanders and of the security of the islands. I do not believe that it is possible for the Government to exclude much greater consultations with other countries. Indeed, we are bound to do so under the resolutions that we have signed. I therefore hope that the Prime Minister will now give an absolute assurance that we shall be prepared to consult other nations according to our commitments under the United Nations Charter to ensure that we provide for future arrangements.

I hope that we shall not exclude the possibility of the trusteeship that was discussed earlier. *[Interruption]* Those hon. Members who wish to exclude that possibility ought to look at some of the changes in the Government's policy that have occurred during this period. The more they examine them, the more I believe that justice will be seen in the case that we have persistently put throughout these discussions.

Even if the Prime Minister will not give a detailed commitment now, I hope that she will say that she intends to carry out to the full, in the spirit and the letter, the resolution that she and her Government proposed at the United Nations in the name of this country. I do not know whether the right hon. Lady is shaking her head, but it would be a breach of faith if she were to abandon that commitment. I therefore hope that she will reiterate our allegiance on these questions.

All these matters will later have to be examined afresh, including the investigation of how the original crisis arose. Much the best course for the Government is to recognise the commitments that they have made in these international obligations and to say that they will uphold them as determinedly as we have upheld the rights of British territory.

The Prime Minister: I am grateful to the right hon. Gentleman for what he said about our Armed Forces. We mourn the loss of those who were killed and we are dedicated to the cause for which they gave their lives.

As to the United Nations resolution, the withdrawal by the Argentines was not honoured and our forces had to go there because they would not withdraw. Indeed, they had to recover and recapture British territory. I cannot agree with the right hon. Gentleman that those men risked their lives in any way to have a United Nations trusteeship. They risked their lives to defend British sovereign territory, the British way of life and the rights of British people to determine their own future.

Mr David Steel (Roxburgh, Selkirk and Peebles): Will the Prime Minister consider allowing the House a special opportunity to pay tribute to our forces after they have returned? I think that that would be appropriate.

Is the right hon. Lady aware that at lunch time the BBC carried allegedly authoritative reports about the form of inquiry in which she would invite the other party leaders to participate? However, she mentioned nothing about that in her statement. Without going into the form of that inquiry, will she give an undertaking that it will be strong enough to include not just the matters leading up to the invasion but such questions as the sale of arms to Argentina and the defence policy decisions that affect the equipment and operation of our Navy?

The Prime Minister: During Question Time, I referred to the form of inquiry and said that I would shortly be writing to Opposition leaders. I do not believe that the form of the inquiry should be anything like as wide as the right hon. Gentleman suggests; otherwise it would never report. I do not believe that it is the general wish to have the inquiry as wide as that. That is a totally different kind of review from the one on which I thought we were agreed. However, I shall be writing shortly to the right hon. Gentleman about the matter. Surely today is a day for congratulation and celebration and not for post-mortems ...

Mr Edward du Cann (Taunton): Is my right hon. Friend aware that the House and the nation will have noted with particular approval the sentence in her statement that indicated that we shall not again allow the Falkland Islands to be the subject of unprovoked aggression? In the meantime, is it not possible to say something about the local inhabitants of Port Stanley and West Falkland? I am sure that many people would be grateful for information on that subject.

The Prime Minister: I am grateful to my right hon. Friend for what he said about defending the Falkland Islands so that they are never again the victim of aggression. At present information about the civilian population is sketchy because of appalling weather and the fact that there were only a few hours of daylight before I came to the House. Initial indications are that the islanders are thrilled to see our forces and that in general they are safe and well, but we have no further details.

Mr J. Enoch Powell (Down, South): Will the Government be careful to ensure that nothing is done or said in the coming days that could be an obstacle to our securing, both in the Falkland Islands and in Britain, compensation and satisfaction for the loss and damage that have been suffered as a result of this unprovoked aggression?

The Prime Minister: I shall try to refrain from saying anything that will prejudice that, but I must point out that we are not seeking compensation. We went to recapture the islands, to restore British sovereignty, which had not been lost because of the invasion, and to restore British administration. That was our objective, and I believe that we have achieved it.

Dr David Owen (Plymouth, Devonport): I wish to express our congratulations to the right hon. Lady and sympathy to the relatives of those who were killed. Will the Prime Minister confirm that it is not the intention to return all the Argentine military until Argentina has confirmed that all hostilities in the South Atlantic have ended? When considering the association that might be developed with other countries for the long-term development of the Falkland Islands, and before making any final decision—it is too early to reach a firm conclusion about how we should handle the future—will the right hon. Lady consult the United States of America, which has been one of our most loyal allies and which has great interest in the Organisation of American States?

The Prime Minister: It was precisely because we believed that we should not return all the prisoners of war until we were certain that we had achieved a cessation of hostilities with the mainland of Argentina that I said that "we hope" to evacuate the prisoners of war. We must send back a considerable number, but we should withhold some, especially the officers and commanders, until we have achieved a ceasefire with the mainland.

As to the long-term future, as the right hon. Gentleman said, we are talking about British sovereign territory and British people. Many people will be interested in the future of the islands, but we must consult the people and then make the best possible arrangements that we can for them. I recognise that that will need the friendliness of other States in the region. It would not be wise to go beyond that now.

Sir John Eden (Bournemouth, West): Following the successful outcome of the campaign, which would not have been possible without the supreme valour displayed by our forces nor without the steady and resolute leadership shown from the start by my right hon. Friend the Prime Minister, will she say whether, in attempting to tackle some of the enormous and immediate logistical problems, especially the shortage of water, it would be practicable to turn to Uruguay, Chile or other Latin American countries for help?

The Prime Minister: I am grateful to my right hon. Friend. We wish to have help with the logistical problems from wherever we can get it, but few places are near and therefore we had to prepare for some of those matters in the supplies and provisions that we sent down with the task force. We shall be all right for water. If we cannot return some prisoners, we shall need some help with food and transport, but I believe that the United States of America will be prepared to help with some of those matters.

Mr Tony Benn: (Bristol, South-East): Apart from the inquiry, will the Prime Minister publish the full text of all the exchanges that took place with the United Nations,

Argentina and the Americans so that we may see what happened and a full analysis of the costs in life, equipment and money in this tragic and unnecessary war which the world knows very well will not provide an answer to the problem of the future of the Falkland Islands? Does she agree that in the end there must be negotiations, and will she say with whom and when she will be ready to enter into such negotiations?

The Prime Minister: The texts of all the negotiations are not mine to publish. We entered into the negotiations in confidence and I do not believe in breaking a confidence. I do not intend to negotiate on the sovereignty of the islands in any way, except with those who live there. That is my fervent belief. The right hon. Gentleman called it an unnecessary war. Tragic it may have been, but may I point out to him that he would not enjoy the freedom of speech that he put to such excellent use unless people had been prepared to fight for it.

Mr Churchill (Stretford): Is my right hon. Friend aware that the nation owes this signal victory not only to the skill and courage of British forces but to her resolute leadership during the critical weeks? Is she further aware that the entire House will wish to be associated with the tribute that she paid to those who will not return from the South Atlantic? Will she associate us with her condolences to the families of those involved, whose grief the entire nation shares?

The Prime Minister: I am grateful to my hon. Friend. Every hon. Member would wish to pay tribute to those who lost their lives, to those who have been injured and to the families without whose support they could never have done such a wonderful job ...

Other titles in the series

The Amritsar Massacre: General Dyer in the Punjab, 1919

"We feel that General Dyer, by adopting an inhuman and un-British method of dealing with subjects of His Majesty the King-Emperor, has done great disservice to the interest of British rule in India. This aspect it was not possible for the people of the mentality of General Dyer to realise."

Backdrop

At the time of the events described, India was under British rule. Indians had fought alongside the British in World War I, and had made tremendous financial contributions to the British war effort. Mahatma Gandhi was the leader of the Indian National Congress party, which was seeking independence from the British Empire.

The Book

This is the story of the action taken by Brigadier-General Dyer at Amritsar in the Punjab in 1919. Faced with insurrection in support of Mahatma Gandhi, the British Army attempted to restore order. General Dyer, on arriving in the troubled city of Amritsar, issued an order banning any assembly of more than four people. Consequently, when he discovered a large crowd gathered together during a cattle fair, he took the astonishing action of shooting more than three hundred unarmed people. Regarding the subsequent native obedience as a satisfactory result, he was surprised to find himself removed from command a year later, and made lengthy representations to Parliament.

ISBN 0 11 702412 0   Price £6.99

British Battles of World War I, 1914–15

"The effect of these poisonous gases was so virulent as to render the whole of the line held by the French Division incapable of any action at all. It was at first impossible for anyone to realise what had actually happened. The smoke and fumes hid everything from sight, and hundreds of men were thrown into a comatose or dying condition, and within an hour the whole position had to be abandoned, together with about 50 guns."

Backdrop

On 4 August 1914, Britain declared war on Germany. Germany had already invaded Belgium and France and was progressing towards Paris.

The Book

These are the despatches from some of the battles of the first two years of World War I. They include action in northern France, Germany, Gallipoli, and even as far afield as the Cocos Islands in the Indian Ocean. They describe the events of battle, the tremendous courage, the huge losses, and the confusions and difficulties of war. These startling accounts, which were written by the generals at the front, were first published in the "London Gazette", the official newspaper of Parliament.

ISBN 0 11 702447 3 Price £6.99

D Day to VE Day: General Eisenhower's Report, 1944–45

"During the spring of 1945, as the sky grew darker over Germany, the Nazi leaders had struggled desperately, by every means in their power, to whip their people into a last supreme effort to stave off defeat, hoping against hope that it would be possible, if only they could hold out long enough, to save the day by dividing the Allies. Blinded as they were by their own terror and hatred of 'Bolshevism', they were incapable of understanding the strength of the bond of common interest existing between Britain, the United States and the Soviet Union."

Backdrop

In 1944 the Allies were poised to launch an attack against Hitler's German war machine. The planning and timing were crucial. In February, General Eisenhower was appointed Supreme Commander of the Allied Operations in Europe.

The Book

The book is Dwight D. Eisenhower's personal account of the Allied invasion of Europe, from the preparations for the D-Day landings in Normandy, France, to the final assault across Germany. He presents a story of a far more arduous struggle than is commonly portrayed against an enemy whose tenacity he admired and whose skills he feared. It is a tactical account of his understanding of enemy manoeuvres, and his attempts to counter their actions. The formality of the report is coloured by many personal touches, and the reader senses Eisenhower's growing determination to complete the task. Hindsight would have had the general take more notice of Russian activity, but that this was not obvious to him is one of the fascinations of such a contemporary document.

ISBN 0 11 702451 1 Price £6.99

The Irish Uprising, 1914–21: Papers from the British Parliamentary Archive

"Captain Bowen-Colthurst adopted the extraordinary, and indeed almost meaningless, course of taking Mr Sheehy Skeffington with him as a 'hostage'. He had no right to take Mr Sheehy Skeffington out of the custody of the guard for this or any other purpose, and he asked no one's leave to do so. . . . Before they left the barracks Mr Sheehy Skeffington's hands were tied behind his back and Captain Bowen-Colthurst called upon him to say his prayers. Upon Mr Sheehy Skeffington refusing to do so Captain Bowen-Colthurst ordered the men of his party to take their hats off and himself uttered a prayer, the words of it being: 'O Lord God, if it shall please thee to take away the life of this man, forgive him for Christ's sake.'"

Backdrop

In 1914 it was still the case that the whole of Ireland was part of Great Britain, under the dominion of the King, and Irish constituencies were represented in the British Parliament.

The Book

This book contains five remarkable documents published by the British Government between 1914 and 1921, relating to the events leading up to the partition of Ireland in 1921. In the first, a report is made into the shooting of civilians following a landing of arms at Howth outside Dublin. The second is of the papers discovered relating to the activities of Sinn Fein and particularly of Sir Roger Casement. The third is the government inquiry into the Easter Rising of 1916. The fourth describes the treatment of three journalists by the British Army shortly after the uprising, and the last is an exchange of correspondence between Eamon de Valera and David Lloyd George prior to the Anglo–Irish Treaty of 1921.

ISBN 0 11 702415 5   Price £6.99

Lord Kitchener and Winston Churchill: The Dardanelles Commission Part I, 1914–15

"The naval attack on the Narrows was never resumed. It is difficult to understand why the War Council did not meet between 19th March and 14th May. The failure of the naval attack showed the necessity of abandoning the plan of forcing the passage of the Dardanelles by purely naval operation. The War Council should then have met and considered the future policy to be pursued."

Backdrop

The Dardanelles formed part of the main southern shipping route to Russia, and was of great military and strategic importance to whoever controlled it. However, it had long been recognised by the British naval and military authorities that any attack on the Dardanelles would be an operation fraught with great difficulties.

The Book

During the early stages of World War I, Russia made a plea to her allies to make a demonstration against the Turks. So attractive was the prize of the Dardanelles to the British generals, notably Lord Kitchener, that this ill-fated campaign was launched. Just how powerful an influence Kitchener was to exert over the War Council, and just how ill-prepared the Allies were to conduct such an attack, are revealed in dramatic detail in the report of this Commission.

The book covers the first part of the Commission's report. It deals with the origin, inception and conduct of operations in the Dardanelles from the beginning of the war in August 1914 until March 1915, when the idea of a purely naval attack was abandoned.

ISBN 0 11 702423 6   Price £6.99

Defeat at Gallipoli: The Dardanelles Commission Part II, 1915–16

"It has been represented ... that from a military point of view, the Dardanelles Expedition, even if unsuccessful, was justified by the fact that it neutralised or contained a large number of Turkish troops who otherwise would have been free to operate elsewhere. Lord Kitchener estimated this number as being nearly 300,000. But in containing the Turkish force, we employed ... a total of at least 400,000. Our casualties amounted to 31,389 killed, 78,749 wounded and 9,708 missing, making a total of 119,846. The expedition also involved heavy financial expenditure and the employment of a considerable naval force."

Backdrop

The naval attempt by the British to force the Dardanelles was abandoned in March 1915. Rather than losing face, the military commanders decided to send a large army to the area.

The Book

Picking up the story from where the earlier volume, *Lord Kitchener and Winston Churchill* left off, this second part of the Dardanelles Commission's report deals with the disastrous military campaign to capture the Gallipoli Peninsula using ground forces. As the story unfolds, we learn how the Allies were unable to make any headway against an enemy who was well prepared and well positioned. Within a few months the Allies had suffered a humiliating defeat, and thousands of men had lost their lives. The realisation of the government's incompetence in handling this affair was instrumental in the removal of Herbert Asquith as Prime Minister in December 1916.

ISBN 0 11 702455 4   Price £6.99

The Siege of the Peking Embassy, 1900

"I cannot conclude this despatch without saying a word of praise respecting the ladies of all nationalities who so ably and devotedly assisted the defence, notwithstanding the terrible shadow which at all times hung over the legation—a shadow which the never-ceasing rattle of musketry and crash of round shot and shell and the diminishing number of defenders rendered ever present. They behaved with infinite patience and cheerfulness, helping personally in the hospital or, in making sandbags and bandages, and in assisting in every possible way the work of defence. Especially commended are two young ladies—Miss Myers and Miss Daisy Brazier—who daily filtered the water for the hospital, in tropical heat, and carried it with bullets whistling and shells bursting in the trees overhead." Sir Claude MacDonald

The Backdrop

The Boxer movement in China was a secret society which preached hatred of foreigners. By the spring of 1900, this movement was out of control. On 9 June, the Boxers launched their first attack against foreign property in Peking by burning down the racecourse. On 19 June, all foreigners were ordered to evacuate Peking within 24 hours. The order was not complied with.

The Book

As events worsened for the diplomats and their families in Peking, Sir Claude MacDonald, the British ambassador, wired the Admiralty in Taku to request the immediate despatch of a relief force. Just how that relief force fared, and how the hundreds of diplomats and their families who were stranded inside the Legation buildings coped with the rigours of the siege, are the subject of the diplomatic papers presented in this book. The central part of the story is the gripping diary of events kept by Sir Claude MacDonald.

ISBN 0 11 702456 2   Price £6.99

Florence Nightingale and the Crimea, 1854–55

"By an oversight, no candles were included among the stores brought to the Crimea. Lamps and wicks were brought but not oil. These omissions were not supplied until after possession had been taken of Balaklava, and the purveyor had an opportunity of purchasing candles and oil from the shipping and the dealers in the town."

Backdrop

The British Army arrived in the Crimea in 1854, ill-equipped to fight a war in the depths of a Russian winter.

The Book

The hospital service for wounded soldiers during the Crimean War was very poor and became the subject of concern, not just in the army, but also in the press. "The Times" was publishing letters from the families of soldiers describing the appalling conditions. This embarrassed the government, but even more it irritated the army, which did not know how to cope with such open scrutiny of its activities.

The book is a collection of extracts from government papers published in 1855 and 1856. Their selection provides a snapshot of events at that time. In particular they focus on the terrible disaster that was the Charge of the Light Brigade, and the inadequate provisions that were made for the care of the sick and wounded. The documents relating to the hospitals at Scutari include evidence from Florence Nightingale herself.

ISBN 0 11 702425 2   Price £6.99

The Siege of Kars, 1855

"We had, up to that date, suffered from cold, want of sufficient clothing, and star-
vation, without a murmur escaping from the troops. They fell dead at their posts,
in their tents, and throughout the camp as brave men should who cling to thei
duty through the slightest glimmering of hope of saving a place entrusted to the
custody. From the day of their glorious victory on 29th September, they had
tasted animal food, and their nourishment consisted of two-fifths of a ratio
bread and the roots of grass, which they scarcely had the strength to dig fo
night and day they stood to their arms, their wasted frames showing the
effects of starvation, but their sparkling eye telling me what they would do were
the enemy to attack them again." W. F. Williams

Backdrop

In 1855, while the British Army was fighting alongside the French and
the Turkish armies in the Crimean War, a little-known but serious siege
was taking place in the city of Kars in eastern Turkey. Set within moun-
tains and overlooking a gorge, Kars is a natural fortress, but its
possession by the Turks was threatened by the Russians.

The Book

During the Crimean War, the British were giving aid to the Turkish
army by lending them generals to help organise and strengthen their
garrisons. General Williams had arrived in Kars in September 1854,
having been appointed British Military Commissioner with the
Turkish Army in Asia. He soon began organising the troops there,
although his repeated requests for supplies and reinforcements were
met with delay and obfuscation. These despatches concerning the siege
of Kars date from May 1855. Their unfolding tells a sorry tale of hero-
ism and frustrated hope.

ISBN 0 11 702454 6   Price £6.99